POLITICAL FOOTBALL

POLITICAL FOOTBALL

Regulation, Globalization and the Market

WYN GRANT

agenda
publishing

First published in 2021 by Agenda Publishing

Agenda Publishing Limited
The Core
Bath Lane
Newcastle Helix
Newcastle upon Tyne
NE4 5TF
www.agendapub.com

ISBN 978-1-78821-350-9 (hardcover)
ISBN 978-1-78821-351-6 (paperback)

British Library Cataloguing-in-Publication Data
A catalogue record for this book is available from the British Library

Typeset by JS Typesetting Ltd, Porthcawl, Mid Glamorgan
Printed and bound in the UK by TJ Books

CONTENTS

PREFACE

This book is dedicated to the memory of my grandmother, Lucy May (1872–1956), who was its original inspiration. Until I undertook the research for this book, I was puzzled by this otherwise Victorian lady's interest in football, but I did not realize how early women's football developed in this country. She was particularly interested in questions of promotion and relegation, but considered one had to look beyond the manager and the teams, important though those were, to explore longer-term socioeconomic trends which is what I have done in this book.

I am a long-standing fan of Charlton Athletic where I am a regular contributor to the fanzine. At my local non-league club, Leamington, I am secretary of the Vice-Presidents' Club and write an article in each home match programme. I have therefore been able to observe changes in football from two ends of the spectrum. Both Charlton and Leamington have had troubled histories, losing their grounds. Leamington disappeared altogether as a club for over a decade and was only revived due to the tireless efforts of fans. Hence, I have direct personal experience of the struggles faced by clubs and their fans to survive, let alone succeed.

Football is being transformed by forces outside the control of the ordinary fan. These may be summarized by one word that offers a central theme of this book: globalization. Clubs are increasingly controlled by foreign owners who usually have no personal or emotional link with the club. They have a variety of motives, ranging from prestige and political protection to making money. Not all foreign owners are bad, indeed the "rogue owner" problem often occurs domestically. However, as the owner of a football club you are a trustee for a community asset and many owners do not understand that.

While this book is written by a football fan, my working life has been as an academic with a broad interest in what has been termed "political economy". In particular, one area of interest has been in the way in which the excesses of a capitalist market economy may be tempered by regulation. Indeed, regulation may be necessary to prevent a market economy destroying itself and its potential benefits.

Regulation is not a panacea for the problems besetting football, but it is part of the solution. However, good regulatory design is not easy. What is a good regulatory design? It is one that achieves the objectives of regulation in a transparent and comprehensible way. It must also be efficient in that it must not be unduly onerous and impose large transaction costs on the regulated. Above all, it must not create new problems that are worse than those it seeks to solve.

Devising an effective regulatory system that wins public confidence is never an easy task. This is particularly the case in relation to football. A variety of stakeholders is involved. This, of itself, is not unusual; it would apply, for example, to the energy industries. However, the interests and perspectives of owners, players, agents, leagues, governing bodies and fans can be particularly divergent. Yet the model of "responsive" regulation requires that they all be taken into account.

A particular problem arises in relation to the "consumer" of football: the fan. The term consumer is itself inappropriate because being a fan of a club is often an important part of personal identity. It is not just a question of the price and quality of a product. If nothing else, fans are characterized by excessive expectations. These could quickly be applied to a regulator. Hence, it is important to set boundaries to what a regulator of football can and cannot do.

There is a complex variety of tasks that needs to be undertaken. Apart from questions of club ownership and fan involvement, these include issues of racism and homophobia. It is also important to ensure that the development of women's football is not held back

An independent regulator is clearly needed because the football authorities have fallen down on the job. Clubs with long histories have been acquired by rogue owners who are able to avoid tests of their suitability. At the international level, the governing body, FIFA, has been beset by problems of favouritism and corruption.

The state therefore needs to intervene to create an effective system of regulation for football. However, the general preference of governments has been for self-regulation. There have been interventions but they have been ad hoc and sporadic and they have certainly not been decisive. The European Union has come closest to making a difference, but it has been distracted by other issues on its agenda.

There needs to be a thorough overhaul of existing governance arrangements for football at the national and international levels. There is an increasing recognition of this urgent need. This book seeks to give further impetus to that welcome trend, but above all it seeks to provide a route map of how effective change could best be achieved.

For the chapter on women's football I made substantial use of the digital British Newspaper Archive of the British Library (www.britishnewspaperarchive.

co.uk). I would like to thank Rick Everitt, editor of *Voice of the Valley*, for giving me permission to quote from a number of articles that have appeared in the fanzine. My granddaughter Victoria Candelent helped me with some aspects of the book that touched on her discipline of psychology. I would like to thank Alison Howson at Agenda for being a very patient and helpful editor. Margaret Hitchcocks became my partner while I was writing this book and was very tolerant of the time I spent working on it in my study.

Wyn Grant
Leamington Spa

1
THE POLITICAL ECONOMY OF FOOTBALL

The excitement of attending a first football match is ingrained in the memory of many fans. They can recall the details of the journey to the ground, who they were with, the merchandise and food being sold outside and the feeling they had on entering the ground for the first time. They can remember the match itself, the emotional involvement of the other spectators around them, the singing and the chanting. I recall catching the number 53 bus from Plumstead Common at the age of six with my parents, walking with the crowds through Maryon Park and standing on the huge East Terrace at The Valley, the home of Charlton Athletic.

For many fans, that first experience begins a lifelong commitment that becomes an important part of their identity. Going to a match is not simply a release from the pressures of everyday life, important though that is, it also represents an opportunity to connect with an extended football family. This may include generations of the same family and old school friends. However, it may also involve "football friends" with whom the only contact is at the game, for a drink beforehand or afterwards. I frequently make the two-hour journey to attend Charlton home games to meet football friends in my birthplace of Greenwich for brunch and a pre-match pint.

Even if after moving away from the club's location, a fan's continuing support for their team can be a means of maintaining and reviving their connection with an area familiar to them. Topophilia, a love of place, and the cultural identity associated with a place, can be a powerful force. Of course, in some ways this is a nostalgic and sentimental interpretation, or at least a constructed version of the experience of football. Many fans never visit the ground of the team they support and simply follow their progress on television and social media. Football is now a global game with supporters of leading teams located all over the world. Inevitably this leads to a tension between a club as a global business, perhaps with foreign owners, and the idea of a club as an expression and embodiment of a particular community. Some fans have become alienated from football as a result, as the business and finances of the sport distance and diminish the importance of the local supporters to the team's success. The need to temper and regulate the globalizing market forces at work in the beautiful game is a central theme of this book.

The challenge of global football

To help understand and explain the forces at work in global football, I draw on the analytical framework provided by the concept of political economy, which is all about the relationship between the market and the state and the governance of that relationship. Unrestrained market forces can damage the functioning of both economy and society so that competition cannot deliver its benefits, and the structure and cohesion of society is undermined. One response to prevent these harmful outcomes by governments has been the increase of regulation to ensure that the market operates within a framework of rules. Football has operated largely outside this "regulatory state" and has relied on self-regulation, which has often been found wanting. The absence of effective regulation has been criticized as football has been transformed by globalization, foreign investment and new technology. The need for regulation cannot, however, be satisfied simply by importing established forms of regulation from areas such as utility company competition and pricing. It requires a more responsive and innovative form of regulation that takes account of the variety of stakeholders in football, not least the fans.

There is widespread discontent about the state of football at a time when it is followed more extensively and intensively across the world than ever before, even making headway in the United States with its own long-established and distinctive sports. It is important to be cautious about falling into the trap of believing in a sepia-tinged golden age of football. There have always been dominant clubs with more resources than others. Players were ruthlessly exploited in the past by owners. Games were played in stadiums that were at best uncomfortable and at worst dangerous, leading to a number of incidents in which spectators were killed. The state of pitches certainly did not encourage the development of silky skills; training was often limited to physical fitness with a belief that keeping players away from the ball would make them hungry for it at the next match; and there was little understanding of diet and nutrition and its relationship with performance: "Objectively, the football of the 1970s was markedly inferior to the tactics, fitness and skill levels of today" (Everitt 2019: 19). In the twenty-first century players are athletes with much higher work rates and better technical skills.

Given that there have been improvements in the standard of player fitness and of playing tactics along with the facilities in which the game is watched, why is there so much discontent? There are many grievances, and some real cause for concern, but among the most prominent is a widely held opinion that players are paid too much, and agents extract too much from the game. Owners are often considered to have little emotional investment in their clubs and to be pursuing agendas that have little to do with football. A small number of top clubs dominate the game such as the "big six" in the Premier League (Arsenal, Chelsea, Liverpool, Manchester City, Manchester United and Tottenham Hotspur), Paris Saint-Germain (PSG) in France, Juventus in Italy and Barcelona and Real Madrid in Spain. This domination is regarded as anti-competitive with top clubs ruthlessly pursuing their own interests and evading rules designed to keep their conduct in check. There is also a troubling symbiotic relationship between football and gambling, which is a theme I explore in Chapter 5.

All these concerns can be summarized as the feeling of alienation that many fans experience from the game they love. Clubs are an important source of identity for fans and their communities. However, they feel powerless in the face of owners who may run a club into the ground and even destroy it, as exemplified by what happened at Bury in 2019. Players are tradeable commodities and may have little real loyalty to their clubs, however much they kiss the badge. The price of attending games has often soared beyond what can be afforded by those on below average or even median incomes. Of course, it should be acknowledged that fans often have unrealistic expectations and are one of the forces leading to overspending on players.

What is evident is that at a time when economic and political resistance to globalization is growing, it remains a strengthening force in football. Leading clubs often have foreign owners and they continued to be active in acquiring clubs during the Covid-19 pandemic. Overseas television revenue is becoming more important to the Premier League while domestic revenues actually diminished in the last settlement. Footballers migrate from Africa and Latin America to play in the European leagues. Football is celebrated as a global game, its appeal resting in part in its simplicity, which means that it can be played for fun with very basic equipment. Yet in many respects it remains highly conservative. This reluctance to embrace change can stand in the way of needed reforms.

Forces for change

Football is not dissimilar to any other economic sector or industry. In assessing what drives the evolution and development of an industry, important considerations would be the role of technology, patterns of ownership, market structure and consumer demand, and how these are changing. To understand what is going on in football, each of these aspects needs to be considered in turn in relation to what has become a global game.

Technology

The adoption of technology has always been mediated by culture, and this is particularly true of the subculture of "the world of football". Football has not undergone many technological changes and those that have come along have often been strongly resisted. Floodlights were initially treated as a novelty with their own special competitions. They were met with resistance from administrators, and it took some time to realize their potential in terms of evening matches and later kick-off times in winter. The concern being that "evening football would keep working men from the family home" (The Away Section 2019). They were not, of course, the only spectators, but their presence at the match was seen as a potential social harm.

Laced leather balls, which were heavy and easily became waterlogged, were replaced with a resultant improvement in performance and a reduced risk of injury to players, in particular the long-run risk of developing dementia. Artificial pitches have been controversial in part because they are seen as giving an advantage to teams used to playing on them, but also because they offend traditionalists. Any non-league team with an artificial pitch promoted to the Football League would have to replace it, as happened to Harrogate Town in 2020. The introduction of video-assisted refereeing (VAR) has been opposed by many fans who believe it spoils the spontaneity of the game. Although some of the problems may have arisen from associated and subsequent rule changes, particularly on handball, and the way in which decisions have been communicated, VAR has also revealed that many refereeing decisions are genuinely borderline.

However, the technological changes that have had a profound impact on football have been external to the game itself. The really transformative technology has been satellite broadcasting. The competition between terrestrial television channels was insufficient to drive up the price paid for coverage to clubs. They were also not very innovative in the way in which they covered football, in terms of utilizing new technology to interpret the game, camera positions and angles, and the range and diversity of commentators used. The involvement of satellite broadcasting in televising matches all over the world has created a new financial dynamic and created a situation in which "followers" become more important than "fans". Satellite broadcasters constantly need new and fresh content that attracts and retains subscribers, and football is ideal for that purpose. Live sport sells subscriptions, particularly to key demographics for advertisers, such as young males. In 1992, "[f]earing stagnation from earlier losses of £14m a week, Sky needed to secure live Premier League football to survive" (Bower 2003: 105). It is satellite broadcasting that has created the riches of the English Premier League. By the end of the second decade of the twenty-first century, however, there were signs that growth in the subscriber numbers was slowing or even going into reverse. In turn this meant that broadcasters were reluctant to increase their bids for exclusive coverage of league games.

The Covid-19 pandemic was an additional complicating factor. The Premier League, the Bundesliga, La Liga and the Champions League all granted rebates to the broadcasters to compensate for spring lockdowns. The Bundesliga was the first major league to conclude a television deal, and it had to take a €200 million – 5 per cent – reduction on a €4.4 billion deal over four years. In retrospect this could be seen as a good outcome. A warning of possible future trends came in the autumn of 2020 when Mediapro skipped one of its payments to France's Ligue 1 and stated that it wanted to renegotiate the deal, arguing that the absence of fans from grounds changed what was on offer. They subsequently withdrew from the agreement and Ligue 1 had to replace it with a much less lucrative deal. The dispute was seen as "the first indicator of a painful correction in the multibillion-euro market for European football's media rights" (Abboud & Ahmed 2020). There had already been indications that peak television revenues for football had been reached, but the pandemic was a final blow to the free-spending era for television executives and football clubs alike.

Patterns of ownership

From the mid-1990s "a new breed of club owner" has emerged in European football, "members of the super rich with little or no connection to the club they had bought ... By the end of 2016 foreign owners had bought, or held significant shares in, 15 of the 20 Premier League teams" (Montague 2017: 6). The motivations for buying clubs range from the commercial to the political and the personal. As a consequence, there is considerable variation in ownership strategies and styles. On the whole, fans are not too concerned about the owner's history, as long as they provide a substantial, steady stream of funding and don't interfere in the affairs of the club in a way that damages the playing side.

This variation is illustrated by five of the "big six" Premier League clubs, all but one of which have foreign owners (see Table 1.1). The exception is Tottenham Hotspur where the majority shareholder is British billionaire Joe Lewis, who lives in the Bahamas.

Having built up his interest in Arsenal over a number of years, Stan Kroenke took full control of the club in 2018. He has extensive sports franchise interests in the United States in American football, basketball, hockey, football and even lacrosse. He is known as "silent Stan" to Arsenal fans because of his lack of communication with them. Unlike other owners, he has put no money into the club. His approach illustrates the limitations of a profit-driven franchise model, although it can be executed with greater skill than has been the case at Arsenal.

Table 1.1 English Premier League club owners 2020/21

Club	Majority owner(s)	Country of origin	Principal business
Arsenal	Stan Kroenke	USA	Sports franchises
Aston Villa	Nassed Sawins, Wes Eden	Egypt/USA	Fertilizers, cement/ investment (Fortress Investment Group)
Brighton & Hove Albion	Tony Bloom	UK	Property, development, real estate
Burnley	Mike Garlick, John Banaszkiewicz*	UK	Management consultancy/Freight Investor Services
Chelsea	Roman Abramovich	Russia	Oil and industry
Crystal Palace	Joshua Harris, David Blitzer, Steve Parish	USA/UK	Private equity investors, sports franchises
Everton	Farhad Moshiri	Iran and UK (Monaco resident)	Steel and energy
Fulham	Shahid Khan	USA	Automotive industry, sports franchise
Leeds United	Andrea Radrizzani	Italy	Global investment company in media and sports sectors
Leicester City	Srivaddhanaprahaba family	Thailand	Airport concessions
Liverpool	Fenway Sports Group	USA	Sports franchises
Manchester City	Sheikh Mansour	Abu Dhabi	Hereditary ruler
Manchester United	Glazer family	USA	Sports franchises
Newcastle United	Mike Ashley	UK	Retail
Sheffield United	Abdullah bin Musa'ed	Saudi Arabia	Manufacturing
Southampton	Gao Jisheng	China	Inheritance
Tottenham Hotspur	Joe Lewis	UK (resident outside the UK)	Currency trading
West Bromwich Albion	Lai Guochan	China	Landscape development and construction
West Ham United	David Sullivan	UK	Print media
Wolves	Fosun International	China	Conglomerate and investment company

Note: * Two bids from potential foreign owners were made for Burnley in the autumn of 2020.

Arsenal is financially successful, having coped with the financial consequences of the move from Highbury to the Emirates Stadium. They have reported profits for 16 consecutive years that total £393 million, averaging £25 million a year, but in 2019 they reported their first loss since 2002. Only four clubs in the Premier League had worse results in 2018/19 than their £32 million pre-tax loss. Even so, Arsenal had the highest cumulative profit of any of the top six clubs in the period since the formation of the Premier League in 1992 to 2020 (£480 million). Fans want to see profits reinvested in the club (Arsenal Supporters' Trust 2020). Arsenal has spent money on new players: they haven't always spent it very well. They became bolder in their spending in the summer of 2019, in part because of the consequences of their failure to qualify for the Champions League, which was hurting the club's bottom line.

The purchase of Chelsea by Roman Abramovich in 2003 heralded the arrival of big-spending foreign owners in the Premier League. For Abramovich, Chelsea was an insurance policy that protected him and his assets from the long arm of Putin. Abramovich bought Chelsea for £60 million in 2003 and took on its £90 million of debts. He had lent the club a total of £1.17 billion by 2018. They made the biggest losses of any of the big six clubs, £797 million in the period from 1992 to 2020. However, the extent of Abramovich's subsidy has been scaled down from the early years of his ownership. Beset by visa restrictions, plans to rebuild Stamford Bridge were abandoned, and it was reported in 2019 that he was willing to sell the club.

The Chelsea business model has been to run large operating losses (driven by a substantial wage bill), offset by big profits from player trading. The 2017/18 season was no exception with a £47 million operating loss more than compensated by a £113 million profit on player sales. Research undertaken by the Swiss Ramble blogger shows that "[t]heir business model is far more reliant on player sales than any other major English club. In the last five years [to 2019], they made a hefty £337m from this activity with only Tottenham Hotspur anywhere near them (£192m in four years)" (*Political Economy of Football* 2019a).

Liverpool FC shows how a franchise model can work well, when there is good judgement and a balance of prudence and ambition. The objective has been to increase the financial value of the club. The Fenway Sports Group, owners of the Boston Red Sox baseball team, acquired the club in 2010. Plans to build a new stadium did not go ahead, but Anfield was expanded, particularly through the provision of more lucrative corporate hospitality seats. Capacity was increased in 2016 from 44,000 to 54,000 with 7,500 corporate hospitality places. The club's 2017/18 profit of £125 million was the second highest ever reported in the Premier League, although admittedly this was reliant on player sales, which can be volatile. Their pre-tax profit in 2018/19 was £42 million, and they have made a cumulative profit of £138 million in the Premier League years since 1992.

In the autumn of 2020, RedBall Acquisitions announced that they planned to take a 20 per cent stake in Fenway Sports Group as part of a plan to develop a portfolio of clubs in Europe. A deal was not reached, but the club started to explore similar options. The implications for Liverpool FC were ambiguous, but on balance a recapitalization was probably beneficial in the middle of an ongoing pandemic when cash flow problems were likely to get worse before they got better.

Manchester City provides the ultimate example of a benefactor club with an owner with unlimited resources at his disposal. The club was acquired by the Abu Dhabi United Group headed by Sheikh Mansour in 2008 (the investment group China Media Capital acquired a 14 per cent stake in 2015). One of the factors in the purchase was "one-upmanship in the intense competition between the UAE's two most powerful emirates" (Montague 2017: 213). They effectively became the richest club in the world overnight. By 2018, £1.3 billion had been invested in the club. In 2018 and 2019 they were top of the Footballex football finance 100. Manchester City topped the global rankings with a Football Finance Index score of 4.71, which factors in five variables – playing assets, fixed assets, money in the bank, potential owner investment and net debt (Footballex 2019). The club made cumulative losses of £636 million between 1992 and 2020.

The contrast with the strategy pursued across the city at Manchester United could not be greater. The Glazer family were already owners of sports franchises in the United States when they purchased Manchester United in 2005 using debt, which the club then had to service. As Montague observes, "Manchester United FC effectively paid for its own takeover, as well as its continued upkeep" (2017: 86). The Glazers' takeover has in fact drained United of more than £1 billion in interest, costs, fees and dividends since 2005, not far off the amount Mansour has invested into City (Conn 2018). In 2019 total interest costs since 2005 amounted to £809 million, exceeding the amount originally borrowed. By 2018 they still had debts of nearly half a billion pounds. The club was listed on the New York Stock Exchange in 2012 as a means of acquiring funds to reduce debt. Their cumulative profit in the Premier League was £266 million.

Manchester United has remained a formidable cash generator, always at the top or near the top of the Deloitte Money League, although their revenues fell by 19 per cent in the year ended June 2020 because of the effect of the Covid-19 pandemic and other factors. Their £1.3 billion earned in revenues over the decade to 2019 is almost twice as much as the next highest, Arsenal with £754 million (*Political Economy of Football* 2019b). Manchester United has remained a highly sophisticated marketing machine, able to exploit its global fan base to keep it financially ahead of rivals and attract a wide variety of sponsorship. In 2018 it earned £666 million in revenues, more than a third of which were from commercial contracts. However, it is no longer true that "[s]ince it was formed in

1992, the Premier League has belonged to Manchester United plc" (Conn 1997: 42). Inevitably Manchester United's dominance would have been challenged by the emergence of well-funded rivals, even if the owners had been different.

The club's struggle to find a satisfactory replacement for Sir Alex Ferguson as manager, who was always building a new team even when he had a great one, is difficult to ignore. A team like Manchester City can afford to hire Pep Guardiola, one the best managers in the world, while Chelsea have been able to fund the compensation involved in their frequent changes of manager, even if the settlements are sometimes contested.

Foreign owners of English clubs have been motivated both by prestige and profit. However, even at the generously funded benefactor clubs, Chelsea and Manchester City, there has been a move towards self-sustainability. The three franchise clubs are run in very different ways, although for all of them long-run profit is the objective.

The big six have enjoyed success both on and off the pitch. Since the start of the Football League in 1888 until 2016/17, the same six clubs had never finished in the top six more than twice (across 117 seasons). Now Manchester United, Manchester City, Liverpool, Arsenal, Chelsea and Tottenham Hotspur have finished as the top six four times in the six years to 2020, five times in the past decade.

The big six have 3.3 times the income of the other 14 Premier League clubs (see Table 1.2). Big six wages are three times those of the other 14. The other 14 have 2.6 times the income of parachute payment clubs. In turn the parachute clubs have three times the income of other Championship clubs, bringing home the distorting effect of parachute payments. The Championship has 2.9 times the income of League One and League One has 1.6 times the income of League Two.

The big six have different financial strategies, but are generally secure. However, they would like an even bigger share of the available funding, and there is a case for them taking a larger share of the available broadcasting money. International deals have taken up a bigger and bigger share of the money earned from broadcasting. Viewers outside the UK want to see matches between the big clubs with a global profile. This led Liverpool and Manchester United to devise in secret the controversial "Project Big Picture" revealed in October 2020. Their plan was to reduce the league to 18 clubs and give greater control to the big six clubs. Just the bottom two teams in the Premier League would be relegated automatically; the 16th-placed team would join the Championship play-offs.

Project Big Picture attracted widespread opposition both from government and from within football, although some, such as crusading football journalist David Conn, saw it as a basis for negotiation.

The plan was quickly dropped, but it is likely that the big six will make renewed attempts to corner a bigger share of football's riches for themselves.

Table 1.2 Comparison of Premier League "big six" with "other fourteen", 2018/19

Metric	Big six	Other fourteen	Difference
Profit (loss) before tax	+£33 million	–£188 million	£221 million
Revenue	£3 billion	£2.2 billion	£845 million
Revenue growth	£240 million	£103 million	£137 million
Match-day revenue	£495 million	£187 million	£308 million
Commercial revenue	£1.16 billion	£295 million	£821 million
Television Europe	£427 million	£1 million	–£426 million
Wages	£1.7 billion	£1.5 billion	£200 million
Wages/turnover ratio	55%	68%	13%
Operating expenses	£631 million	£387 million	£244 million
Gap between 6th and 7th highest Premier League clubs by revenue	Arsenal	West Ham	£204 million
Revenue gap 2012			£373 million
Revenue gap 2019	Revenue share 58%	Revenue share 42%	£845 million
Player sales	£193 million	£241 million	–£48 million

Source: From data collected by Swiss Ramble.

Many analysts think that the real agenda here is the formation of a European Super League. Indeed, veiled threats to proceed in that direction have been made. However, the European Super League idea has been around for a long time and has never got anywhere near being made a reality, although it acquired new momentum in early 2021.

At the core of the plan was a special voting status for the big six, alongside three other clubs with a long-term Premier League record (Everton, Southampton and West Ham United). Changes could be made with the support of just six of these nine long-term "shareholders", effectively allowing them to set the future course of the Premier League.

The English Football League (EFL) would get a £250 million bailout package and 25 per cent of all future revenue. However, as with many aspects of the plan, the devil is in the detail. In the Project Big Picture calculations the value of EFL television rights were assumed to stay at the present level of £119 million per year, ignoring the fact that the deal covers both EFL matches and the league cup (currently sponsored by Carabou). The league cup would be dispensed with under the plan, along with the Community Shield, although few fans would miss that. It has been estimated that the league cup is worth two-thirds of the value of the broadcast rights, as the leading clubs draw the big viewing figures. With no league cup, the value of the rights could fall by about £80 million a year. In addition EFL clubs would lose the chance to play one of the big teams, denying those clubs money and their fans the chance to see their club play a more famous opponent.

A key feature of Project Big Picture is that Premier League clubs would be able to sell their own television rights for eight games a season internationally. This anticipates the likelihood that streaming, or selling via Amazon, could account for a bigger share of revenues in the future. This would have the effect of reducing the value of the centrally negotiated television deals and concentrate more money in the hands of the big clubs. It would also mean that the value of the 25 per cent of revenue going to the EFL would go down.

One aspect of the plan, which many found attractive, was that the highly distorting parachute payments would be scrapped. These mean that there is not a level playing field in the Championship. Another sweetener was that fan away tickets would be capped at £20. Although this particular plan was dropped, the big six are likely to continue to pursue their agenda in a different form and changes that are in their interest are likely to come eventually.

Market structure

Football's market structure has two principal elements: the clubs themselves and the competitions in which they take part. These competitions are principally leagues with cups, including the FA Cup, of declining significance. A cup run can still be a very significant source of revenue for a cash-strapped lower-league or non-league club. For example, Newport County income increased by £900,000 to a turnover of £3.2 million in 2017/18 due to its FA Cup matches with Leeds and Tottenham Hotspur. Cases such as these may provide some justification for references to the "magic" of the FA Cup, but cup revenues are of secondary importance to leading clubs, which is why so many of them put out below-strength teams. For example, in 2017/18 Tottenham Hotspur received almost 23 times the income from the Champions League as they did from the FA Cup. The club banked £63.2 million as a result of qualifying for the last 16 of the Champions League in 2018/19, compared to £2.8 million for reaching the FA Cup semi-finals.

If a league structure were being designed today, it probably would not consist of 92 clubs in the Premier League and EFL. Indeed, almost all clubs in the fifth tier of the National League, and some in the sixth tier competitions, have full-time squads. Some clubs constantly struggle to survive, for example those in the Greater Manchester conurbation where two leading Premier League clubs are available. This surely contributed to Bury's recurrent financial difficulties.

The situation in Scotland is even more challenging with "the highest number of professional football clubs per capita in the world", although given that it also had an attendance per capita exceeded only by Cyprus it could also be seen as one of the "most easily quantifiable signs of a still deep and rich football culture" (Goldblatt 2019: 297).

A possible solution that would make positive use of the competitive imbalance between clubs is prohibited by the rules of the competition. A club cannot be a "nursery" or "feeder" club for a larger one; although for many years there was an informal relationship of this kind between Liverpool and Crewe Alexandria. Linked clubs were banned from entering the FA Cup after 1937 leading to the dissolution of a mutually successful relationship between Arsenal and Margate (Arsenal History Society 2019).

The normal response to overcapacity in an economic sector would be mergers. These have occasionally occurred among non-league teams, such as Solihull and Moor Green merging to form National League Solihull Moors. On the rare occasions they have been proposed for league teams, there has been a furious reaction from fans, as happened when the late Robert Maxwell proposed to merge Reading and Oxford United to form the Thames Valley Royals, possibly to play at Didcot (BBC 2019a). The importance of clubs as a source of identity for their fans means that a merger is not possible even if a stronger team for a particular city was the result. Ground sharing is unusual and usually temporary, although stadiums may be shared with rugby clubs. Hence, Dundee and Dundee United continue to play in their separate stadiums a few hundred metres apart.

American sports, including Major League Soccer (MLS), are organized in a different way from football across the world. The league allocates franchises to a group of owners with an exclusive territory and in some cases, such as baseball, it also controls the allocation of players through a draft system, which "operates so that the weakest team from the previous season gets the first choice of the college players coming through to the professional leagues for the new season" (Gratton 2000: 14). Franchises can and have been transferred from one city to another. In 2006 the San Jose Earthquakes football team moved to Houston and became the Houston Dynamo, but the franchise was revived at its original location in 2008.

The franchise system is anathema to British football and European football more generally. Wimbledon FC were playing at Crystal Palace's ground Selhurst Park and attracting poor attendances. Consideration was given to moving to Ireland, either to Dublin or Belfast. Eventually, the club was allowed by the Football Association (FA) to move to Milton Keynes where it was reconstituted as the MK Dons. This decision attracted considerable criticism and Wimbledon fans formed a phoenix club, AFC Wimbledon, which rose through the non-league pyramid to play in League One of the Football League alongside MK

Dons. The unpopularity of this decision means that it is highly unlikely to be repeated.

American owners of football teams find it difficult to come to terms with the system of relegation, which is entirely unknown in the United States. Despite generous parachute payments for teams relegated from the Premier League to the Championship, relegation can be a significant financial blow to a club. It can result in a substantial deterioration in its value, undermining any hopes of selling it on at a profit. However, the Premier League is aware that the annual relegation battle helps to stimulate interest in the competition at a time when the outcome at the top of the league may have been decided.

The market structure of English football was fundamentally altered by the formation of the Premier League in 1992. In 1990 a secret meeting of the self-appointed "big five" clubs (Arsenal, Everton, Liverpool, Manchester United and Tottenham) sought "FA support for the big clubs' divisive and devastating plan to break away from the other three divisions of the Football League and form their own elite, the Premier League" (Conn 2005: 4). Motivated by their long-standing and rather petty rivalry with the Football League, the FA were prepared to go along with this scheme regardless of the impact on lower-league clubs. Without the FA's support the breakaway would not have gone ahead. Apart from anything else, the clubs would probably have been excluded from European competitions. The FA was outmanoeuvred by the big clubs who appropriated the lion's share of the money for themselves.

The year 1992 also saw the transformation of the European Cup into the Champions League. This represented another victory for the biggest clubs. Szymanski (2015: 118) argues that:

> the Champions League has done much to increase the inequality of revenue distribution in football. Between 2003 and 2012 almost half of all prize money paid out by UEFA from the Champions League went to just ten clubs ... And it has largely been the traditionally dominant clubs that have benefitted most from the unequal distribution of the new European TV money.

Of a total of €1.8 million paid out by UEFA in 2017/18 in distributions for the Champions League and the Europa League (a much smaller component) two-thirds went to clubs in the "big five" leagues (Deloitte Sports Business 2019: 8).

The total amount distributed to clubs in the 2018/19 Champions League in-creased by 54 per cent (€681 million) from €1.269 billion to €1.950 billion. This was split: participation €488 million (25 per cent), performance €585 million (30 per cent), television pool €292 million (15 per cent) and coefficient rankings €585 million (30 per cent). In 2018/19 each of the 32 clubs that qualified for the

Champions League group stage received €15.25 million plus €2.7 million for a win and €900,000 for a draw. Additional prize money was awarded for each further stage reached.

The new UEFA coefficient distribution method clearly benefits traditional big clubs like Real Madrid, Barcelona and Bayern Munich at the expense of clubs from countries with large broadcast pools (i.e. England and Italy). However, the overall increase in Champions League prize money, driven by booming television and commercial deals, meant that English clubs still earnt more in 2018/19 than 2017/18, if one assumes similar progress in the competition: "The lucrative value of this competition to the "big six" ... has resulted in clubs spending more of their revenue on wages to obtain and retain the best playing talent" (Deloitte Sports Business 2019: 2).

The Swiss Ramble blogger estimated that the English clubs have earned the following revenue to April 2019 from the Champions League (previous season in brackets):

- Liverpool €92 million (€81 million)
- Tottenham Hotspur €86 million (€61 million)
- Manchester City €93 million (€64 million)
- Manchester United €94 million (€40 million).

The Swiss Ramble commented:

> It has also become clear that it pays to have a good history in Europe, as shown by the case of Manchester United. Clearly, this has implications for those clubs in the Premier League that have not qualified for Europe, as it's once again a case of "the rich getting richer," which poses yet more questions about competitive balance in football.
>
> (*Political Economy of Football* 2019c)

A constant topic of discussion for at least 30 years has been the evolution of the Champions League into a European Super League. In its most developed form, the participating clubs would cease to take part in domestic competitions, although most versions are less radical than that. One view is "that the Champions League is already a super league in all but name" (Szymanski 2015: 27). Often, however, the threat of a super league is used to extract concessions in relation to the format of the Champions League.

In 2019 proposals were put forward by the European Clubs Association (ECA), representing over 200 top European clubs, to restructure the Champions League to create what might be termed a Super Champions League. The intention was to make it a more exclusive competition in which top clubs would have a more or less permanent place. The top 24 clubs in the Champions League would automatically qualify for the next year's competition, creating an effective elite cartel. Four places would be given to teams "promoted" from the Europa League. Just four sides would qualify based on performances in their domestic competitions. In some ways it represented an adaptation to European circumstances of an American model of professional sport in which the same franchises stay in place.

One of the main backers of the proposal was Andrea Agnelli, chairman of the ECA and president of Juventus. It was also backed by FC Barcelona. However, seven other Spanish clubs, although not Real Madrid, had criticized the plan. All 20 Premier League clubs also opposed the plan as they feared it would detract from the value of their lucrative broadcast rights. At a meeting of the ECA in Geneva in September 2019 progress on the plan was halted because of a lack of support, although that does not mean that it could not reappear in one form or another. The commercial logic is that such a competition would appeal more to global television audiences, who are the spectators that really matter.

One aspect of market structure that has attracted criticism from both clubs and fans is the role of players' agents. Intermediaries are never popular in any market, think of lawyers or estate agents, but they often perform a useful function. However, agents have been accused of taking money out of the game, lining their pockets at the expense of clubs and in some instances engaging in dubious practices. Clubs nevertheless feel obliged to deal with them to obtain the best players they need to be successful.

Having admitted that it was a mistake to deregulate agents in 2015, FIFA announced the introduction of new regulations in 2021. The amount agents earn from transfer deals will be made public. Commission will be capped at 3 per cent of a player's salary when representing a player, 3 per cent of a player's salary when representing the buyer and 6 per cent when the same agent represents both the player and the buyer. An agent representing a selling club can earn a maximum of 10 per event of the transfer value (BBC 2020a).

Consumer demand

The redefinition of the fan as a consumer has important implications for the discussion of how football can be regulated. Domestically the fan becomes an object of marketing efforts designed to turn his or her allegiance into a flow of money. However, the global fan becomes an increasingly important source of funds through television revenues and merchandise (albeit a revenue stream that is undermined in some countries by counterfeit goods).

UK domestic Premier League television rights actually dropped 7 per cent (£0.4 billion) from £5.4 billion to £5.0 billion in the 2019–22 payment cycle, but this decrease was more than offset by overseas rights, which increased by 34 per cent (£1.1 billion) from £3.1 billion to £4.2 billion. Overseas rights are now worth almost as much as UK domestic rights: 45 per cent compared to 55 per cent. In 2001–4, they only accounted for 11 per cent of the total. The increase in Premier League overseas broadcast rights is particularly striking in terms of encouraging clubs to orient towards a global fan base (an ambition, for example, of Wolverhampton Wanderers) and it is anticipated that they may overtake domestic rights in the 2022–5 cycle. These now average around £1.4 billion a year, up from £1.1 billion in the 2016–19 cycle. As recently as 2007–10 these were only worth £200 million a year.

Overseas broadcasting rights have always been distributed as equal shares by the Premier League, but this was changed in the 2019–22 deal. Originally the big six clubs asked for 35 per cent of overseas broadcast money to be distributed according to final league position, arguing with some justification that it was their matches that drove overseas television sales. If that proposal had been adopted, every club finishing below 13th would have been in a worse financial position. The agreement arrived at was that clubs will continue to share current levels of overseas revenue equally, but any increase will be distributed according to where they finish in the league. This was the result of pressure from the big six with the constant threat of a breakaway to a European Super League or replacing collective rights negotiation by individual rights negotiation in the background.

These trends increase the distance between the fan and the club. The notion of a club implies the idea of a like-minded group of individuals with a common identity and goal forming a bond of allegiance, whereas in fact clubs are in large part corporate entities concerned with boosting revenues and increasing market share. The brand loyalty of the fan makes him or her susceptible to marketing ploys. Fans located in other countries are both geographically and culturally distant, and some might argue that they are not really fans at all, any more than a domestic fan that follows a team on television but never visits its stadium. However, "[t]he overwhelming majority of fans of football in Britain are armchair fans in the sense that they hardly ever go to games" (Kuper & Szymanski 2012: 244). They quote data that shows that 45 per cent of British adults are interested in football, but only 3 per cent make up average weekly attendances in England and Scotland. Armchair and overseas fans are potentially even more susceptible to the manipulation of image through marketing techniques. The cultural distance may actually increase the appeal of the marketing message. It allows them to attach themselves to something that is "world class".

If you listen to radio phone-ins or read a book like *Fever Pitch* (Hornby 1992), it is easy to imagine that the typical fan stays loyal to a particular club their whole life, often having been introduced to it by parents or older relatives, and continue to travel long distances to games even if they move away from their home area. Such fans do, of course, exist, but they are not typical. In fact, "it has always been the case that the majority of people who go to English football matches go only once in a while, and are often quite fluid about who they choose to watch" (Kuper & Szymanski 2012: 251). Success is a big factor in attendances, which generally fall when a club is relegated. The amount of "churn" among fans only increases the importance of successful marketing and treating them as a consumer.

A common complaint made by fans and some journalists is that the demographic base of football is changing. High ticket prices exclude traditional working-class supporters and also cannot be afforded by younger people, leading to an ageing support base. According to Wood, "In 1960, tickets at Chelsea's Stamford Bridge cost 1% of the average weekly wage, which rose to almost 3% by 1990 and in 2010 stood at 10%" (Wood 2018). Supporters have become more affluent with clubs particularly keen to sell lucrative corporate boxes. Nevertheless, observations of this kind often overlook the fact that society as a whole has become more middle class and affluent with a decline in the number of those in manual occupations: "Spectatorship is something of a neglected area in sports research" (Malcolm *et al.* 2000: 129). The surveys that are undertaken often have a marketing focus looking at such issues as which devices fans use or their "brand engagement". Conn concludes that "the excluded are a minority; most people who always went to the football will somehow find the wherewithal to go" (2005: 11).

How do these forces for change interact? Satellite broadcasting has transformed the audience for football, accelerating its globalization and creating unprecedented wealth at the top of the game. Foreign owners have poured their fortunes into the game for a variety of motives, boosting the dominance of top clubs. The Premier League and the Champions League have interacted with pay-per-view television to reinforce the gap between the biggest clubs and the rest. These clubs are always seeking new opportunities to enhance their wealth, whether by moving the Champions League towards a "super league" format or taking a bigger slice of television revenues. This environment encourages marketing techniques directed at the fan as consumer and some see this as producing an alienated supporter. However, attendances are increasing. Attendances in the EFL reached their highest levels for more than 60 years with more than 18.3 million supporters watching league fixtures in 2018/19. This was the third consecutive year that the 18 million barrier had been broken, with the average gate at all three divisions at over 11,000. Premier League attendances were 9.7 million in 1992/93; 12.5 million in 2000/01; and 14.5 million in 2018/19.

The need for effective regulation

Left to their own devices, markets can destroy themselves and the benefits they can confer. This was evident in the global financial crisis when the creation of a pyramid of assets based on insecure debts led to a cataclysmic financial market collapse with wide-ranging repercussions for the economy as a whole. Although there are many small and medium-sized clubs, football has developed many of the characteristics of an oligopoly in which a few big companies can collude to their mutual advantage and to the detriment of both smaller clubs and consumers.

Consumers are always notoriously difficult to organize because they are so heterogeneous: for example, they vary in their averseness to or acceptance of risk. The Consumers' Association in Britain manages to fund its campaigns through its magazine, *Which?*, and selling a range of advisory services to members. The challenges are even greater in relation to football because fans tend to focus on issues relating to their own club, or even particular matches, rather than being concerned with a broader agenda about football as an industry. However, the formation through merger of a single national fans' representative organization, the Football Supporters' Association, in 2019, is a step forward. It seeks to be a representative body for football supporters in England and Wales, campaigning on a wide range of issues related to the game.

The governance of football clearly needs to improve, but this is unlikely to happen from within for a variety of reasons. The primary aim of the Premier League and the Football League is to run a competition for the benefit of their member clubs. They have undertaken regulatory measures such as the Owners' and Directors' Test, but these are widely regarded as falling short of what is needed. At an international level, FIFA has been beset with problems of corruption.

Hence, external intervention is required by the state, both at a domestic and an international level in the form of the EU. The dysfunctional aspects of free market capitalism have been tempered by the development of a regulatory state, which provides a framework of rules, backed up by sanctions, in which the economy operates. This has been particularly important at the EU level where, given its limited budgetary resources, its main mode of operation has been to issue regulations in the form of directives. EU directives range over all aspects of economic activity, from the safety of toys to the environmental performance of white goods to the hours we work.

However, regulation by the state has been largely absent from football which, sporadic and ad hoc interventions aside, has largely been left to regulate itself despite evident deficiencies in its regulatory arrangements. Measured against the advance of the regulatory state, it has continued to enjoy considerable autonomy in its governance arrangements: "Historically, sport in Britain was a quintessential example of an activity regulated autonomously in the sphere of civil society" (Moran 2003: 73).

The privatization of nationalized industries gave a substantial boost to the regulatory state in the UK, leading to the formation of a number of regulatory bodies. These were initially focused on particular industries such as telecommunications or electricity, but some of them were subsequently merged to create bodies with a wider remit across related industries. Beyond these innovations made necessary by privatization, there was a more general appetite for the regulation of economic activity: "[The] consensus held that [regulatory support] should be provided not primarily by politicians, driven by the vicissitudes of the electoral cycle and the distortions in the market for votes, but by regulators, operating within a well-understood statutory framework, and supported by evidence and analytical rigour" (Tyrie 2019). However, this technocratic vision was never completely fulfilled. The regulatory state evolved in a very different way from the depoliticized regulatory state envisaged in the 1980s and 1990s. There has been a move away from a model based just on market efficiency and consumer welfare and curbing the activities of monopolies and oligopolies. Regulators became politically salient in a way that had not been envisaged.

There were a number of reasons for these developments. Faced with asymmetry of information problems, utility regulators were often disappointed with their levels of performance. This was particularly apparent in the water industry, which often seemed to offer a combination of higher charges, deteriorating service and a failure to achieve environmental objectives alongside greatly increased profits. Thames Water has had a particularly chequered industry. It was acquired by a German utility company in 2001 and then sold on to an international consortium. It has a bad record of dealing with water leaks and in 2017 was fined £20.3 million after repeated leaks of untreated sewage. It attracted a further fine of £2 million for spilling raw sewage into a river in 2018. It was criticized by the regulator, Ofwat, in 2019 as "the water giant's costs were 25% higher than justified and customers were at risk of poor service. It also questioned whether Thames could meet leakage reduction targets" (Bow 2019).

The global financial crisis highlighted the shortcomings of financial services regulation, particularly in terms of the treatment of vulnerable customers. It enhanced awareness of the way in which markets could fail and the limitations of "light touch" regulation. There was more pressure to consider the distributional implications of regulatory activity, particular in terms of the impact of less well-off sections of the population. There is an increased awareness of individual and societal harms and a demand for more citizen engagement in the regulatory process. MPs started to focus more on regulatory issues and developed new tools of oversight. Government departments paid regulators more attention, issuing more strategic directions.

The challenges that have emerged to the conventional idea of the regulatory state have led to a revival of interest in the concept of "responsive regulation" first advanced in 1992. It is not a simple means of overcoming increased complexity or the fact that regulatory objectives may conflict with one another, as "Responsive regulation is not a clearly defined program or a set of prescriptions concerning the best way to regulate. On the contrary, the best strategy is shown to depend on context, regulatory culture, and history" (Ayres & Braithwaite 1992: 5). As far as football is concerned, this implies a need to identify the specific objectives to be achieved and sensitivity to the special features of the sector, and "Responsive regulation does not provide a complete answer to the problems of designing tools for regulation or of applying tools in different combinations, nor was it intended to" (Baldwin & Black 2007: 11).

It should not be thought that responsive regulation involves privileging any one stakeholder, as "Responsive regulation involves listening to multiple stakeholders" (J. Braithwaite 2019). In the case of the UK, this would involve the parent department; the regulated industry; Parliament; and the relevant public, in this case football supporters. It has to be recognized that there is a tension between acting responsively and acting responsibly. Regulation cannot serve one particular agenda, and it should be rule based in an effort to make it as impartial as possible. This is a particularly difficult task in such a partial arena as football and it would be important to specify which tasks were excluded from the remit of the regulator, for example, the behaviour of game officials.

The purpose of regulation and creating regulatory capacity

Without a clear objective it is difficult to set up an appropriate institutional framework for regulation. The particular challenge in the case of football is that "its regulatory and competitive structures were formed in the nineteenth century when the economy in which football operated was totally different to that of today" (Banks 2002: 32). External interventions in the game were often driven by considerations of crowd control, and "Much of the legislation has been generated in response to disasters, and [therefore] contemporary policy has been driven by the twin factors of public safety and public order" (Greenfield & Osborn 2001: 37). Ground safety has improved beyond recognition, and although football hooliganism has not disappeared there is no lack of legal mechanisms to deal with it and greatly improved surveillance technology within grounds.

The principal preoccupation of fans in demands for the regulation of football is the "rogue owner" problem, someone who by his or her actions, intentionally or not, undermines the viability of a club. This is not as easy to resolve as might first appear to be the case. More stringent tests could be devised and applied, but reducing the number of prospective bidders could make it difficult to find own-ers for some clubs. It is possible to scrutinize a prospective owner's past record in terms of their financial track record and the absence of criminal convictions or regulatory penalties. It should also be possible to assess whether they have the funds they claim to have. It would also be reasonable to ask new owners for a business plan setting out their objectives for the club and how they intend to achieve them, including how they propose to engage with fans.

The real challenge arises when an owner deviates from announced plans once ownership has been secured. One question that arises is how to test whether there has been sufficient deviation to give rise to legitimate concern. Fans may be disgruntled with a new owner, but that is not sufficient reason to deprive him/her of control. Fans often have unrealistic expectations about what can be achieved within a given time period. One consideration would be whether there had been sufficient consultation with fans about plans for the club and their im-plementation. If an owner is found to be unsatisfactory, the question then arises regarding what any regulator can do about it. A club is a privately owned entity, and it cannot be readily expropriated.

Another issue is the level at which regulation should take place. This needs to reflect the different arenas in which football is played. Most football games are played domestically and clearly the national associations and leagues have a key role, even if they have been reluctant to assume their responsibilities. Similarly, government has been keen to leave football to put its own house in order. The House of Commons Digital, Media and Sport Committee (2016) noted that

> [it] has repeatedly urged the football authorities to improve self-gov-ernance. Although the Committee's recommendations have been backed by successive Sports Ministers and progress has been promised by the FA, in practice very little has changed: the governance of football is cumbersome, and power lies with the clubs, especially in the Premier League. Real reform in relation to the ownership of clubs, transfers of players, the influence of fans, the role of agents and investment in the grassroots – amongst other issues – has stalled.

Regulation and governance at an international level have been undermined by endemic problems of corruption. Given the centrality of Europe in the world of football, it did seem at one time that the EU as the premier regulatory body might play a key role in the establishment of a regulatory framework. However, its initiatives were not sustained as it was overtaken by other, more pressing issues on its agenda. Its role, and that of UEFA and FIFA, is explored more fully in Chapter 7.

2
GLOBALIZATION

On a summer's day in 2008 I was walking around Reykjavik when I heard football chanting. Following the sounds, I located the ground of KR Reykjavik and went in to watch the match. Without knowing a word of Icelandic I was able to understand immediately what was happening in the game and to respond to the local fans around me. Football is a universal language, shared everywhere, and participating in a game whether as a spectator or a player creates mutual understanding.

Football has become a global sport and is subject to the forces of globalization that have shaped the world economy over the last 40 years. The experience of globalization has sparked considerable debate and led to the creation of a variety of theoretical perspectives that seek to explain the phenomenon and understand its effects on the economy and society. Globalization itself is a contested concept, not least because it has been used normatively as well as analytically. Competing definitions of globalization abound and it is important to note that it has a number of dimensions: principally economic, cultural and political. In broad terms, it is a process that reduces the significance of national boundaries as an impediment to the free movement of capital, goods and services and (to a far lesser and more contested extent) of labour. It is a process in which international trade grows faster than national output; foreign direct investment grows faster than national trade; and there is a transformation in response of international financial markets. These trends have been facilitated by advances in communication and digital technology, which Goldblatt (2019: 26) argues "have been the key to the economic globalization of football, multiplying the game's audience many times over, and forging the basis of the phenomenal income it now generates". However, it is more than a single economic dynamic, or even a set of them, but "a syndrome of changes of social relations that also produce deep tension" (Markovits & Rensman 2010: 27n).

How far football has been globalized is a more complex and nuanced question than it may first appear. Goldblatt (2019: 26) puts the case for pervasive and damaging globalization: "[Twenty-first] century football has experienced a profound globalization of its player and coach labour markets, the ownership of clubs and its patterns of consumption and fandom, and its immersion with the global television industry and the huge global money-laundering, gambling, gaming and leisurewear markets".

Scholte (2000: 15–16) set out five alternative definitions in terms of internationalization, liberalization, universalization, Westernization and deterritorialization. He prefers the last definition, which regards globalization as the spread of supraterritoriality: "globalization entails a reconfiguration of geography, so that social space is no longer wholly mapped in terms of territorial places, territorial distances and territorial borders" (Scholte 2000: 16). This immediately sets up a tension in terms of the way in which football has been historically framed. Supporting a club was about identification with a particular geographical territory, albeit in some cases religious divisions within a given territory may have also been significant dividers, as in Glasgow (Rangers FC being Protestant and Celtic FC being mainly Roman Catholic, and together known as the "Old Firm").

The Covid-19 pandemic has raised the question of whether globalization is over. O'Sullivan (2019: 55) had no doubts: "Globalization … is in retreat and will not return". Of course, this is an argument that has been made before in the context of the 9/11 terrorist attacks in 2001; the global financial crisis of 2008; and, more recently, the trade wars between the US and China. In the context of the pandemic, emphasis has been placed on the fragility of long and complex supply chains. The supply chain in football is far simpler: it consists of getting a signed player to the club. It may, of course, be the case that the composition of globalization is changing. Economic globalization has slowed: even before Covid-19, "global trade had stagnated for a decade. By [2019] foreign direct investment (FDI) as a share of GDP [gross domestic product] had fallen by two-thirds compared with its peak in 2007" (*The Economist* 2020). It can be argued that "[t]he kind of growth in physical goods that marked recent waves of globalisation is indeed slowing. But cross-border activity in other areas, for instance in knowledge services or flows of data, continues to expand, suggesting that new forms of cross-border integration can develop even as the traditional ones decline" (Crabtree 2019).

Even if globalization in general is halted or even reversed, this may not apply to world football. It became evident that the pandemic would not slow foreign direct investment in football in the form of merger and acquisitions activity. Private equity groups saw it as an opportunity to buy distressed assets in the form of clubs with long-term growth opportunities given that the consumer appetite for football was unlikely to diminish. In August 2020, the US-based Friedkin Group acquired effective control of AS Roma. The price was €591 million, a considerable reduction on a €750 million offer made before the Covid-19 pandemic.

It is not often that there is a chance to buy a league, but that is what happened with Italy's Serie A in the summer of 2020. The whole competition was effectively put up for sale because already debt-laden clubs hit by the Covid-19 crisis were desperate for cash. Serie A used to be one of the world's top competitions, but it fell behind its rivals. The €1.2 billion it secured in television rights is well behind the amount secured by the Premier League. In the 2018/19 season Serie A generated €2.5 billion in revenues compared with €5.8 billion for the Premier League. Serie A clubs made a collective loss of €318.3 million last season, whereas those in La Liga made a collective profit of €230.8 million.

Luxembourg-based buyout group CVC started the ball rolling with a €2.2 billion offer for a 20 per cent stake in a new company to manage the league's broadcast rights and its commercial development. They teamed up with Advent International and worked with Italian investment fund Fondo FSI to take a 10 per cent stake in a new company managing Serie A's broadcasting rights. The eventual deal could be worth €1.6 billion. Fifteen clubs voted in favour of the offer and five abstained. Some club executives think the league is worth more than the €11 billion implied by CVC's original bid. The pandemic could actually stimulate further globalization in football even if it is in retreat elsewhere.

How would this increased globalization affect the relationship between fans and clubs? As supporters become geographically and socially mobile, this identification can remain important to them, indeed in a sense it may become more important to them. It becomes a way of showing that they have not been separated from their origins, that they still remain true to a particular image of themselves. In many ways this is a highly constructed image, but that does not diminish its psychological importance. Michael O'Sullivan, who describes himself as a "passionate supporter" of Manchester United, grew up in Ireland and has never lived in Manchester but complains that, "like many other clubs that used to express the ethos of their local regions, Manchester United has now largely become a consumer brand, with a global base of supporters and a set of players disparate in background and spirit". He evidently feels no cognitive dissonance in stating: "It has lost touch with its roots, its culture and its winning ways" (O'Sullivan 2019: 27). Following a team "is about family and friends, about business and politics, about wealth and identity" (Everitt 2019: 19).

The idea of the fan as a passionate self-identifier unconstrained by geography may not be completely in conflict with the conception of football clubs as brands that need to be marketed globally, often in conjunction with the multinational providers of sports equipment such as Adidas and Nike (Bridgewater 2010). These can be substantial commercial deals. Nike negotiated a £50 million deal with Chelsea and Arsenal, and a £71 million deal with PSG in the summer of 2019.

In October 2019 the question of whether Liverpool should continue with a deal with New Balance was resolved in the High Court. Liverpool's proposed kit deal with Nike was worth £15 million less a year than their existing deal with New Balance. However, on top of the £30 million a year agreement on offer there was a commitment to pay the club a 20 per cent royalty on net sales of Liverpool products. They would also promote the club through stars such as Serena Williams, illustrating a global crossover with other sports. The club thought the deal would allow them to tap into Nike's global marketing reach and distribution. New Balance alleged that Liverpool was in breach of a matching clause agreement allowing it to extend its contract. The court ruled that the Nike offer was the better one.

Liverpool supporters were no doubt satisfied that their club got the best deal on offer. The more general point to emerge is that globalization and local identities may sit alongside one another, at least as far as the fan is concerned. The fan's primary concern is with the success of the club. If that means attracting followers in, say, South Korea, who will buy merchandise and lead to local sponsorships, all well and good. It does not prevent supporters maintaining their traditional identity; it simply helps to enhance the team's performance on the pitch.

Glocalization

Glocalization – a merger of "globalization" and "localization" – has become an important element in the analysis of globalization in football, offering an alternative interpretation of the inexorable march towards a homogeneous global game. Glocalization is in evidence when "social actors combine globally circulating culture to pre-existing cultural frameworks at the local level" (Jijon 2017: 83). Some analysts "locate the cultures of glocalisation at the heart of the sociology of football" (Giulianotti & Robertson 2004: 562). Steger presents the concept by using the example of the men's football World Cup "as a way of exploring complex 'glocal' dynamics" (Steger 2017: 2). Some analysts go so far as to argue that international football "has essentially a *glocal* nature, and is guided by a glocalisation process" (Andersson *et al.* 2011: 189).

Glocalization offers the possibility of resistance to globalization, but it is more likely to represent the mediation and adaptation of global forces. The process of globalization comes to be seen through local cultural lenses that can interpret it in different ways. Thus, "local cultures and groups may absorb, transform and reject certain dimensions of globalization" (Markovits & Rensman 2010: 27*n*). There are, of course, limits to this process, and in some ways it could be a means of tolerating and accepting the burden of globalizing forces. Seen as a marketing rather than an intellectual challenge, the objective of glocalization "is to balance the global/universal with the local and particular", by offering "a mid-path between total standardization and local adaptation of the marketing offer" (Bridgewater 2010: 143). Internationally owned football clubs thus "possess strong degrees of glocality" (Giulianotti & Robertson 2004: 562).

As Jijon notes (2017: 83), some scholars in the literature are sceptical about the value of descriptions of "glocal culture", arguing that "they do not reflect the creative agency of social actors, but are 'facades' hiding global homogenization". An alternative perspective is that "glocalization is marked by social actors' fluid and critical engagement with, and reconstruction of, local and global phenomena" (Giulianotti & Robertson 2006: 173). It opens up the possibility of the invention and construction of particular traditions by the fans themselves which they believe they own. Particularism becomes universal so that "[s]pecific local cultures worked inside football's universal rules to establish their own football 'traditions', as illustrated by distinctive corporeal techniques, playing styles, aesthetic codes, administrative structures and interpretative vocabularies" (Giulianotti & Robertson 2004: 549). They may even allow migrants to retain their own distinctive football cultures when no longer living in their own home country, although they may become more tolerant of supporters of rival teams living alongside them and the subcultures may not persist across generations. This was evident in a study of Scottish football supporters living in North America (Giulianotti & Robertson 2006).

How far glocalization is more than a local adaptation that offers a means of coping with the impersonal forces represented by globalization processes is a matter for debate. One benign view is that glocalization offers a means of reconciling supporters to the sometimes harsh realities of a global football landscape. Andersson *et al.* (2011: 203) "put forward the glocalisation of supporters as the trend that is most adapted to the transformation of the football landscape". This is an area that is beset by admittedly often instructive paradoxes and ambiguities. It is possible for the same author to argue that "football is not the same everywhere" and admit that "all teams play by the same rules, work with the same global organization, and (ostensibly) understand football in the same way" (Jijon 2017: 82–3). The similarities in the way the game is played are more important than the differences, but the differences make the game more culturally acceptable. This does make it easier in some ways to offer fans a marketable and hence commercially profitable version of reality, but it also opens up potential channels of resistance.

The concept does sensitize us to the two-way flow of cultures and perceptions between the global and the local. It alerts us to the possibility that "local politics and cultures (and sports cultures) may have global impact" (Markovits & Rensman 2010: 27*n*). However, perhaps the most important take-away message from this debate in terms of the concern of this book with issues of regulation is political rather than cultural or social: "Glocalization describes the parallel shifts towards global *and* local scales of political relationship" (Giulianotti &

Robertson 2006: 173). It also calls forth new political structures that attempt to bridge the gap between the global and the local, notably the EU.

It is possible to have two contrasting views of the EU in relation to globalization. One is to see it as facilitating globalization by creating an internal market that removes barriers to the operations of multinational companies. The other is to see it as an entity that offers its citizens some protection against the worst effects of globalization by creating a distinctive social space. These perspectives are not, of course, incompatible with each other: the actions of the EU might do something to reconcile its citizens to globalization. What is clear is that the EU is potentially an important actor in relation to football as its territory contains the richest clubs and the most expensive players, although admittedly this has been diminished by Brexit with the Premier League now outside the EU. Its actions in relation to football have been somewhat sporadic and ad hoc, but they have had a considerable impact, which is discussed later in the chapter.

When we add in the role of national football competitions and authorities, we are faced with four intertwined dimensions: global, regional, national and local. Steger reminds us that "the global should not be rigidly separated from the national" (Steger 2017: 2). That is not to deny that what happens locally may be substantially influenced by global forces.

One manifestation of glocalization is the way in which high-profile football clubs can boost their local economies, particularly given the development of football tourism, in which tours of top matches are organized for visitors from, say, Norway. These are admittedly easier to organize in London where it is possible to offer more than one top-flight match over a weekend, or at least a Premier League and a Championship game. A major football club also helps to raise the profile of a city, facilitating the attraction of overseas investment.

A report commissioned by Liverpool from Deloitte Sports Business Group highlighted the positive impact the club's activities had on the city and its immediate region, amounting to just under £500 million gross value added. The club's activities support more than 4,500 full-time equivalent jobs across the Liverpool economy (2.3 per cent of jobs in Liverpool):

> More than 1.5m football fans came to Anfield in the 2017–18 season and the impact of visitors from outside the local area is reflected in their £102m contribution to the visitor economy of the Liverpool City Region – broken down into £42m spend on accommodation, £28m in the area's restaurants, cafes and bars, £15m on travel, £12m in the region's retail, and a further £5.4m on groceries and other items.
>
> (Liverpool Football Club 2019)

Liverpool calculated that 140,000 spectators who attended Anfield during the course of the 12 months were from overseas, with visiting fans increasingly spending several days in the city.

An earlier study completed in 2013 by Cambridge Econometrics looked in greater depth at the impact of football on Greater Manchester. It was estimated that football supported 5,000 full-time equivalent jobs in Greater Manchester, and that the gross value added associated with footballing activities was £330 million per annum in 2011. In addition to the positive impact on tourism, and not just on match days, it was noted that "Missions looking to attract trade and investment to the Greater Manchester area use football in a number of ways. The most direct method is co-ordinating mission dates with Manchester United and Manchester City on their summer tours to major overseas markets" (Sport Industry Research Centre 2019: 40).

Even smaller clubs can have a significant economic impact. A study that was commissioned by Brighton and Hove Albion – "and carried out by Marshall Regen and the University of Chichester – shows that the club's economic contribution in 2017/18 to the local economy was valued at a staggering £212 million". It also showed that the club was "one of the most significant contributors to the economic growth of the Greater Brighton City region" (*Brighton & Hove Independent* 2019).

Globalization can clearly bring local economic benefits through the medium of football. Its relationship to questions of supporter identity is more problematic. It is possible to have a global football presence and still maintain and nurture specific identities, FC Barcelona and Catalonia being an important example. Elsewhere in Spain, in the Basque country, Athletic Bilbao shows how a very distinctive identity can be maintained alongside success commercially and on the pitch. For more than a century only those born or raised in the Basque country have been eligible to play for the club, the only one in top-flight European football to restrict itself to local players. Nevertheless, the club is one of Spain's most successful, having won the league eight times. Over the past decade they have performed well enough to qualify for European competition on seven occasions, reaching the Europa League final in 2012. They are one of La Liga's wealthiest clubs with revenues of €134 million in the 2017/18 season, almost double what they earned five years earlier.

However, they could be regarded as the exception that proves the rule. The relationship between culture and globalization is complex and contested. Culture can provide a means of resistance, or at least a prism through which the experience of football is refracted in different countries and locations. A football match in Buenos Aires, Glasgow, Liverpool, Milan or Islington offers very different cultural experiences, but for most of those watching it is experienced second hand and in a diluted, even censored form, on television.

Resistance to globalization

The aftermath of the financial crisis

Globalization has been presented by its proponents as a benign force, an opportunity rather than a challenge, a promoter of economic efficiency that benefits consumer welfare. Even those who were more sceptical about its benefits were inclined to take a deterministic view of it as an irresistible force. The prevalence of neoliberal thinking in which markets are permitted to operate in a largely unconstrained fashion with only "light touch" regulation meant that its critics faced an uphill battle.

All this was called into question by the global financial crisis of 2008 which was the most severe economic crisis since the Great Depression of the 1930s. Although there were widespread economic consequences, the political effects were slow to emerge. In part this was because there was an absence of alternative paradigms in the way that the crisis of the 1930s had led to Keynesianism or the crisis of 1970s had popularized the concept of government failure.

The political paradigm that eventually emerged was populism, although it took many forms and its definition was contested. However, one of its key characteristics was the emergence of demagogic leaders with authoritarian tendencies who challenged or disregarded the conventional rules of the political game. They enjoyed electoral success based on an appeal to at least some parts of the population. They particularly emphasized the need to control migration but had a wider economic nationalist agenda which represented a direct challenge to globalization. One consequence was a turn towards protectionism with a resurgence of trade wars, most notably between the United States and China, and a weakening of the authority of the World Trade Organization (WTO).

The limits of resistance in football

None of this, however, really shook globalizing trends in football. The television-based model of the Premier League increased its reliance on overseas markets. One of the major impacts of globalization on football was the growth of foreign direct investment, stimulated by the growth of a new super-rich global elite. Football attracted "a new breed of club owner, one that had been largely unseen in world football until the mid-1990s: members of the super-rich with little or no connection to the club they had bought" (Montague 2017: 6).

Just consider the case of Serie A in Italy, perhaps not the most attractive destination for international investment given issues with crumbling stadiums, the presence of "ultras" and a not particularly lucrative domestic television deal. In

2011 Thomas DiBenedetto, a US private equity magnate, led a group of US investors to buy a controlling stake in AS Roma, making them at the time the first foreign owners of a top Italian club. At the time Serie A had slipped financially behind other leading European leagues.

In 2017 Li Yonghong acquired AC Milan from Silvio Berlusconi. After Li defaulted on high-interest loans, US hedge fund Elliott Management gained control of the club in 2018. In 2016 Suning Holdings, a Chinese retail conglomerate, paid €270 million for a 70 per cent stake in Inter Milan. In June 2019 US billionaire Rocco Commisso acquired ACF Fiorentina for an undisclosed sum. As noted above, AS Roma changed hands again in 2020.

The continued viability of a globalization model is illustrated by the case of City Football Group (CFG), the parent company of Manchester City which is 78 per cent majority owned by the Abu Dhabi United Group. CFG has more than 1,000 players at its disposal and a club presence on every continent. New York City FC is jointly owned by the Yankees and CFG. A 20 per cent stake in the Yokohoma Marinos in Japan was purchased in 2014, while 44 per cent of La Liga side Girona was acquired in August of that year. Melbourne City in Australia was bought in 2014. In 2017 CFG acquired the Uruguayan side Club Atletico Torque, which they describe as an investment that "enables CFG to build on existing connectivity in the country and helps to expand the currently limited options for identifying and developing local Uruguayan and South American talent" (City Football Group 2020). In 2019, with China Sports Capital, they acquired Chinese League 2 Sichuan Jiuniu as the seventh club in their global portfolio. This was followed by the acquisition of a majority stake in Mumbai City. In May 2020, CFG agreed a deal to acquire a majority stake in Lommel SK in the Belgian Second Division, a club with a strong academy and youth development record. In September 2020, CFG announced that France's Ligue 2 club Espérance Sportive Troyes Aube Champagne had become its tenth club.

It is interesting that they portrayed the Mumbai City purchase as very much part of a glocalization strategy. CFG chief executive Ferran Sorriano said: "We are a global organization and now we have football clubs in eight countries. But we are and we want to be very local. The best clubs in the world are embedded in the societies of their cities" (ISL media team 2019). Globalization has to be adapted to local circumstances if it is going to succeed. Sorriano emphasized: "The first thing we will do is learn. We need to learn about India, we need to learn about Mumbai, about Mumbai City" (ISL media team 2019).

CFG "is a global resource that provides help to each club with everything from scouting and recruitment to analytics and innovation" (Hughes 2017). It has also globalized the style of play: "All clubs in the global network are directed to play in the attractive, attacking footballing style pioneered by Manchester

City manager Pep Guardiola. They also benefit from shared sponsorship deals and youth player development programmes" (Vandevelde & Ahmed 2019).

In November 2019 CFG sold 10 per cent of the group for £389 million to American private equity house Silver Lake in a deal that values CFG at £3.75 billion, more than a billion pounds higher than Manchester United which at that time had a market capitalization of $2.8 billion, and far outweighing Juventus at $1 billion. This gave CFG a valuation of $4.84 billion, a record for a sports group. Five-sixths of the $782 million revenue in 2017–18 came from Manchester City (Lex 2019).

The valuation did seem on the high side given that CFG had been losing £1 million a week over the previous couple of years. However, Silver Lake would not have put in such a large sum of money unless they were confident that City would succeed in avoiding a Champions League ban for its breaches of financial fair play rules (the outcome is discussed further in Chapter 7). Silver Lake reckoned that even if City were given a Champions League ban, they would still be worth the valuation.

Group chairman Khaldoon Al Mubarak said: "We and Silver Lake share the strong belief in the opportunities being presented by the convergence of entertainment, sports and technology and the resulting ability for CFG to generate long-term growth and new revenue streams globally." Silver Lake said its investment would "help drive the next phase of CFG's growth in the fast-growing premium sports and entertainment content market" (BBC 2019b). The emphasis on entertainment in relation to football is interesting. A more traditional view would be that supporting a team involves as much suffering as entertainment, but perhaps that does not apply to teams like City.

Silver Lake is best known for its technology, investing in companies such as Alibaba, Dell and Skype. However, in recent years it has pivoted towards entertainment and its acquisitions include a Hollywood talent agency. They had approached other leading English and European clubs, including Chelsea: "The firm was attracted by the multibillion-dollar prices paid for football media rights by broadcasters and internet groups" (Ahmed 2019a).

Braithwaite questioned the statement by Silver Lake boss Egon Durban that CFG is "an impressive global platform of marquee football clubs across five continents" (T. Braithwaite 2019). Admittedly, they are second- or third-rank teams, but what is important is the capacity for growth in cities like New York, Mumbai and Melbourne. The smaller clubs provide an opportunity to identify and develop promising players. Braithwaite argues that the fan base for Manchester City is "thin". It is the case that at one time they were more of a city-oriented club than Manchester United, but they are catching up in terms of global presence. He also argues that the entire media rights market is on shaky ground. Admittedly the last auction for domestic television rights saw a 10 per cent decline but it was outpaced by overseas rights sales which account for an increasing share of the total sum, although possibly also starting to plateau. He makes no mention of streaming rights, which are seen as a lucrative new market.

CFG believed that the Silver Lake deal provided a vindication of its business strategy. However, making money through CFG, with City the only profitable club in the network, will take many years. Some think that CFG has as much to do with the exercise of soft power by Abu Dhabi as it does with making money, in particular using "sportswash" to offset a poor human rights record. Soft power is an idea introduced by thinker Joseph Nye (1990) and is used to describe the move away from coercive forms of power – such as military power – at the end of the Cold War. Nye argued that a "state may achieve the outcomes it prefers in world politics because other states want to follow it or have agreed to a situation that produces such effects. In this sense, it is just as important to set the agenda and structure the situations in world politics as to get others to change in particular cases" (Nye 1990: 166).

Grix and Brannagan (2016: 252) comment that "[a]s part of the strategic shift from employing 'hard' to 'soft' power, states have increasingly used sport in general and sports mega-events ... in particular". Such events "provide national governments with significant opportunities to increase their soft power, through cultural showcasing on global television, 'attracting' tourists and augmenting national pride" (Brannagan & Giulianotti 2015: 706).

It has been argued that, notwithstanding its extensive deployment, soft power is "a highly confusing and problematic concept with which to work" (Grix & Brannagan 2016: 256). Its precise definition is unclear, as is the mechanism by which it is acquired. Nevertheless, it is capable of refinement and does tap into a significant phenomenon. In many respects it may be portrayed as a form of persuasive power, based on enticement and attraction, and Nye used co-optive power as an alternative term, "getting others to want what you want" (Nye 1990: 167) and argued that it is just as important as "hard command power". Events in the post-Cold War era turned out rather differently than anticipated and hard power remained important. However, soft power was another route for achieving foreign policy goals and sport generally, and football specifically, was one possible mechanism.

There are, however, reputational risks that can lead to soft disempowerment, as happened in the case of Qatar and the World Cup. The country's soft power strategy ran into difficulties with critical international comment about its role as a host for the global tournament. Attention was drawn not to Qatar as a well-run modern state but "to bribes surrounding the acquisition of the tournament itself; the state's controversial laws concerning gay rights; concern [about] a winter World Cup ... and finally, and most significantly, Qatar's severe lack of human rights for its migrant workers" (Brannagan & Giulianotti 2015: 716).

The Pozzo family have developed a more modest version of the globalization model, owning both Watford in the UK and Udinese in Italy. They also owned Granada in Spain from 2009 to 2016. The Pozzo model is based upon an extensive scouting network across the world that buys young and upcoming talent for relatively small sums and, when they turn into stars, sells them on for a large profit which is then reinvested in the club and other signings. However, another attempt to develop a network model ended in failure. Belgian millionaire Roland Duchâtelet acquired Standard Liege in Belgium and Charlton Athletic in England, as well as clubs in Germany, Hungary and Spain. However, his stewardship of the clubs attracted criticism and he eventually disposed of almost all of them.

RedBall Acquisition Corp, a special purpose acquisition company set up by baseball executive Billy Beane and Gerry Cardinale, founders of the private equity firm Redbird Capital Partners, raised $575 million in August 2020 with the aim of acquiring a sports franchise. They are interested in building up a portfolio of European football clubs, demonstrating the continuing attraction of the sector to international financiers.

Cultural globalization

Cultural differences can be a source of resistance to globalization, yet football has been able to overcome cultural differences to become a universal object of attention. According to Goldblatt, "Football is first: the most global and most popular of popular cultural phenomenon in the twenty-first century" (Goldblatt 2019: 3). All that is needed for a game is a ball and some improvised goal posts. It is a universally accessible sport and readily played almost anywhere in the world.

There are countries with allegiances to long-established sports that football has to compete with. Australia has been a stronghold of cricket and rugby, but also has its own distinctive game, Australian rules football, played across the country but with particularly strong roots in Victoria. While it can be an entertaining game to watch, its rules can be baffling to outsiders, and it has not been exported on a significant scale elsewhere in the world. Soccer was for a long time predominantly associated with migrant ethnic groups, which affected its image negatively. The A-league, established in 2005 as a successor to earlier football competitions, has had its challenges, but is slowly gaining traction. It is helped by the success of the national team, the Socceroos, most of whose players are with clubs outside Australia: "The A-league, in its own terms, has been a success. Although it has struggled to find the right balance and distribution of clubs and owners, attendance and television ratings have been respectable and rising, without seriously challenging the country's other professional sports leagues" (Goldblatt 2019: 401–2).

Cricket has to date been the most popular mass sport in India. However football, as Goldblatt writes, "is emerging from beneath a blanket obsession with cricket of the last few decades as a new marker of cosmopolitanism and class distinctions" (Goldblatt 2019: 2). When CFG bought a stake in Mumbai City in 2019 their chief executive said: "the step was following careful consideration and research, which convinced the group of India's bright future in football … ten years from now, we'll be here talking about a lot of people playing good football in India, a very good national team, a good league, good teams and Indian players who are going to be stars on the world stage" (ISL media team 2019). Rather unusually, India has two recognized top-tier leagues, the I-League, founded by the governing body, and the Indian Super League (ISL). I-League teams often have good local support, but the ISL, which has just eight clubs, is a highly commercial, media-oriented operation using an American-style franchise system.

In the United States baseball, basketball and American football dominate the sporting scene, and ice hockey also attracts many fans. At one time the commonly held view was that "football would never catch on in America and that it was just a game for 'ethnics' or high school wimps that could not make the football, baseball or basketball team" (Hopkins 2010: 29). The first attempt to create a national football league in the United States, the North American Football League, lasted from 1968 to 1984. The signing of Pelé in 1975 by the New York Cosmos created much greater interest in the competition. However, even his signing and that of other foreign stars failed to create a sustainable basis for the development of football in the USA, although it did demonstrate the game had potential and not just among Hispanics. The foreign players could not be afforded with the revenues the teams generated and the league succumbed to financial failure. Nevertheless, it left a legacy of enthusiasm for the game, particularly among younger fans. It was "a failed league, yes; a failed experience for many, no" (Hopkins 2010: 29). It also helped the game to develop a substantial following among women. The success of the American women's national team in the 1999 World Cup also made an important contribution: "In the United States, women entered into a soccer space that was marginal at best and managed to construct a level of excellence in it in two decades that really has few parallels in any sport practiced by either gender" (Markovits & Rensman 2010: 159).

A new league, the MLS, began playing in 1996; initially with ten teams, by 2019 it had 26 teams with plans to expand to 29 and then 30. Goldblatt (2019: 470) suggests that "football has finally found a place in the mainstream of American sports culture". Success enjoyed by both the men's and women's national teams has undoubtedly helped, and although "[S]occer in the United

States remains some way short of the big three, [it] is certainly challenging ice hockey for number four" (Goldblatt 2019: 472). This is, of course, still very different from the majority of countries where football is the number-one sport. The interest shown by the Hispanic population has been important to football making inroads in the United States. Although there has been a considerable expansion in the numbers of home-grown quality players, some of whom play for well-regarded European clubs, there is still a reliance on marquee players in the form of overseas stars as a marketing device, such as David Beckham at LA Galaxy who subsequently became involved in establishing an MLS franchise in Miami.

Football has made adaptations to the specific features of United States sports culture, particularly in terms of the way in which competitions are organized. Changes to the game itself such as a countdown clock and shootouts in place of draws did not find favour with fans and were abandoned. However, the league operates on a franchise system with no team subject to relegation. Each team is owned by the league and operated by investors. New teams have to pay an entry fee. The two most recent expansion additions, St Louis and Sacramento (California), each paid $200 million entry fees, but this could increase to $300 million for the next entrant. Taxpayers often find themselves contributing funds for the prestige of having a football team. In the case of Charlotte's bid for a franchise in North Carolina, the bid "is contingent upon $100 million worth of taxpayer money that would be used to make football-specific improvements at the NFL stadium and to help pay for a team headquarters" (Charlotte Business Journal 2019). The team is expected to begin playing in 2022.

Japan was another country that distanced itself from football in the twentieth century with baseball and sumo being the country's dominant sports. The presence of baseball demonstrates that Japan is a country willing to import innovations from elsewhere. Whether football is "likely to replace baseball and sumo as the country's twenty-first century central sport" remains to be seen. The national team has reached the round of 16 in the World Cup on three occasions, losing narrowly to Belgium in 2018 and further success will consolidate the popularity of the game. The very global character of football serves as an attraction, however, compared with baseball "framed primarily as a binary with American baseball … By contrast, football is the only major team sport that is truly global in expanse, and it allows Japan to position itself in a far wider and more complex field of world sports competition" (Kelly 2013: 1236).

The motivations for overcoming cultural resistance to globalization in football vary from one country to another. In the USA the main driver was the perception of a new commercial opportunity demonstrated by the involvement of franchise owners also involved in other sports. This overcame notions of American exceptionalism, which at one time were seen to be prevalent, leaving the USA aloof from the world's most popular sport (Markovits 1990). In India commercial motives have also been important, with the success of cricket's premier league being a stimulus, although involvement from outside the country has been more important than in the USA. In Australia migrants were important in the early development of football, which affected its image, but in the longer run success in football was seen as part of Australia's identity as a sporting nation. For Japan the global nature of football was of itself a positive factor, allowing the creation of a broader sense of national belonging (Kelly 2013).

What is evident in all these cases is that although football encountered some cultural resistance or antipathy, it was able to entrench itself through its global appeal, made available through new forms of media. Admittedly, this story is most unambiguous in the case of the men's game. The women's game encountered different resistances and higher barriers, which are discussed in detail in Chapter 6.

The globalization of football has required it to adapt to local cultural circumstances. However, countries that are behind the curve in terms of their involvement in football are generally keen to catch up. It is also used as a means of exercising "soft power" and one way of promoting the game is through state intervention.

Promoting football: state intervention

China: promoting domestic football and restraining foreign investment

China's economic reform in 1993 started a process of the professionalization and commercialization of football. A league system modelled on that of Western countries was launched in 1994. Private ownership of clubs became possible but "the football league remained under the tight control of the government" (Hong & Zhouxiang 2013: 1650). A series of match-fixing and corruption scandals led to disillusionment among fans and a new competition, the Chinese Super League (CSL), was created in 2004, which "pushed modernisation and globalisation further, and partially reduced top-down, centralised national management" (Connell 2018: 8).

In some ways there are parallels between the CSL and MLS in the United States. Both have a penchant for signing marquee players – big or fairly big names that are past the peak of their careers – that attract the crowds. China "rapidly joined in the ... 'sports grab' of players, analogous to global land grabs, that represents market participation on a grand scale" (Connell 2018: 13). However, the political environment is very different in China with the Communist Party exercising considerable control over the trajectory of football development.

For President Xi, football offered a means of exerting soft power, alongside the development of the economic might of the People's Republic. China's long march into football saw substantial investment in European clubs. It was hoped this would be a means of learning about the playing and coaching skills required in the game, as well as raising China's international profile. However, it was also hoped, rather optimistically, to make money from the investments. An important motivation was to win political credit with Xi and the party hierarchy. It was thought that the overseas investments would help China gain experience and expertise to develop its domestic game. Some purchasers had a more commercial motivation. They hoped to use cheap financing to buy clubs before selling them on for a profit. By 2019 China owned 13 per cent of the top hundred clubs in the world with only the United States owning more (Footballex 2019).

However, it did not all go to plan. The big capital outflows concerned the Communist Party at a time when the economy was slowing and there was not enough investment in developing local talent to build up the national team. Hence, clubs were reined in and the global impact of Chinese spending in the transfer market is no longer as great as it was.

The Chinese Football Association, which is under government control, introduced a tax of 100 per cent on transfers worth more than $7 million. Consequently, Javier Mascherano's transfer to Hebei China Fortune was just below the $7 million threshold. In the two previous winter transfer windows the CSL had spent more on transfers than any other league, but in 2017/18 they only spent $86 million, down from $500 million, and well behind the $700 million spent by Premier League clubs.

Aston Villa became the fifth European football club in which a big Chinese investor has sold all or some of its stake following the introduction of investment restrictions by the Chinese authorities. Others include AC Milan, Atletico Madrid, Slavia Prague and Northampton Town. The Chinese government set out new criteria for overseas investment in August 2017, placing sports clubs on a list of "restricted" sectors. The investment curbs made it more difficult for Chinese owners to pump money into their often loss-making clubs.

The initial deluge of Chinese money had led to a "Wild West" environment in which some investors were significantly overpaying for clubs, and advisers were cashing in. Between 2014 and 2017 Chinese investors pumped more than $2.5 billion into European clubs. Leading investors included Fosun, the tourism to finance conglomerate; China Media Capital, the media and sports group; and, until it sold its stake in Atletico Madrid, the Wanda Group.

The case of AC Milan is instructive. As mentioned earlier, AC Milan was acquired in April 2017 by a Chinese businessman, Li Yonghong, for $840 million from Silvio Berlusconi, the disgraced Italian prime minister. Li hoped to exploit the club's large Chinese fan base. The takeover was funded by $340 million of high-interest loans from Elliott Asset Management, a $38.2 billion hedge fund. In July 2018, Li defaulted on the loans, losing nearly $600 million in equity overnight. Elliott effectively acquired AC Milan for $472 million, just half of what the club had been valued at months earlier.

An even stranger situation beset Northampton Town and demonstrates how enthusiasm for football in China can displace commercial judgement. Chinese investors 5USport sold back their 60 per cent stake to the club's directors in 2018. The new overseas investment restrictions by the Chinese authorities were cited as the reason and certainly there had been a clamp down on speculative investments in football clubs. However, it was never clear how linking up with a League One club was going to help 5U's educational offering in China, even given their ambition to develop products and services in the area of sports training.

Fosun's $58 million acquisition of Wolverhampton Wanderers in 2016 was probably the most successful deal, as Wolves went on to win promotion to the Premier League and establish themselves there as a significant force in Europe. The Chinese owners of Aston Villa and AC Milan got their fingers burnt after taking on big debts as part of their acquisitions, hoping success on the pitch and favourable financing in China would help them pay off their loans. At Atletico Madrid Wang Jianlin's Wanda group made a small profit when he sold his 17 per cent stake.

European clubs were also interested in the potential of the Chinese market for broadcasting and merchandise sales, although one challenge is that Chinese fans often tend to follow individual star players rather than teams. Manchester United will open three so-called "experience centres" in China by 2020. One of them will be adjacent to Beijing's iconic Tiananmen Square. The objective is to capitalize on the club's fan base in the world's most populous country. Arsenal got ahead of them as they opened a Shanghai bar festooned with sports memorabilia in 2018.

CFG added a third-tier Chinese club, Sichuan Jiuniu, based in Chengdu, to their global football portfolio in 2019. Club executives had considered acquiring teams in the CSL but were put off by sky-high valuations at elite Chinese clubs, few of which are being run profitably. Instead, CFG hopes to build the Sichuan Jiuniu team with the aim of being promoted into China's top division, while also using the club to find and train young players capable of taking part in Europe's leading leagues. The group jointly acquired the club alongside China Sports Capital. This is a group co-founded by China Media Capital, which holds a 13 per cent stake in CFG, illustrating the two-way investment flow between China and Europe. In essence, football in China "demonstrates how sport is affected by globalisation, how football contributes to globalisation, and how the search for soft power and the dynamics of state intervention add additional levels of complexity, where both globalisation and the dissemination of soft power are contested processes" (Connell 2018: 13).

China's use of soft power in football

China has been experimenting with the use of soft power since the mid-2000s, the 2008 Beijing summer Olympics being an important milestone. It "is viewed as one of the elements necessary to realize the 'Chinese Dream' – the revitalization of Chinese society and achievement of national glory. The concept of soft power is also prevalent in Chinese academic discourse, with works by Chinese intellectuals forming a large part of the body of literature on Chinese soft power" (Kalimuddin & Anderson 2019: 116).

The Premier League game between Arsenal and Manchester City on 15 December 2019 was pulled by Chinese state television after the Arsenal player Mesut Özil made remarks on social media about the treatment of Uighur Muslims in China (claims denied by China). A Chinese state newspaper described Özil's comments as "false" and claimed he had "disappointed" the football authorities. In addition, the Chinese Football Association denounced Özil's comments as "unacceptable" and that they had "hurt the feelings" of Chinese fans (BBC 2019c).

Arsenal was quick to distance itself from their player's remarks on Chinese social media, saying that they were those of an individual and not the club, emphasizing that the club was apolitical. Any exclusion from the lucrative Chinese market would be a commercial blow for Arsenal. In this instance, China took action against an individual club rather than the Premier League as a whole in contrast to its treatment of the National Basketball Association in October 2019, when a team manager in the United States tweeted support for the democracy protests in Hong Kong. Chinese firms suspended sponsorship and telecast deals leading to substantial commercial losses.

The BBC's Beijing correspondent Robin Brant commented in relation to Özil: "The NBA's crisis in China showed how serious and how immediate the impact on commercial interests could be. So important is football to the UK and its soft power that very senior British diplomats have pondered the impact on UK China relations of something like this" (BBC 2019c).

Clearly this matter raises some troubling issues. China is very quick to react to what it sees as unjustified criticism of its domestic or foreign policy. They are ready to use such occasions as a means of emphasizing their commercial power. In terms of how football should react, one view would be that clubs need to think about the commercial consequences of what are seen in China as unwelcome interventions in its domestic affairs. The alternative view would be that the ability to speak out against claimed human rights abuses should not be curtailed. Whether footballers (like actors) should use their celebrity to intervene in politics is a matter for debate.

The Gulf states

Although the Gulf states have experimented with establishing largely unsuccessful domestic leagues, their main involvement in football has been at an international level, both through the acquisition of clubs and with Qatar's successful bid to stage the 2022 World Cup, a controversial episode that is discussed more fully in Chapter 7. The soft power of football has enabled the Gulf states to use their wealth to project themselves onto the world stage and improve their international image.

Sheikh Mansour, a member of the Abu Dhabi royal family, was behind the acquisition of Manchester City by the Abu Dhabi United Group in September 2008. For Abu Dhabi, the success of Manchester City "has helped to promote a vision of the Gulf state to the world – of a progressive, Western-friendly, pro-business beacon of stability in a turbulent neighbourhood" (Montague 2017: 205). However, there has been criticism levelled at City's ownership, describing it simply as a "a means of projecting Abu Dhabi's soft power and damping criticism of the United Arab Emirates' human rights record" (Ahmed 2019a).

There has also been a willingness to acquire clubs outside the Premier League that have potential. In November 2020 a senior member of the Abu Dhabi royal family, who had recently failed with high-profile bids for Liverpool and Newcastle United, agreed in principle a takeover of Championship club Derby County, but in early 2021 it seemed unlikely to proceed. Sheikh Khaled bin Zayed Al Nehayan, 62, is the cousin of Sheikh Mansour and owns the Bin Zayed Group, a Dubai-based conglomerate.

Competition between the constituent parts of the seven-member federation of the United Arab Emirates has been a factor in the race for football club ownership with Abu Dhabi, the capital and wealthiest member, "keen to manage its image and avoid comparisons to brasher Dubai" (Kerr & England 2019). One should not underestimate the importance of "the intense competition between the UAE's two most powerful emirates" (Montague 2017: 213). Dubai's airline Emirates has been extensively involved in stadium sponsorship, as at Arsenal and Real Madrid, but has generally refrained from buying clubs, although Getafe was bought by the Royal Emirates Group in 2011.

Qatar Sports Investments (QSI) is a subsidiary of Qatar's sovereign wealth fund, the Qatar Investment Authority. It has close links to the Qatari royal family. It is best known for its purchase of PSG in 2011, and its lavish spending on the club, although it also bought KAS-Eupen, a relatively obscure Belgian club, and has been engaged in discussions about purchasing a stake in Leeds United, leading to complete ownership. However, this seemed less likely when the San Francisco 49ers increased their stake in Leeds in January 2021.

QSI made PSG the richest club in France and one of the wealthiest in the world, spending hundreds of millions on it, but in doing so found themselves in conflict with UEFA over financial fair play (FFP) rules. The club was generally sponsored by Qatari firms and it was argued that the sponsors had been paying inflated sums to boost the club's income artificially, something which PSG denied. In 2014 PSG were fined after being found guilty of breaking the FFP rules. A sponsorship deal with the Qatar Tourism Authority was deemed to have an unfair value by UEFA's independent investigation panel. The club were also forced to play with a restricted 21-man squad in European competition for a season.

Media attention on the club's spending intensified over the summer of 2017 when they bought the Brazilian forward Neymar for a record-breaking €222 million (£198 million) from Barcelona, and then secured the teenage France winger Kylian Mbappé from Monaco. Mbappé was signed on a season-long loan followed by a €180 million (£160 million) payment, an arrangement that critics argued helped the club to circumvent FFP spending limits.

In June 2018 UEFA, to some surprise, dropped a further investigation into PSG, but reopened it in September 2018. PSG appealed to the Court of Arbitration for Sport which upheld the appeal on the grounds that the renewed investigation was out of time.

Saudi Arabia, in contrast with its neighbours, has not generally followed a strategy of investing in football clubs elsewhere in the world, but instead seeks to attract top clubs to play there. In January 2020 a Spanish Super Cup was staged in Jeddah with Spain's top four teams including Barcelona and Real Madrid taking part. This will earn the Spanish Football Federation €35–40 million over three years. They may also follow other Gulf states in acquiring a top club. There have been persistent rumours that Crown Prince Mohammed bin Salman "wants to buy Manchester United" (England & Ahmed 2019). In 2020 the country's Public Investment Fund (PIF) was involved in an unsuccessful attempt to buy Newcastle United. Premier League approval for the deal was delayed as it sought information about the links between the PIF and the Saudi state and amid controversy over Saudi Arabia's human rights record.

The lavish spending of the Gulf states reflects their battle for regional supremacy, exemplified by the tensions between Saudi Arabia and Qatar. The soft power strategy has arguably been successful in giving the regimes a favourable international profile through their involvement in the world's most popular sport. However, it has also had a distorting effect on the competition between clubs, which UEFA seems able to control to only a limited extent.

The limits of globalization

The role of the European Union

As I mentioned in Chapter 1, it is a matter of debate as to whether the EU is a check on the impacts of globalization or a facilitator that accelerates the phenomenon. What is undeniable is that decisions by the EU have affected the global football game, if only because the EU encompasses all of the world's richest clubs and global brands, apart from the Premier League, whose games are watched all over the globe and whose buying power has a profound effect on the labour market for players. Attempts that have been made to organize clubs on a basis broader than Europe encounter resistance. The potential tensions between the global and regional level are shown by the formation of the World Football Clubs Association (WFCA) in 2019: "[Its] inclusion of clubs outside Europe could set it on a collision course with the powerful European Club Association (ECA), which is headed by Juventus chairman Andreas Agnelli, and is opposed to the enlarged FIFA Club World Cup, and the expansion of FIFA-run competitions in general" (Forbes 2019).

The EU's involvement in the football world is politically important as it again enables the exercise of soft power. The EU is often regarded as a technocratic, remote entity that fails to connect with its citizens. Football appeals to rich and poor, old and young, and every ethnic group in Europe's diverse society. Through its role in football, the EU has an opportunity to enhance its legitimacy and efforts at deeper integration: the Champions League and, even more, a European Super League could be seen as a means of forging a European identity by creating a European sporting space as part of a larger European public space. This could give citizens a more European frame of reference and hence promote an integrationist project. Whether fans perceive the EU as their friend and defender is open to question. What is evident is that football's governing bodies, and in particular the Premier League, have resented the EU's interventions to date.

As far as the European Commission is concerned, football is a multi-billion euro economic activity that is not exempt from competition rules that are designed to deal with abuses of dominant position or the formation of cartels. State aid rules are also relevant when it comes to subsidies for the building of stadiums. The introduction of transfer windows from the 2002/03 season was UEFA's response to an EU ruling that the existing transfer system was against its labour laws and restricted the movement of players. The compromise that was arrived at was that transfers could only take place during two periods in the summer and midwinter.

The Commission was less successful in influencing the broadcasting regime. If, in its activist phase of policy in relation to football, the Commission had been able to substantially fragment the live broadcasting of games in the UK, it would have undermined BSkyB's dominance and hence the Premier League model, which is based on television revenue. At one time the Commission appeared to be aiming at a 50/50 split between Sky and other companies, but it failed. This failure is discussed further in Chapter 7.

The controversial "Bosman ruling" by the European Court of Justice had far-reaching consequences for football, and not just for out-of-contract players in Europe like Marc Bosman. The court found that the operation of the international transfer system for players and the use of nationality restrictions in club football were incompatible with the free movement provisions of the European Commission Treaty. This had several consequences. It became more attractive in England to hire foreign managers, because of their familiarity with players outside the domestic clubs and because of their contacts for signing foreign players (Carter 2006: 126). Agents gained in importance and number because of their relevant knowledge of players and their contacts (Carter 2006: 133). Inequalities in the game were reinforced, with big clubs able to "more easily lure players away from the small clubs … The ruling hits the small clubs hardest; they receive less money from transfers than would have been the case without the ruling" (Van Der Burg 2014: 94). The ruling also had a globalizing effect. It meant that there could be no "restrictions on the numbers of EU players in a squad or a league … The global pool of talent available widened even further as clubs' scouting networks began to look at Africa, Latin America and Asia" (Goldblatt 2019: 28).

Although the EU may aspire to regulate football, its capacity to do so is another matter. In 2019 it added professional football to the list of money-laundering risks, for example. This followed an investigation in Belgium into illicit fees paid to players and referees. The European Commission stated that "[p]rofessional football's complex organisation and lack of transparency have created fertile ground for the use of illegal resources. Questionable sums of money with no apparent or explicable financial return or gain are being invested in the sport" (Brunsden 2019).

Organized, international criminal activity involving money laundering is one of the unsavoury dimensions of globalization, but can it be effectively tackled at a European level? The Commission "admitted that it faced 'structural problems' in its fight against illegal financial flows" (Brunsden 2019). There are many ways in which this can be done in relation to football, for example through betting and fixing matches as discussed in Chapter 5. Criminals can also take over financially unstable clubs and put money through the club structure to make it "clean". Gathering information on these illicit activities is difficult, let alone taking action to curb them. Checking some of the more harmful effects of globalization is far from easy.

Unsuccessful attempts at globalization

Leading clubs typically go on pre-season tours to Asia or the United States to connect with their fans there. The FIFA World Cup Club was staged in Qatar in December 2019. As noted earlier in the chapter, Saudi Arabia was the host for a Spanish cup competition in 2020. However, the Premier League, and more recently La Liga, have had a long-standing interest in playing regular fixtures overseas, but the proposals discussed below have encountered considerable resistance both in the home countries and from international governing bodies and the fixtures have not taken place. The objective of such matches would be to increase the broadcasting and merchandise appeal of leading clubs and leagues in new markets.

The Premier League first put forward the idea of a so-called "39th match" in 2008, an idea particularly favoured by their then chief executive, Richard Scudamore, who was a strong advocate of globalization in football. Premier League clubs agreed in February 2008 to explore the option of playing an extra round of ten matches overseas at five different venues, with cities bidding for the right to stage them. The additional fixtures would be determined by a draw, but the top five teams could be seeded to avoid playing each other. The Asian Football Federation opposed the proposal, but Hong Kong and the United Arab Emirates were interested. However, probably the real target for the Premier League was the USA, but it was seen as a potential threat to the development of soccer there. Scudamore was still pressing for a 39th game in 2019 but it was opposed by FIFA, no doubt concerned about sponsorship revenues.

In 2018 La Liga pursued the idea further, hoping to appeal to Hispanic audiences in the USA. La Liga sought permission from the Spanish Football Federation to move a regular fixture between Girona and FC Barcelona to Miami's Hard Rock stadium, home of the Miami Dolphins NFL team. MLS objected and the game did not go ahead. However, in 2019 Relevent Sports, the organizer of the proposed La Liga game, brought a legal case against the United States Football Federation for anti-competitive behaviour. The anti-trust case was dismissed by a federal judge in July 2020, but Relevent considered that it had not exhausted possible legal remedies. So there is a chance it could appeal the decision or pursue it by other legal routes.

In 2019 CVC Capital Partners, one of the world's largest private equity groups with $82.5 billion of assets, was approached by Real Madrid about creating a new global football league contest. Two leagues of 20 teams each were being considered. Florentino Pérez, the Real Madrid president, is also president of this newly created WFCA.

Founder members of the WFCA include Real Madrid, AC Milan, Auckland City, Boca Juniors and River Plate in Argentina, Club América in Mexico and

Mazembe in the Democratic Republic of the Congo. Significantly no Premier League clubs were involved in the set-up, although the intention is to expand and attract new members. The association aims to be a platform for clubs from around the world to discuss issues with FIFA, with which it seems to have something of a symbiotic relationship, both the WFCA and FIFA pursuing a global agenda. There are not many economic sectors that are organized on a global basis, suggesting that globalization is a real force in football.

Meanwhile, CVC was involved in talks with FIFA about acquiring the commercial rights to the revamped Club World Cup. The present eight-team Club World Cup is to be replaced by a 24-team contest featuring at least eight teams from Europe and taking place every four years. China will host the first expanded tournament in mid-2021. CVC has a long history of acquiring and selling sports franchises, including Formula One. Its 2005 bet on Formula One generated $7 billion in returns by the time it sold out in 2016. It has also done deals in rugby union. Investment in tournament franchises offers less volatility than bets on the big clubs themselves.

The proposal for the revamped contest provoked a strong reaction. Aleksander Ceferin, president of UEFA, condemned it as an "insane plan" and went on to claim that "[i]t would clearly ruin the game around the world; for the players and the fans … all for the benefit of a tiny number of people" (Ahmed 2019b). It would, of course, present a threat to the Champions League, where discussions about securing more involvement for top clubs were taking place. Premier League clubs derive 44 per cent of their revenue from broadcasting and would be concerned about anything that might threaten this income stream.

However, there is evidently an appetite for deals in football, the world's most popular sport, by top investors. How this plays out, along with the idea of a 39th game, will be an interesting test of the limits to globalization in football and how far big, footloose capital can call the shots.

Conclusion

Recent reports suggest that globalization is becoming undone or defunct (Diamond 2019; O'Sullivan 2019). It is true that flows of overseas direct investment have fallen and trade restrictions are increasing. However, football seems largely exempt from these trends. The Covid-19 pandemic created new investment opportunities for international capital. Although Chinese investors have been less active of late, this is not the case for investors from the Gulf states or the United States. The overwhelming majority of Premier League clubs continue to have foreign owners, while foreign investors have become more active in Italy. Admittedly, some of the more ambitious globalization projects that involve relocating matches or creating new leagues have not yet succeeded and may never materialize. The forces of globalization in football are driven both by considerations of soft power and prestige as well as profit, meaning that to a certain extent football operates outside the normal field of play for other economic sectors with a more complex set of objectives for club owners. Nevertheless, it can be argued that the game is being treated as a commodity rather than as a sporting activity with its own worth.

3
NOT BUSINESS AS USUAL

According to FIFA there are some "five billion football fans around the world, with Latin America, the Middle East and Africa representing the largest fan bases". Over three billion people watched some of the 2018 World Cup with more than a billion tuning in for the final (Goldblatt 2019: 551). However, the money in the game is concentrated in Europe. No club from outside Europe ranks in the top 30 for revenue generation. In the 2018–19 season the top 20 clubs in the world were all European, raking in a combined revenue of €9.3 billion (FIFA 2020).

Football's consumer appeal is huge, with its younger consumers being the most important commercially. It is ostensibly an industry, and some clubs attempt to operate in a business-like fashion, but with one important exception: it is a business unlike any other. The overwhelming majority of football clubs do not make any profit. As a result, many conventional forms of economic analysis do not apply. When interrogating the data, however, it should always be remembered that this is "a unique industry because the investments made are frequently emotional or political instead of just financial" (Maguire 2020: 169).

The absence of profits

In a capitalist or free market economy businesses are normally run with the expectation of making a profit. Stock markets pass judgement on companies and increasingly feature predatory hedge and private equity funds. Companies that are seen to make insufficient profits are highly vulnerable to buy-outs and takeovers.

Often an investor or company specializing in acquisitions takes over the company for a nominal amount in the hope of securing a turnaround by disposing of underperforming assets, as in the case of Mike Ashley and the UK department store House of Fraser. Hedge and private equity funds may perform a similar role. Whether this is good for the company, its employees or the wider economy is beyond the scope of this book. It is, however, worth noting that an economy without mechanisms for dealing with failing companies would soon start to underperform at a macro level.

This does not mean, however, that the exit mechanism necessarily works efficiently in a market economy. Efficient firms that have recently invested in new equipment may exit before less efficient ones operating with outdated machinery. In part what happens will depend on the flexibility of bankruptcy laws, although if they are too flexible then administration may simply be used as a reorganization device at the expense of creditors, something that has certainly happened in football. For example, Leeds went into administration in 2007 after years of mismanagement. Local small businesses and charities like the St John's Ambulance often lose out from insolvency given that football creditors are treated preferentially.

Football clubs may be in a better position than most companies to overcome inefficiencies in exit because purchasers may be prepared to take a long-term, often overly optimistic view of their long-term potential. This is good news for the supporters of a particular club, but arguably means that the market as a whole is overprovided with clubs. Clubs that have become financially distressed can be acquired at a price that is attractive in relation to their potential. The motives of the purchaser may vary from a genuine concern for a club they supported when they were young, to using them for asset-stripping properties with great value for development.

It is frequently the case that football clubs rely heavily on benefactors for whom profits are a secondary consideration (see Table 3.1). There are, of course, exceptions where the investor hopes to make money, for example through capital appreciation or even by being paid dividends as in the case of Manchester United and the Glazer family. They were already invested in sports franchises in the USA and saw scope for applying the model elsewhere, despite the different competitive structure. However, as noted in Chapter 2, there are a variety of motivations for acquiring a football club that may include prestige and the exercise of soft power by a state. That does not mean that the owner is not interested, after heavy investment, in making the club sustainable in the longer run, Manchester City being a case in point.

Nevertheless, owners may be willing to pour large sums of money into a club, proving the applicability of the adage, "If you want to make a small fortune, start with a large one and buy a football club". Consider the case of Malaysian entrepreneur Tony Fernandes, who became the majority shareholder of Queens Park Rangers (QPR) in 2011. Fernandes was actually a fan of West Ham United but his bid for a majority shareholding was rejected, so he turned to QPR. Losses since then have exceeded £287 million. Most of the spending has gone on operating losses and player acquisitions, with relatively little spent on infrastructure,

Table 3.1 Finances of top European clubs, 2019

Club	Pre-tax profit/loss	Comments
AC Milan	−£124 million	Lost nearly £500 million in last six years
AS Roma	−£13 million (+ £112 million player sales)	Losses ten years in a row
Barcelona	+£15 million (+ £876 million player sales)	Profits eight years in a row
Bayern Munich	+£65 million	Profits for 27 years
Inter Milan	−£34 million	Debt of £400 million would be higher without £126 million equity swap
Juventus	−£24 million (£111 million player sales)	Big growth in commercial revenue (Ronaldo factor)
Manchester United	+£18.18 million	Debt £203.6 million
Real Madrid	+£46 million (£86 million player sales)	Debt £72 million

Note: Player sales figures are profits. Reliable figures not available for PSG.

Source: Swiss Ramble and own data.

although the long-term ambition is to replace the ground at Loftus Road. QPR's owners lent the club an additional £11.4 million cash in 2019 interest free. Their pattern of spending attracted the attention of the EFL who lodged proceedings against them for breaches of FFP rules, but they reached a settlement that imposed an effective cash cost of under £10 million to be paid in annual instalments. Football finance expert Kieran Maguire commented, "[t]o show just how nuts football is in this country, during the whole of the last decade QPR had [an] income of £435m and a wage bill of £457m, despite three years in the Premier League and five years of parachute payments" (*Political Economy of Football* 2020a).

Maguire (2020) provides a classification of different types of owner. The first category is the local fan made good who has enough money to buy and develop the club he/she has supported all his/her life. The classic case is Tony Bloom at Brighton. By the time Brighton & Hove Albion was promoted to the Premier League he had provided £280 million in the form of shares and loans. Maguire points out that the "advantage of having a genuine fan as [the] owner is that if they do loan money to the club it is likely to be interest free … The downside of such a relationship is that the owner-fan may have a limited amount of money to invest" (Maguire 2020: 171). However, having a few million pounds at your disposal is not sufficient, even for an ambitious non-league club. You really need to be a multi-millionaire on a big scale to take on an EFL club, ideally a billionaire.

As Maguire points out, if "the owner's money runs out they may sell the club to simply get rid of it and not pay much attention to who takes over" (Maguire 2020: 171). The classic example is Bolton Wanderers: once riding high in the Premier League, by 2020 it had been relegated to League Two. As his health failed and his funds ran out, Eddie Davies sold the club for £1 to former player Dean Holdsworth and Ken Anderson, the latter having been banned from being a company director for eight years, not that this proved a barrier to passing the EFL's Owners' and Directors' Test. A period of great difficulty for the club ensued.

The category of the owner as "butterflies", flitting from one club to another, is based around one case, David Sullivan and David Gold, who owned Birmingham City and then bought West Ham United. Moving West Ham to the London Stadium produced only a 6 per cent increase in match-day income and left West Ham still well behind the leading London clubs. Maguire comments, "Without substantial extra money coming from the move to the new stadium, the attitude of many fans is that they sacrificed their beloved Boleyn Ground for a larger but soulless home which was never designed for football in the first place" (Maguire 2020: 173).

Much more common is the owner who acquires the club as a "trophy asset". Such an owner may be in a position to pour money into a club, but "The biggest downside is that if things don't go according to plan, they may lose interest and stop backing the club" (Maguire 2020: 175). Of course, that would degrade the resale value of the asset, and this is perhaps most likely to happen when owners who are not mega rich have hopelessly ambitious but still expensive plans for non-league clubs, Billericay Town being a case in point. The club lost £122,000 in the final full year of ownership by controversial Glenn Tamplin, taking total losses to nearly £1.4 million (*Political Economy of Football* 2020b).

Perhaps more importantly, if a club is "a rich person's plaything … the owner is not answerable to anyone apart from themselves as they have total control of the club" (Maguire 2020: 176). Another downside is that an owner may want to have a say in the playing side of the club. Since acquiring Chelsea Roman Abramovich has invested over £1.1 billion in the club. However, he has intervened over decisions about players and, more significantly, has proved impatient with managers. He has been through 13 managers since he bought the club, Frank Lampard joining their number in 2021. Plans for developing Stamford Bridge had to be shelved after Abramovich encountered issues with his UK visa.

Many UK supporters would like to see fan-owned clubs. Some Spanish clubs are owned in this way, but as Maguire observes, such an arrangement can mean that club "presidents spend a lot of time campaigning for re-election and making populist promises that are not always in the club's long-term interests" (Maguire 2020: 177). In England the history of fan-owned clubs is mixed. Even with a prosperous fan base, raising sufficient capital can be challenging as phoenix club AFC Wimbledon found with their move back to a new stadium near to their historic home in Plough Lane. They were successful, but other fan-owned clubs – such as FC United, started as a protest following the Glazer acquisition of Manchester United – have encountered greater challenges. Despite a one-person one-vote constitution regardless of the sums invested, there have still been "fall outs between the club board and membership, which has resulted in conflict in terms of the future direction of the club" (Maguire 2020: 178). A more general problem is that fans cannot afford to underwrite losses and this may lead to an overly cautious financial strategy.

Wycombe Wanderers was acquired from the Supporters' Trust in 2020 with American businessman and sports team owner Rob Couhig acquiring a 75 per cent stake. Manager Gareth Ainsworth later commented on his arrival at the club: "The Trust had just taken over and they were as wet behind the ears as I was" (Football League Paper 2020). Former chairman Trevor Stroud commented, "Without [Couhig's] contribution [in 2019], we were facing an extremely precarious position and I don't believe the club would be in the position it is now had Rob not come forward." Kieran Maguire commented that Wycombe Wanderers "lost £868,000 in 2018/19 and are technically insolvent as liabilities exceed assets. This may further explain why the supporters' trust sold the club to a private investor" (*Political Economy of Football* 2020c). The fans did the best they could, but providing the finances to run the club, let alone develop it, proved a challenge. Similarly, Wrexham fans voted overwhelmingly in November 2020 to sell their club to two Hollywood actors who were able to promise £2 million of investment, a sum the fans would have had difficulty in raising themselves.

Although those with relevant skills in law and accountancy can usually be found within the fan base, they can still be outmanoeuvred by sophisticated financial operators. At Swansea the Supporters' Trust played a key role in rescuing the club from near oblivion and took a 21 per cent stake, but "When a majority stake was bought in the Trust by two American investors, the Trust claimed that it had been bypassed and other investors made millions of pounds in the process" (Maguire 2020: 178).

Dominant clubs

Once asked what he thought was the best club in the world, Liverpool manager the late Bill Shankly responded: "I always said we had the best two teams on Merseyside … Liverpool and Liverpool Reserves." One respect in which football is not different from other sectors of the economy is that it tends to experience the emergence of dominant producers with oligopolistic tendencies. This is what has happened with the big six in the Premier League where new owners have played an important role. These dominant producers tend to resort to typical cartel behaviour by creating barriers to new entrants into the sport, which many see as the real function of FFP rules.

Indeed, Ware argues that the pursuit of domination can become the primary goal for a firm or club: "This is akin to positional competition, where relative position matters" (Ware 2020: 52); "One team can improve its league position only if at least one other does worse. Competition is for position and is therefore necessarily zero-sum … Thus positional competition intentionally creates unequal outcomes." If a competitor takes what you see as your position you must seek to do more than you did previously to reclaim it, for example by spending more: "There is a spiral to this form of competition which, unless checked by either natural or artificial factors, is continuous" (Ware 2020: 30). There is a risk of social waste.

One consequence of positional competition is that the top producers pay whatever it takes to ensure that they have the best staff, leading to the phenomenon of talented young players sitting on the substitutes' bench at best. Ware notes that "a strategy for domination has been evident in football, where the salaries and transfer fees paid by those in a financially dominant position – such as Barcelona, Real Madrid and Manchester City – have escalated in recent years" (Ware 2020: 52).

Ware argues that the demise of localized economies provides one of the conditions in which "winner-take-all" markets can thrive. At one time "the British economy was institutionally more 'bottom heavy' in the sense that it included proportionally more locally based firms and relatively few truly international ones". The predominant smaller firms "had fewer resources to find the 'best' employees, and for them it was rational to 'satisfice' when recruiting" (Ware 2020: 34). In the case of football, where clubs were often owned by local business persons, this was underpinned by the maximum wage system which prevented outbidding from other clubs making a better wage offer.

Until the dawn of the Premier League there was a particular type of locally based football club chairman: "They were self-made men, like meat packer Louis Edwards at Manchester United, Littlewoods Pools magnate John Moores at Everton and furniture retailer Manny Cussins at Leeds United. Men who enjoyed a bit of football on a Saturday afternoon and wanted to put something back into the club they supported as boys" (Thomas & Smith 2019: 13). It was a very different world from that of Sheikh Mansour or Roman Abramovich, a world in which it was possible for the team of the Burnley butcher, Bob Lord, to win the league title.

Of course, one must not exaggerate the extent to which it was a level playing field. There were always clubs that were consistently at the top of the game and a cut above the rest, for example Arsenal with its marble halls at Highbury. Of the top ten clubs in the first division in the 1919–20 season, eight were in the Premier League in 2020–21. The exceptions were Bolton Wanderers and Sunderland, both clubs that had been in the Premier League but encountered financial difficulties. The top ten clubs by average attendance in 1919–20 were all in the Premier League a century later apart from Sunderland (Tabner 1992: 74).

Does it matter in terms of the attractiveness of the game to fans and followers if there is a lack of competitive balance in football? As Szymanski observes, "There is a large literature in economics devoted to this topic, seeking to define what is meant by competitive balance, to measure it, and to see what effect it has on demand for a given league" (Szymanski 2015: 235). For example, would fans be more deterred by the domination of La Liga by two clubs for a long time or the recent domination of the French league by one club compared with the six-club oligopoly in England? The original argument was that "fans will not go to watch a game if the outcome is known in advance – uncertainty of outcome is a defining characteristic of attractive sporting competition" (Szymanski 2015: 236). Yet when Manchester United were in their pomp their fans turned up to Old Trafford in the expectation of seeing the visiting club soundly beaten with great flair.

Of course, that experience only relates to a single match, even if the anticipation was that it would be repeated at Old Trafford. Overall "Three types of outcome uncertainty can be identified: match outcome uncertainty, seasonal outcome uncertainty and the absence of long run domination" (Szymanski & Kupers 2000: 256). A league with outcome uncertainty appears to be more attractive to both fans in attendance and television viewers, but the formula of "several strong teams competing for honours" (Szymanski & Kupers 2000: 257) is somewhat vague, although the Premier League would satisfy it. In reality, "Statistical research attempting to isolate this kind of uncertainty and the demand associated with it has been surprisingly inconclusive. It is simply not clear that fans want a balanced competition" (Szymanski 2015: 236).

Certainly, in England the football authorities have shown little interest in competitive balance, reflecting the influence of the top clubs. Between 1920 and 1983, 20 per cent of the home gate was paid to the home side. Even this weak form of cross-subsidization was removed under pressure from the big clubs. In 2019 the Premier League agreed to give a bigger share of increasing overseas television revenues to the top clubs. Practice in the United States has in contrast been based on competitive balance, but the underlying sporting culture and competitive structure is very different.

The distinctive character of investments in football

Stadiums

Football stadiums are expensive capital assets, where matches are staged relatively rarely during the season but cost a lot to maintain. In the USA it is custom-
ary for local authorities to provide a substantial portion of the cost of a stadium
for a new franchise and in many parts of Europe the local authority owns the
stadium and rents it out to the club. In England new stadiums or stadium en-
largements have usually to be funded by the club borrowing money, which can
then constrain the amount of money it has available to pay players. In 2020
Bournemouth, which had by far the smallest stadium in the Premier League,
stated that the club's board had put its proposed new stadium on hold, as they
did not want to "take away our ability to perform at our strongest levels on the
pitch" (*Political Economy of Football* 2020d). They were, nevertheless, relegated
from the Premier League.

A further constraint was that money was required for a new training ground
at Canford Magna. A modern, fully equipped training ground can also be very
expensive, but is needed to support academy programmes and also to attract
the best players. Some clubs, such as Everton, have been successful in attracting
commercial sponsors for their training grounds.

Iconic stadiums can easily become tired and worn. There has been no mod-
ernization at Manchester United's Old Trafford since the Glazers took over in
2005, apart from the mandatory expansion of disabled facilities and enhance-
ments to corporate hospitality. So much so that "[w]hen the Manchester rain
poured hard last season the Sir Bobby Charlton Stand leaked. The seating is
crammed and WiFi patchy. The directors' box has an antiquated feel and the
bars and suites a faded glamour" (Jackson 2019). Meanwhile, Liverpool have
substantially enlarged their stadium, Arsenal and Tottenham Hotspur have built
new ones and Everton are moving ahead with ambitious and costly plans for a
new location

There are some partial solutions to the intermittent revenues that stadiums
generate themselves on a match day. Some have been built so that shops, res-
taurants and small business premises can be fitted in around the periphery, as
at Utrecht in the Netherlands or Real Madrid's Bernebau. Ground shares between football clubs are rare though, and often temporary, but shares with rugby
clubs are more common, although the damage to the pitch can be a problem.
Tottenham Hotspur's new stadium is specifically designed so that lucrative
American football games can be played there. It is also possible to use the stadium for boxing or pop concerts and conference business can be generated.
Nevertheless, clubs are invariably carrying a costly asset designed for a very specific purpose, which is used relatively rarely.

For fans the ground is often bound up with their identification with the club. Charlton fans fought hard, including a local election campaign, to overcome council opposition and return to The Valley. Fans have come to accept moves to more modern and convenient stadiums as at Arsenal, Middlesbrough, Southampton and Sunderland, to name just a few examples. Nevertheless, there is considerable nostalgia for old-style grounds compared with modern stadiums, as reflected in comments made on the popular Facebook group "Football Stadia and Grounds".

There is no doubt that "the way we experience football is being reshaped. Stadium architects build stands so enormous that they entirely block out our view of the surroundings." Grounds thus become detached from their geographical and cultural settings, although "they are part of our wider socio-political ecosystem and are permeated by the concerns and conditions of the communities in which they are enmeshed" (Gheerbrant 2019). Stadiums present clubs with a financing challenge, but they are also highly symbolic venues.

Players and managers as assets

Important though stadiums are as assets, it is the case that "football clubs can be described as knowledge-based organisations where most of the value is generated by talent rather than capital equipment" (Carter 2006: 155). Fans often urge owners to "invest" in players, but players are a very risky, uncertain and often costly investment. They may get injured and be out of action for long periods of time. They may not fit in with the manager's plans or turn out to be a disruptive influence in the dressing room. They may then have to be loaned out or sold at a loss.

Nevertheless, player sales have become an increasingly important if highly volatile source of income for leading clubs. Arsenal made a £170 million profit on player sales in the five years to 2020, having recorded a loss in 2018/19 largely because of player purchases outweighing sales. In any case their five-year profit was only around half of Chelsea's £332 million. Liverpool and Tottenham have made £260 million and £161 million respectively, although this only covers the last four years. Celtic generated a £102 million profit from player sales in the eight years to 2020. There is an increasing reliance on player sales as a revenue stream across Europe.

Better players simply cost more. There is a clear relationship between wages paid and success on the pitch. One consequence is that Championship clubs chasing promotion often have wages-to-turnover ratios well above the 70 per cent recommended by UEFA: "78 per cent of the total variation in league position can be accounted for by wage expenditure. By most standards this is a high percentage: the correlation is very close" (Szymanski & Kuypers 2000: 162–3). What is more, "the relationship between league performance and wage spending is even stronger over a period of time than for a single year" (Szymanski & Kuypers 2000: 165).

Another key investment a club makes is in the manager. After all, managers carry substantial responsibility, albeit variable between clubs, for recruiting the team. He/she selects the players, decides on tactics and makes decisions about substitutions. The manager is also effectively responsible for media relations and hence the image of the club. Another managerial skill is that of the "mind games" with prospective opponents. It is therefore understandable that there is a focus on the skill set and decision-making abilities of the club's manager.

One consequence has been an increase in managerial turnover. In the ten years to 31 December 2019, "103 different men have been in charge of Premier League clubs in the last 10 years, holding 153 posts between them" (Ridge 2019). Lower-league clubs are also unforgiving of managers that are perceived to be underperforming. There is often a brief improvement in performance after a manager is replaced. However, "eventually results regress to the mean" (Kuper & Szymanski 2012: 129).

A manager's success may well be affected by luck, such as refereeing decisions or injuries to key players. This, however, does not excuse what has often been a lack of professionalism in the recruitment process. Simon Kuper notes that in hiring managers, as a rule "research is usually hasty. A club owner rings a man's mobile and offers him the job, typically days after sacking the previous incumbent" (Kuper 2020a). The process of recruitment is slowly becoming more professional. Jürgen Klopp was the subject of a 60-page report by Fenway Sports Group, and he was then interviewed for several hours at a New York law firm before his appointment at Liverpool. However, the Covid-19 pandemic may change the emphasis on external recruitment. Less well-financed clubs "will tend to give top jobs to internal hires with briefs to sell players and develop cheap youngsters" (Kuper 2020a).

The manager may not be as key a factor as some popular discussions of football assume, but that does not mean that they have no impact at all on performance. Examining data on managers that have been in charge for 30 games or more, which would tend to exclude the worst-performing managers, Szymanski (working with Thomas Peeters) found that about 20 per cent of a population of over 1,000 managers had a positive impact on their club that was statistically significant. Any fan could produce a list of managers they considered to be outstanding and this is consistent with the finding that "most managers made little difference, while a few have a significant impact" (Szymanski 2015: 183). There are exceptional managers, but there are fewer of them than is generally supposed which helps to explain why there is so much disappointment with the performance of managers. This is magnified by the perception of the manager as "some kind of dream maker, who 'gives hope' to fans" (Carter 2006: 154).

Disposing of a manager can be expensive. Chelsea paid out £96 million in compensation to departing managers and their staffs in the 15 years to 2019. It cost Chelsea £23.1 million to sack the "special one" in 2007/8 and £8.3 million in 2015/16. It cost Manchester United £19.6 million to sack him in 2018/19. That's a total bill of £51 million.

Dealing with demand: the fan as consumer

Every club has a hard core of fans: those supporters who never miss a match even if they are ill or have a pressing family engagement. However, they are in the minority. When fans change their support to another club they often keep quiet about it as it "is the football equivalent of an extra-marital affair: it happens all the time but is seldom talked about" (Szymanski 2015: 146). Once a club is relegated there is invariably a drop in attendance and when it is promoted again attendances increase. The evidence suggests that "support is about as fickle as the average player: both are driven by success" (Szymanski & Kuypers 2000: 190).

From the perspective of the club, or at least its commercial arm, it would be preferable if fans behaved more like typical consumers, as passive and grateful purchasers of a product or service. From this perspective the ideal fan would purchase a season ticket and perhaps even hospitality packages; buy a programme; eat and drink in the ground; buy merchandise from the club shop rather than street sellers; and refrain from criticism of the club, the manager and the team. Perhaps the ideal customer is the football tourist from overseas. As Maguire observes, "Some clubs deliberately restrict season ticket sales in order to maximise income from football tourists, who pay more for tickets for individual matches and are more likely to spend money on merchandise in the club megastore" (Maguire 2020: 80).

Football tourists aside, a commercial ideal is seldom attainable because of the high level of commitment associated with football: attendance is driven by support for the team and this necessarily makes the numbers a subset of the available consumer group. A further difficulty is that although fans "consume" football, "it is difficult to define what is supply, demand and product" (Carter 2006: 150). Nevertheless, what is evident is that demand for football tickets is highly price inelastic, that is to say demand for them is maintained regardless of the price charged (although this applies less at lower levels). Indeed, between 1966 and 2018 prices "outstripped inflation ... by over 2000 per cent for the cheapest tickets, and a mere 750 per cent for the most expensive" (Maguire 2020: 75). Of course, in part this reflects a wealthier population with greater discretionary income. Moreover, football has become more attractive to the more prosperous section of the population as the hooligan element largely disappeared and stadiums were made safer and more comfortable.

The commercial department of a club may consider that the fan base can be treated simply as consumers, who can be targeted by marketing. Even so, "Because of changes in society the twenty-first century football supporter is probably less tolerant of failure than his or her counterpart fifty years ago" (Carter 2006: 151). One only has to listen to a radio phone-in after a day's games to have this view confirmed. This makes managing expectations difficult, particularly when they are amplified by the echo chamber of social media which is replete with abuse of players and the manager and allows the continuous and rapid spread of fake news. Clubs are dealing with a critical audience who demand more than just consumption but also interaction. Stories in the programme, on the club web page or via social media are an attempt to meet this need, but often fall short because their tone is either bland or overly enthusiastic.

Expectations in society generally of private or public services have increased, but this is particularly acute in the case of football where there is an immediate measure of success or failure in terms of results and tables. "It's a results business" is one of the most familiar clichés used in relation to the game, although fans also complain about managers who grind out results with a style of play they find lacking in entertainment value, particularly if it is seen as too defensive. One could dismiss this as so much "noise", but some of it does reach managers and players. It also has important implications for the central theme of this book as it makes it challenging to devise a system of regulation that incorporates fans as stakeholders in a way that allows them to make constructive and well-founded criticisms. If the arrangements are too responsive clubs may become overloaded.

Leagues as competitive structures

The pioneers of football soon discovered that friendly matches or even cup competitions were insufficient to maintain the interest of fans and the enthusiasm of players. A more structured and regular competition with a standardized fixture list was required, leading to the formation of the English Football League in 1888.

Over time some changes in the format had been made to make it more attractive to spectators and hence to increase revenues. These have included more promotion and relegation: at one time just one club could go up from the regionalized Third Divisions North and South. Play-offs for promotion were seen as a means of sustaining interest in the latter part of the season, as well as offering an additional source of revenue. Rather than waiting for the rare event of a bottom club not being re-elected by its fellow members or a club going bankrupt, non-league clubs have the chance of automatic promotion to the EFL. This means that a club can start way down in the non-league pyramid and reach the EFL, something which has encouraged optimistic investments by benefactors who see it as a route to glory. The number of points awarded for a win was increased from two to three in 1982 in an attempt to make matches more entertaining, "leading to a dramatic jump in the number of goals scored by away teams" (Dobson & Goddard 2001: 50).

Leagues have been concerned not just with the structure of the competition itself, but with the conduct of the individual clubs who are members. According to Szymanski and Kuypers, "From its foundation the Football League set out to control competition between clubs (by fixing minimum admission prices), competition for players (through the transfer system) and competition for profits (by fixing a maximum dividend)" (Szymanski & Kuypers 2000: 12). In Germany, and to a lesser extent Spain, special decision-making structures for clubs have been developed which seek to protect them as distinctive structures with particular forms of ownership.

The notion of a *Verein* or association is deeply embedded in German culture and it is possible to characterize Germany as an "associative state" (Grant 1993: 15). Leaving aside a couple of company-owned teams such as Bayer Leverkusen, football clubs in Germany were *eintrager Verein* (*e.V.*) or member associations. In 1998 the German Football Association adopted the 50+1 rule, much admired by reformers in Britain, which "allows the club to become a commercially run entity (such as a limited liability company) and distribute profits to its investors. At the same time 50 per cent plus one of the voting shares must remain in the hands of the e.V., so that ultimately the members' associations retain control" (Szymanski 2015: 163).

In the case of Spain overspending by elected club presidents led to a number of bankruptcies. The Spanish government intervened and forced the introduction of limited liability companies, albeit with a sporting rather than a profit-making objective. However, four clubs were allowed to retain their democratic structures: Real Madrid, Barcelona, Atletico Bilbao and CA Osasuna. As the smallest of the clubs, and one that has alternated between the first and second divisions for most of its history, Osasuna might seem to offer the best prospects for genuine club democracy.

In practice, the blend of "ownership, governance and community" has worked less well: "Beneath this veneer … the power of the *socios* to influence the club's governance was more symbolic than real" (O'Brien 2017: 133). Apart from anything else, anyone wanting to run for the key office of president had to have a minimum of €1 million, "thus retaining power within a small, wealthy provincial business elite" (O'Brien 2017: 134). It is therefore tempting to conclude "that the *socio* model will not easily translate across other football cultures. It remains quintessentially Spanish in nature, deeply embedded in the cultural, political and regional factors which have shaped the Spanish game" (O'Brien 2017: 136).

In any case the advocates of reform have looked mainly to Germany as an example to be emulated, reflecting a broader tendency in Britain to see German institutional arrangements as a model to be replicated. To some extent this is based on a rather uncritical admiration for the German model discussed further in Chapter 8. For example, "the gap in ticket prices between Britain and Germany is not as large as many imagine" (Szymanski 2015: 101). Fan disorder is often overlooked and in particular the copying of the ultra movement from Italy, even if they "have followed a predominantly carnivalesque, less ideology-driven interpretation of being ultra in comparison to their Italian counterparts" (Ziesche 2017: 91). The evidence suggests that

> member clubs in Spain or even in Germany, which is normally acknowledged as the beacon of supporter activism, see the impact of the fans in the decision-making of the club severely reduced when properly scrutinised. Whereas the structures might be prone to participation, the ways in which they are implemented are not always as conducive to "supporter power" as we are led to believe. (Zheng & Garcia 2017: 282)

Putting it more bluntly, Szymanski (2015: 168) states that "Fan democracy at Barcelona and Bayern Munich is to a significant extent illusory."

In any case the German model is encountering domestic difficulties and increasingly being undermined. At Hamburg club rules go beyond the 50+1 rule which stops a single investor owning a majority of a club. Shipping magnate Klaus-Michael Kuhne is limited to a 24.9 per cent stake. He has pumped over £50 million into the club in terms of direct investment and low-interest loans, but does not have much say: "Decisions at board level involve a large group of people, most of them fan appointed. The result is a process that is very democratic, but also slow, unwieldy and leaky which means that information often comes out that sabotages deals" (*Political Economy of Football* 2020e).

The rise of a "franchise" club in the shape of RB Leipzig presented a challenge to the 50+1 model. They were formed in 2009 by acquiring and renaming an existing fifth-division club. They evaded the 50+1 rule since their handful of members is largely drawn from executives of Red Bull GmbH, the manufacturers of the energy drink which also has a team in Austria.

Particular resentment is directed by fans at Hoffenheim, a village with a population of just over 3,000 in southern Germany, and their president Dietmar Hopp. A billionaire, Hopp made his fortune in IT. He is a divisive character in

German football, having bankrolled Hoffenheim up from the fifth tier to the Bundesliga between 2000 and 2008. He is seen as a symbol of the commercialization of German football.

In 2015 Hopp was allowed to take a majority voting share – one of three exceptions (the other two are works teams) to the 50+1 rule which means members must own more than half the shares in their club. This is because of the Leverkusen rule developed to take account of the case of Bayer Leverkusen which has links with the chemical company but was founded by factory workers. "Lex Leverkusen" allows scope for investors who have been funding the parent club "continuously and substantially" for more than 20 years to bypass the 50+1 regulations. In February 2020 opposition to Hoffenheim by ultras led to bizarre scenes at a match against Bayern Munich when both sides withdrew their keepers for the last 13 minutes and passed the ball around after an offensive banner about Hopp had been displayed by fans.

Szymanski argues that "Within the model of football that we have, the position of the members' association seems increasingly anachronistic while the model of the wealthy owner willing to sink his fortune into running a successful team seems to be more and more the norm" (2015: 172). Nevertheless, in 2018 Bundesliga clubs voted to retain the rule despite Bayern Munich chief executive Karl-Heinz Rummenigge taking the view that the rule is a "luxury", outdated in the modern world. Whether the distinctive German ownership model can withstand the pressures of globalization remains to be seen.

Conclusions: the consumer paradox

It is evident from this chapter that football is a very distinctive business, although many fans would prefer it not to be seen as a business at all. Looking at the football business as an aggregate can blur differences between clubs and leagues. In the Premier League, 59 per cent of revenue comes from broadcasting and 26 per cent from commercial, although much of that is stimulated by broadcasting coverage. Match-day revenue contributes only 13 per cent, although it is important to emphasize that the figure varies considerably from one club to another with Arsenal and Manchester United most reliant on match-day revenue (including hospitality packages). In the Championship, match-day revenue contributes 21 per cent of the total (which is affected by parachute payments). The way in which accounts are drawn up in League One and League Two does not permit the extraction of reliable figures on the match-day share of revenue, but it could be around 40 per cent. Indeed, it is 48 per cent in the Scottish Premier League.

These are revenue figures and for many clubs the difference between making a profit and a loss is player sales. This is, however, a volatile source of funds and may be considerably affected by one or two big sales. However, some clubs have managed to derive consistent net profits from this source. For example, Juventus made an average profit of €132 million a year on player sales in the four years to 2019/20. At Swansea City profits on player sales averaged £38 million in three years to 2018/19, enabling the club to balance the books. In 2018/19 all the big six reported a profit on player sales, ranging from £11 million at Tottenham Hotspur to £60 million at Chelsea.

Nevertheless, football clubs in general do not make a profit and often cost their benefactors a great deal of money. One reason the Premier League was reluctant to bail out Championship clubs during the Covid-19 pandemic was the extent to which they were underwritten by generous benefactors such as Stephen Lansdown at Bristol City. He wrote off £71 million of debt owed by the club in 2019. Despite all their financial challenges, professional and semi-professional clubs invariably manage to survive so that the overall landscape of clubs changes very little. Clubs are also sustained by the inelastic character of demand by fans for tickets and merchandise. Are fans exploited consumers?

Consumers are notoriously difficult to organize for political purposes because they are heterogeneous and fragmented whereas business interests are more homogeneous and concentrated. They differ considerably in how risk averse they are. Football supporters have an unusually strong identity with the product or service they are consuming, which makes them easier to mobilize, but their views about their club and football generally are often highly divergent.

Football supporters are very open to exploitation because "Customers make choices, supporters do not" (Horton 1997: 111). They come up against "the generalized bias of the market: to cater to those particular consumer demands that are amenable to commercialization" (Hirsch 1977: 91). The marketing operations of leading football clubs are very sophisticated. The very idea of being a supporter may be in jeopardy if the fan defines himself or herself as a consumer so that football becomes "a financial transaction between a seller and a buyer" (Horton 1997: 112). Self-definition as a consumer offers the promise of autonomy but can facilitate sophisticated forms of manipulation.

The answer does not reside simply in better organization of supporters, although the merger of the Football Supporters' Federation with Supporters Direct in 2019 to form the Football Supporters' Association was a welcome step forward towards more effective representation. This is a very active campaigning group across a range of issues that affect fans. It is in regular contact with the government and with the FA, the Professional Footballers' Association (PFA) and the leagues. It regularly provides evidence to parliamentary enquiries and provides the secretariat of the All-Party Parliamentary Group (APPG) for Football Supporters. It has made headway on a number of issues such as safe standing and better engagement. It provides an important representative mechanism through its links with supporters' trusts for dialogue with organized fans, but what is more important and necessary is external intervention to provide more effective regulation of the game in the interests of all stakeholders (discussed in Chapter 8).

4
THE PLAYERS

In 2020 the Manchester United star Marcus Rashford successfully persuaded the UK government to reverse its stance on the provision of vouchers for free meals to children in poorer families during the school holidays. Rashford's experience of poverty during his own childhood motivated his campaign and his status as a football star gave him the platform to effect change at the highest level. Although football is organized around clubs and national teams, the footballers themselves are the celebrities. They have the power to pull in spectators and to gain the support of media and the general public. Players have taken a leading role in the fight against racism, not just in football but in society more generally. The practice of "taking the knee" before the start of matches in support of the Black Lives Matter movement highlighted the symbolic importance of football and the players themselves as a force for social change.

A club's success is dependent on the acquisition and deployment of skilled talent, encompassing coaches and support staff as well as players. As Szymanski observes, "The main activity of a professional football club is the acquisition of playing talent" (Szymanski 2015: 29). This is an expensive activity, and "since 1992, the average cost of a player has risen 565%" (Tomkins *et al.*: 10). Transfer fees have continued to rise, as have wages. Accounts for 2018/19 showed that total income in the Championship was £796 million but the wages paid were £855 million.

Assessing the skill level of any one player is no easy matter, however. Agents put together videos featuring a player's outstanding moments, but these are no guide to how a player will perform over a gruelling season. Football is a team sport and it is not easy to estimate how a player will fit into a team and whether they will be a disruptive influence in the dressing room. Some players turn out to be injury prone, but that is difficult to forecast, although sometimes clubs will take a risk on a player with an injury record who can be bought at a discount and whose problems might be resolved with better medical attention.

As transfer fees and wages rise relative to inflation, clubs have attempted to become more sophisticated in the judgements they make about players. Scouting networks, generally staffed by retired players, have long played an important role in analysing prospective signings. However, the acquisition of data and its analysis has become more sophisticated and central in the task of recruitment, as well, of course, as being used in relation to existing players.

The use of data has developed rapidly, and "Analytics is sport's cutting edge, and in football it is growing exponentially" (Anderson & Sally 2013: 6). It enables clubs to understand how fast a player is, how much time he or she spends on the ball and how good they are at passing. In the past this was gathered by scouts observing matches and this practice has its value. However, data provides much harder information enabling players to be compared in a systematic way. Gathering the information is just the first step: the vital one is knowing how to make effective use of it. The "garbage in, garbage out" rule applies if anything more in football than in other economic sectors, because it can be more difficult to know what kinds of information are required and how they relate to success on the pitch. Those involved in data analysis have "to work out what they need to be counting, and to discover why exactly, what they are counting counts" (Anderson & Sally 2013: 7). The cost of acquiring the information and analysing means that the competitive edge possessed by wealthier clubs is reinforced.

The search for the best players increasingly leads clubs overseas in the hope of discovering hidden talent that might also be less expensive than established domestic players. Although migration by footballers has a long history, it has accelerated in recent years. It has given opportunities for development to many players, but it also has a darker side with the exploitation of players from the Global South

Players, whether domestic or international, continue to be subject to discrimination and unequal treatment. Racism has blighted football both on and off the pitch. It persists both among fans and at the institutional level. Racism is reflected in the different ways in which BAME (Black, Asian and minority ethnic) players are judged and the very low numbers of BAME football managers. In the men's game, homophobia has led to the almost complete absence of declared gay male players. I return to these issues later in the chapter.

The labour market for players

Some economists argue that the labour market in football works well. Kuper and Szymanski (2012: 98) claim that "football is one of the few markets that indisputably meet the conditions in which competition can work efficiently: there are large numbers of buyers and sellers, all of whom have plenty of information about the quality of the players being bought and sold". On the last point, possession of a substantial quantity of information is by itself not enough:

one needs to interpret that information in a way that facilitates good decisions. Information asymmetries are present and agents as intermediaries in the market compound rather than remove distortions. Maguire notes (2019: 73) "that the sullied reputation of agents has some justification, but that as in all occupations there are both good and bad exemplars". Although labour market theory offers useful insights, its focus is very specific. A political economy approach has to take account of a broader range of factors in terms of the complex interactions between the state and the market and the structure of the market itself. It also needs to take account of the cognitive biases that intrude into decision-making.

Labour markets rarely work perfectly because of the ability of firms or workers to set or influence wages. However, football labour markets have their own distinctive features, notably the payment of transfer fees to sign players who are in contract. Furthermore, "It seems that high wages help a club much more than spectacular transfers. In short, the more you pay your players, the higher you will finish" (Kuper & Szymanski 2012: 14–16). Although there is powerful evidence to support this relationship, one always has to be a little careful about inferring cause and effect relationships from correlations. It may be that the more successful clubs have more leeway to pay higher wages. At the very least there may be a causal flow from success to wages, which could, of course, become a virtuous circle. Marquee transfers may be a way of increasing the profile of a club globally and improving its ability to acquire sponsorships and sell merchandise. For example, the signing of Ronaldo substantially boosted the commercial income of Juventus, as was the intention.

In practice, many factors influence the decision of a player to join a club. Wages and any signing-on fee may be crucial, whereas release clauses or a player's ability to exploit his "image rights" also come into the decision. A player may seek experience at the highest level and therefore look for a club that is likely to qualify for the Champions League. It is also evident from player autobiographies that the possibility of winning trophies is a powerful incentive. Location may also come into the calculation. A harsh winter climate may deter some players and language could also be a factor, although these may be influenced by whether there are players already at the club who speak the player's native language. Indeed, such players may perform an important role in the recruitment process.

Clubs recognize that helping to settle players into an unfamiliar environment is important if they are going to succeed, so they increasingly appoint player liaison officers or relocation consultants to carry out a wide range of "hand-holding" tasks for players such as finding suitable accommodation. Compatibility with, or respect for, the manager may also be an important consideration. Indeed, managers often recruit players who they know from other clubs they have managed.

What all this demonstrates is the complexity of the decision to move from the player's perspective. In practice, players will depend considerably on the advice offered by their agents, which may only serve to increase resentment from clubs at their powerful role. Clubs may thus identify a player who appears to meet their needs but be unsuccessful in their recruitment attempt. This may not be because of the money on offer but because of a variety of other factors, often psychological in character, which cannot readily be captured by statistical models. For example, a player may want to return to his home area to be near to his or her family. A global city like London can be a major draw, even for lesser clubs located in the capital.

This is not to argue that the recruitment process fails because of contrary or seemingly irrational decision-making by players: "While the market for players' wages is pretty efficient – the better a player is, the more he earns – the transfer market is inefficient. Most of the time clubs buy the wrong players" (Kuper & Szymanski 2012: 16–17). One reason is that despite the increasing amounts of information collected, and the greater resources and sophistication applied to the analysis of that data, there are considerable information asymmetries. For example, an agent may be aware of weaknesses in a player's character that are only apparent off the pitch, but that can have a significant effect on his performance. These are exploited by agents whose objective is to maximize their income and that of the players they represent (which are closely tied together).

An exception to this rule of agents putting their own financial interests before those of the club has been the contribution of "super-agent" Jorge Mendes to the success of Wolverhampton Wanderers. He is known as a "super" agent because of his ability to recruit high-quality Portuguese players for Wolves who have contributed considerably to the club's playing revival. The Chinese owner of Wolves, Fosun, has a stake in Mendes's company Gestifute. The Wolves head coach, Nuno Espírito Santo, was Mendes's first client. The closeness of the relationship led to complaints from other Championship clubs and an EFL investigation, but the league ruled that Mendes's involvement did not amount to a formal role.

There are, of course, alternative understandings of efficiency. Mourao (2016) focuses on how efficient a club has been in securing money flows from the sale of players. This is a perfectly valid approach as it is evident that player sales have formed an increasing contribution to the financial sustainability of clubs across Europe. Mourao examined data on 183 clubs playing in the major leagues of England, France, Germany, Italy, Spain and Portugal for at least two continuous seasons between 2007 and 2013. One finding is that "top-ranked teams are usually more successful in transferring players with more significant values than low-ranked teams" (Mourao 2016: 5521). Any player can benefit from their association with success, although their individual value may be overrated, creating another source of market distortion. It also reinforces the relative financial success of already successful clubs.

Successful clubs may also be more adept at playing the transfer market. This links to a finding that could already be found in the literature that "[o]lder clubs tend to exhibit more significant experience in trading players, leading to more efficient scores" (Mourao 2016: 5518). This is confirmed by Mourao's result that "'old' European clubs can be more efficient in having more positive net football transfers than 'younger' football clubs" (Mourao 2016: 5521). Ambitious newer clubs seeking to catch up their more established rivals, such as PSG, may be more reckless in their spending and then have to offload players who do not make the grade at a loss.

It is also the case that a "team's presence in the main European competitions (UEFA Champions League or UEFA Europa League) is associated with an efficient allocation of football transfers ... teams playing in these most competitive competitions tend to receive higher stimulus for being efficient on trading players" (Mourao 2016: 5521). Players taking part in these competitions achieve a higher profile and may be more attractive to teams hoping to play in the Champions League or improve their performance in it. Once again this phenomenon tends to improvements in the financial positions of the wealthiest clubs.

It was also found that "being an English or French football team tends to generate more efficient values in trading players" whereas Italy tended "to have teams with more inefficient values in receiving money" (Mourao 2016: 5521). This is consistent with the overall finding that European football teams "exhibit a very heterogeneous pattern of efficiency scores" (Mourao 2016: 5523). It is also evident that teams fall well short of total efficiency in terms of securing value from their player trading.

Can clubs operate in the transfer market more efficiently? Mourao suggests that apart from the obvious suggestion of acquiring good players, they "should try to generate sustainable cycles of transfer balances" (Mourao 2016: 5523). This may come up against the objective of using net player sales as a means of improving the club's overall financial position. Teams without a long history should seek to stabilize their squads. This can be thwarted by the intuitive appetite of managers for a particular player or a falling out with a talented player. Mourao is surely right when he argues that "football teams must try to reconcile the competitiveness cycle of their squads to the sustainability of their finances" (2016: 5523). The obstacle that stands in the way of this objective is the pressure for short-term success from fans and owners, which tend to overcome the pursuit of a viable medium-term strategy.

Loans of players have become an increasing feature of the football labour market in Europe in recent years. In 1992 loans made up just 6 per cent of transfers in the so-called "big five" leagues. By 2009 they had risen to 20 per cent of all transfers and this figure increased to 29 per cent in 2019 (Ahmed & Burn-Murdoch 2019).

There is a variety of motivations for using loans. One is to avoid paying the high fees demanded in the transfer market. Another is to see whether a player will fit into the team. They can also serve as a means of offloading a player who has underperformed, while recovering some of the cost. They can also be used as a mechanism to evade FFP rules, although UEFA has tightened these to cover cases where there is an obligation to buy.

It is also an important way of giving younger players valuable experience by loaning them out to smaller clubs. Increasingly the loaning club insists that they play a certain proportion of games. From the perspective of the smaller club, they are acquiring a player who may make a considerable contribution to the team and also excite fans, even boosting attendances. They do not usually have to pay the player's full salary, just paying a proportion or even nothing at all. The downside is that the player may be taken back by the loaning club at very short notice, potentially unbalancing the team.

"Try before you buy" or "loan to buy" deals are becoming increasingly common. Ten years ago there were only 28 loans that led to a purchase by the borrowing club within 12 months. In 2019 there were at least 101 in the "big five" leagues (Ahmed & Burn-Murdoch 2019). This serves as a form of insurance, allowing more reliable trading in player values. However, critics argue that they create an unstable working environment for players, reducing the incentive for clubs to train and develop players. Short-term loan deals serve as a risk reduction mechanism for clubs but are less good for player career development. Generally it is the players who are perceived to have the upper hand in dealings with clubs, but here one is dealing with a category of players who are in a weaker position because of indifferent performance or being at an early stage in their careers.

An alternative way of proceeding is to develop players through the academy. All major clubs invest considerable sums of money and expertise in their academies. In part this is also a contribution to the transfer market. Particularly for smaller clubs, selling on promising academy players may be a significant source of revenue. Academies sign up players at a young age in part to prevent rival clubs acquiring them. The overwhelming majority of these academy trainees will never become professional players, although some may find their level in non-league football as semi-professional players.

As far as the functioning of the labour market is concerned, the decision whether to offer an academy player a preliminary professional contract is a crucial one, not least for the player. Once cast out, relatively few find their way back into the professional game by demonstrating their ability at non-league level, Jamie Vardy being one of the few exceptions. From the club's perspective they know everything they need to know about the character, ability and potential of the player. However, in relation to some players the judgement is a finely balanced one, particularly given that some players develop more quickly than others. There is no doubt that some promising players are let go. The selection process is unavoidably imperfect.

The structure of the labour market

Labour markets do not exist in a vacuum. They operate within a framework of rules and norms and, given the distinctiveness of "the world of football", it has developed its own rules which influence the way in which the labour market for players operates. However, this inward-looking world can also be influenced by exogenous shocks, most notably the Bosman judgement of the European Court of Justice (ECJ).

Football was originally played by amateurs for the love of the game and the arrival of professionals was initially resented in some quarters. This was reflected in tensions in England between the Football League and the FA with the latter much more resistant to professionalism. In the pre-modern era, "In the days of maximum wage and the retain-and-transfer system, relationships between club and player were simple. Once hired, the footballer was more or less the captive of his club, and his wage was limited, no matter what club he played for" (Szymanski & Kuypers 2000: 158).

The abolition of the maximum wage in 1961 led to inflation in player wages. The weekly wage of Fulham and England captain Johnny Haynes went up to £100 a week, the equivalent of £2,250 at 2019 prices. According to Dobson and Goddard, "During the 1950s the inflation-adjusted increase in wages and salaries was 10 per cent. Between 1961 and 1974 the real increase was around 90 per cent" (Dobson & Goddard 2001: 92).

Once players were granted freedom of contract in 1978 they could seek the best deal available and the labour market in football functioned much more like a normal market. However, "in practice the out-of-contract player was still constrained to some extent". In order to move, the player "had to find a new club that would either agree a fee with his existing club, or be willing to take the risk of going to arbitration at the Football Association" (Dobson & Goddard 2001: 93).

The Bosman ruling of the ECJ in 1995 was important in ending many of the restrictive practices in the European football labour market and opening it up to greater internationalization. This found that the requirement to pay compensation to the former club of a player who was out of contract was incompatible with the freedom movement of labour provisions of the Treaty of Rome. Restrictions on the number of foreign players permitted in a team were also found to be incompatible with the treaty. In other words, football could not have its own special rules in the labour market, although it did not mean that transfer fees were unlawful under all circumstances.

In an internationally competitive market with club revenues growing, levels of reward for the most sought-after players rose sharply. Truly outstanding world class players are in short supply and the demand for them is high. This is then reflected in the labour price they can command. This applies to any other valued good in short supply, such as a painting by a famous artist. However, the wages paid to top footballers command particular critical attention. For example, during the outbreak of the Covid-19 pandemic, politicians were quick to tell football players that they had a duty to accept substantial cuts in their wages.

Others employed in the entertainment industry do not seem to attract the same level of criticism, for example actors in film and television and popular musicians. Those in other sports such as baseball and American football are also less criticized for their high salaries. It may reflect the fact that football players receive even more continuous media attention across the world than even leading entertainers or those in other sports.

Football players also point out that their playing careers tend to be relatively short and they may only earn relatively high salaries for one part of it. Many players never have particularly high salaries. Some retired players are able to obtain positions in the game as coaches or media pundits. Others work in related professions such as physiotherapy. However, many end up in relatively mundane and not particularly well-paid occupations such as postal worker, taxi driver or builder.

Player migration

One way in which players maximize their lifetime income is to move from one club to another, securing signing-on fees and better wages. At one time these moves were largely domestic, but the labour market for players has become increasingly international. Applying the concept of globalization to player migration is not a straightforward matter and a certain amount of caution is necessary: "much of the writing on football migration has tended to employ 'globalization' uncritically as if it were an established fact rather than a contested concept" (Taylor 2007: 4). Indeed, "For historians of migration, the concept of globalization can be particularly problematic" (Taylor 2007: 5). One complication is that a "simple, straightforward definition of the term 'migrant' is non-existent" (van Campenhout et al. 2018: 1072). However, for the purposes of this discussion the focus is on broad flows over time and their impact on football and society more generally.

Migration has occurred in football since the start of the professional game in the late nineteenth century. Players from Scotland were valued because of their understanding of the passing game whereas many English players were preoccupied with the art of dribbling, which came to be seen as outmoded. Because the most lucrative professional contracts were to be found in England, this drew in players from Scotland and then from Ireland. As such, "By 1910, Scots accounted for 168 (19.3 per cent) of the 870 players in the Football League and even 45 (11.7 per cent) of the 385 in the rival Southern League. By 1925 the figure had risen to 302 Scottish players in the Football League's four divisions" (Taylor 2007: 14). South Africa was an important source of players in the inter-war years and immediately after the Second World War for clubs like Charlton and Liverpool. More generally in continental Europe clubs were largely founded as a result of the activity of migrants: "The defining feature of the first football clubs in continental Europe was their cosmopolitanism" (Taylor 2007: 7).

Expatriates played a key role in disseminating the game throughout the world. By the outbreak of the First World War there were 40,000 British citizens living in Argentina looking after the UK's substantial investments there which in some respects made it like an economic colony of Britain. The headmaster of the English High School in Buenos Aires established a football league there in 1893. Tours by English clubs played an important role. Southampton visited in 1902 and then both Merseyside clubs four years later, followed by Swindon Town and Exeter City. The game became more authentically Argentinian, and "By the end of the First World War the game in Argentina had been overtaken by home-grown Argentinians, most of whom were of Mediterranean origin" (Downing 2003: 21). Over the next half century, scores of Argentinian players went to play for clubs in Italy or Spain, but in 1978 Osvaldo Ardiles and Ricardo Villa were signed by Tottenham Hotspur. This was in the face of opposition from the PFA who argued that young players would be crowded out by the arrival of foreign stars.

Despite forecasts that they would not be able to adapt to the English game, the Argentinians showed up its limitations. A decline set in from the late 1970s in British or Celtic recruitment to English clubs: "Whereas 80.3 per cent of the non-English and Welsh players in the Football League between 1976 and 1985 came from Scotland, Northern Ireland or the Republic of Ireland, this figure dropped to 56.5 per cent in the subsequent ten years" (Taylor 2007: 15). Foreign players were virtually unknown when the Premier League was formed with just 11 of them in the 1992/3 season, but the number quickly increased, reaching 166 by the 1998/99 season. Players were drawn from all over the world and "by 2005/06 there were 60 nationalities represented in the Premiership alone" (Taylor 2007: 17).

Across Europe the Bosman ruling made a difference by allowing players to move to other EU countries once their contracts had ended. Quotas remained in place in teams for non-EU players. However, it was only part of a broader picture in which "a range of technological, structural and economic developments … combined to facilitate the increasing volume and speed of football player migration during the 1990s" (Taylor 2007: 12). Expanded television coverage was probably the most important factor in the spread of the game, and it certainly stimulated awareness of the existence of a "global game". It also gave youngsters outside Europe role models and the hope of a pathway, however illusory, out of poverty.

Analyses of data on players taking part in the men's World Cup confirm the picture of an increasing flow of migrant football players. At the 2014 World Cup, "478 of the 736 players (almost 65%) selected for this tournament lived and worked (played) outside the country of which they wore the national jersey. Furthermore, 85 footballers (nearly 12%) represented a country in which they were not born, the highest number in its history" (van Campenhout *et al.* 2018: 1071). Not only has the World Cup become more migratory during its history, football migration has apparently exceeded general rates of migration: "With an average of just over 6%, the *volume* of foreign-born footballers in the World Cup seems to be notably higher than the more steadily increasing trends in international migration; which historically oscillates between the 2 and 4%" (van Campenhout *et al.* 2019: 7). Moreover, "developments in the *diversity* of foreign-born players in the World Cup basically reflects general tendencies of a *globalisation of migration*" (van Campenhout *et al.* 2019: 15).

The process of player migration has increasingly been interpreted "as a form of neo-colonial exploitation of the developing world by the developed world". It is sometimes claimed that the skills acquired by African players in Europe boosts the performance of their national teams in international tournaments, but "player migration can mitigate against putting together a cohesive, well prepared and successful national squad" (Darby 2007: 496). For those who see the relationship between football in Africa and Europe as essentially a reproduction of colonial relations, it is certainly the case that the typical pattern of migrant flow is between former colonial countries and the colonial power for reasons of language, culture and established links. For example, players from Mozambique would typically move to Portugal. There is more evidence of player undervaluation in relation to African countries than those in Latin America: "While the recruitment of players from Latin America can cost more than €20 million, transfers carried out from sun-Saharan Africa rarely attain more than €1 million, even for the most promising players" (Poli 2010: 1002). Most African players either come from North Africa or the coastal states on the sub-Saharan west of the continent.

The process of recruitment for many African players is deeply flawed. Agents maintain scouts in a particular area: "You arrive in the area, you dress well, shrug on a good jacket and you carry some false headed notepaper with maybe the Manchester United or Paris Saint-Germain crests on them. You go over to speak to five small players, and you fire up their dreams" (Wolter 2019). Once offered "the promise of a shot at European football, they and their families were required to come up with the thousands of dollars necessary for passports, visas, airports and fees and they found themselves abandoned on arrival" (Goldblatt 2019: 54). Parents often push the decision at the prospect of undreamed-of riches, committing their life savings to the agent: "Parents are excited by the prospect of future earnings and they are ready to gather together significant amounts of money in order to get their child to Europe where they can start earning. Parents will remortgage their house or sell land or ask everyone in the village to lend them money in order to pay the sums demanded by the agent" (Wolter 2019).

Once they get to Europe, the few African players that enjoy huge success obscure the plight of the majority: "Although difficult to estimate, the proportion of African players coming to Europe and who succeed in signing a professional contract seems to be, in reality, very low" (Poli 2010: 1002). Their working conditions are very difficult and often they cannot survive on their football earnings and are forced to take second or third jobs: "Those who don't succeed are just abandoned in appalling conditions or are left to eke out a miserable existence. Some 'agents' will just disappear, pure and simple. Some of them will confiscate passports and identity cards from young players" (Wolter 2019). For some abandoned players the only possible move seems to be sideways into the sex industry.

Concerns about trafficking led FIFA to ban transfers of African players younger than 18 years old in the mid-2000s. However, this had an unintended and perverse consequence. It meant that most top clubs soon recalled their scouts from Africa, as they prefer to train and develop young players in their own academies. Instead, teams from lower-level football leagues in Europe entered the player market in Africa. In any case, according to Culture Foot Solidaire, "98 per cent of those would-be footballers who make it to Paris are illegal immigrants, and 70 per cent are under the age of 18" (Rowe 2018). For all the increase in player migration, it should be borne in mind that capital flows more readily and faces fewer obstacles under conditions of globalization than labour.

Racism

Racism disfigured English football in the 1980s, and although it had started to ebb it has experienced a revival after the 2016 Brexit referendum, which for some people served to legitimize the public expression of racist views. Indeed, the emergence of populism across Europe emboldened those with far-right views to strengthen their links with football. With the extensive use of closed-circuit television in stadiums, it is easier to identify culprits, prosecute them and ban them from attending matches. However, the anonymity of social media has provided a new vehicle for racists to express their views: "Social media, particularly Twitter ... has become a kind of conduit for some of the vilest racist smears conducted anonymously via smartphones and computers" (Cleland & Cashmore 2014: 646)

More generally, a measure of complacency, even denial, exists in football about the problem, with a tendency to see it as a historical phenomenon that is now largely under control. This overlooks the existence of more covert, institutionalized or embedded forms of racism, reflected in the underrepresentation of BAME fans in football crowds or the almost complete absence of BAME managers from the game. The Black Lives Matter movement challenged these assumptions and saw players and officials adhere to the symbolic gesture of "taking the knee". Football authorities have, however, seemed reluctant to take punitive action against clubs or national teams involved in racist incidents: "Looking across football, it is clear that football remains a white institution – from the heads of FIFA, UEFA and the FA through to club owners, directors, players, referees and fans" (Cleland & Cashmore 2014: 640). The forced resignation of the chair of the FA in November 2020, after he used an unacceptable racist epithet, only served to underline the problems at the top of the game.

Overt racism in the 1980s was associated with an era of mass hooliganism and with serious violence inside and outside grounds as fans tried to take the "end" of their rivals. Organized gangs such as West Ham's Inter City Firm meted out violence. Racism in the form of prejudice based on skin colour was endemic in the game at that time. Black players were stigmatized as lacking "bottle" or being of no use in defensive positions. Since then, "the baying crowds, monkey chants and bananas of the old era have been banished from the nation's football stadiums by an apparent successful raft of anti-racism campaigns" (Goldblatt 2014: 147). Black players became widely accepted "because the market in players is transparent. It is pretty obvious who can play and who can't, who's got 'bottle' and who hasn't" (Kuper & Szymanski 2012: 112).

There is some evidence of a decline in racist incidents. One survey found that between "1990 and 1999, 67 per cent of those who watched football at that time witnessed or experienced racism; between 2000 and 2009, 61 per cent and 50 per cent since 2010" (Cleland & Cashmore 2014: 641). A resurgence of racist incidents from 2018 onwards was therefore worrying, although one must be cautious about the construction of isolated incidents into an overarching narrative. Haringey Borough had to walk off the pitch in a FA Cup qualifying match because of racist abuse. More than 150 football-related racist incidents were reported to police in the 2018/19 season, a rise of more than 50 per cent on the year before and more than double the number from three seasons ago. Some of this could be attributed to reduced tolerance of racist abuse by fans and a greater willingness to report incidents. However, it also represented a normalization of divisive language in society. England's Euro 2020 qualifier in Bulgaria had to be halted twice. At the game in Sofia a large group of white men dressed in black clothing gathered in the stands. As the game kicked off they made Nazi salutes.

Around 30 per cent of professional footballers in England are BAME, just over twice their representation in the population, but this percentage is not reflected either in the composition of the fan base or the number of BAME players who become managers. It is difficult to obtain reliable figures on the ethnic composition of the fan base, but football crowds look overwhelmingly white. This is the case even in areas which have a high BAME population. For example, the BAME population of Leicester is around 50 per cent, but estimates of the BAME share of the crowd at Leicester City's King Power Stadium is around 10 to 12 per cent (Robertson 2019: 13).

As far as football managers are concerned, a maximum of four out of 92 in the top four leagues have been BAME at any one time. In the 2019/20 season no Premier League team had a Black British manager or a Black majority shareholder. The England football team has never had a BAME manager. Only Chris Hughton, Chris Powell and Keith Curle have accumulated a total of more than five years in management in the English game, and "Clubs traditionally hire from an old-boys network of male white ex-players" (Kuper 2020a). The EFL had adapted the so-called "Rooney Rule" from the NFL in the United States and requires that clubs must interview at least one BAME candidate when recruiting a first-team manager. The FA also includes a BAME coach in each of their national teams. Whether these initiatives go beyond tokenism and lead to a significant increase in the number of BAME managers remains to be seen.

The Premier League, PFA and EFL launched a new coach placement scheme in June 2020 aimed at increasing the number of BAME players moving into full-time coaching roles in the professional game. The BAME player-to-coach placement scheme, open to BAME PFA members at any age or stage in their careers, will provide up to six coaches per season with a 23-month intensive work placement within EFL clubs.

Racism is, of course, not a problem confined to England, although there is a temptation to point to it being worse elsewhere as an excuse for not taking effective action. Italian football has long been plagued by racist incidents and the football authorities have been reluctant to take effective action in response. Indeed, a campaign against racism that was launched by Serie A teams in 2019 that used images of three monkeys was widely criticized as being at the very least in poor taste and displaying a lack of understanding of the nature of the problem. However, "There are signs this may be slowly changing, driven by the commercial considerations of clubs competing for international television and marketing revenues against rivals in Europe" (Johnson 2019).

Perceptions can be affected by the way in which the print media portray white and BAME players. A tabloid newspaper had stories about two young players who had bought homes for their mothers. Phil Foden, who is white, was portrayed in a positive light while the angle on Tosin Adarabioyo, who is Black, was that he was overpaid. The white player's actions were presented as motivated by generosity while the Black player's wealth and his £25,000 a week salary was depicted as "unearned" with reference made to the fact that he had never started a Premier League match. This story led Manchester City player Raheem Sterling to take a stand on the issue of the racist portrayal and abuse of players. His initial post on Instagram about the newspaper story received 650,000 likes. In February 2020 Sterling announced that he wanted to create a Premier League task force composed of leading current players to combat what he said was the rising tide of racism in football. His panel would work with the Premier League on anti-racism and anti-discrimination strategies and be available for consultation when incidents of discrimination occurred.

Those in positions of authority in football sometimes argue that racism is a wider social problem that happens to find one outlet in the game and hence is not particularly football's responsibility. However, Raheem Sterling has commented, "There's never a time in my life in England I've received racism outside of football. It's just purely to do with football" (quoted in Mance 2019). Some fans seem to think that the football stadium is outside society, that they have a licence to behave there in ways that they wouldn't elsewhere, claiming that it is "just banter" or an expression of passion. For some analysts, "a 'colour blind' ideology permeates through British football as the relevant authorities or personnel refuse to acknowledge the extent to which racism remains present" (Cleland & Cashmore 2014: 640).

The football authorities often seem reluctant to take strong action against instances of racist behaviour by fans. Requiring a national team to play behind closed doors and/or imposing a fine is an insufficient deterrent, whereas expulsion from a competition would have a much bigger impact. UEFA suggests that a match should be abandoned if fans have been warned to cease racist abuse twice. One can understand why officials are reluctant to abandon matches because of the disorder that could follow. However, point deductions might concentrate the minds of clubs. Measures such as the "No Room for Racism" campaign and the BAME Participants' Advisory Group launched by the Premier League after the Bulgaria incident are helpful steps, but by themselves they are insufficient.

Cleland and Cashmore argue that "Kick It Out and another analogous organizations have contributed to a culture of complacency – the interests of football's governing authorities and media corporations were best served by creating the impression that racism was a feature of football's historical landscape" (2014: 651). When player Jonathan Leko successfully brought a complaint of racist language against another player in 2020 he stated that "I had minimal contact from the PFA of which I am a member, and no contact in the way of support from leading anti-racism bodies such as Kick It Out and Show Racism The Red Card. Some support or guidance would have been very welcome" (West Bromwich Albion 2020).

Cleland and Cashmore conclude that "Racism remains culturally embedded in the British game and through social media and other social forms, it is becoming a lot harder to tackle" (2014: 651). This pessimism may be justified but it could also discourage effective action by placing racism in a "too difficult" box. There has to be recognition that the problem goes beyond a minority of individual supporters who can be dealt with by being excluded from games. It is a collective problem that requires action by the football authorities to hold clubs and national teams and associations to account as part of a more effective regulatory response.

Homophobia

Gay players in the men's game usually only come out when their playing careers are over and even then not many of them do. Those that do declare their identity often do so reluctantly and with some trepidation. Historically football developed in an industrial working-class setting, where narrow definitions of masculinity were prevalent and went unchallenged. Football chants suggested "male heterosexuality as the highly prestigious norm and gay men's sexuality as the trivialised 'Other'" (Caudwell 2011: 126). This allowed homophobic language to be normalized. Homophobia was prevalent in football stadiums in the 1980s and 1990s, in part stimulated by the outbreak of the AIDS virus.

However, substantial progress has been made towards greater tolerance and acceptance since then: "From a period of high homohysteria in the 1980s and 1990s … there is now a growing body of empirical evidence illustrating a changing cultural context in professional football where homophobia is challenged across a range of populations" (Cleland 2018: 419). Traditional conceptions of masculinity remain in football culture, but their influence is declining as more inclusive forms take their place: "Perhaps the appeal and metrosexual nature of footballers (most notably David Beckham) … and the increasingly fluid social structures in which fans operate in has aided a change towards a more inclusive masculinity" (Cashmore & Cleland 2012: 375). Nevertheless, much remains to be done, and "At a time when the game has shown such impressive solidarity with the anti-racism movement … the question was reasonably asked whether enough thought and exposure is given to the LGBTQ cause" (Dickinson 2020).

Cleland *et al.* analysed over 5,000 internet responses by football fans towards the decision by the former German international footballer, Thomas Hitzlsperger, to publicly come out as gay in January 2014. According to their analysis, "From a period of high homophobia during the 1980s and 1990s, just 2 per cent … of the comments contained pernicious homophobic intent", illustrating "a significant decrease in cultural homophobia than was present when Justin Fashanu came out in 1990" (Cleland *et al.* 2018: 91). This development reflects wider attitudinal change in society as a whole, but there is always a risk that football stadiums may be seen as settings in which voice can be given to attitudes which would be unacceptable in other contexts. Nevertheless, homophobic language "is now recognized and discouraged by more enlightened fans" (Cleland *et al.* 2018: 104). In a notable turnaround, "Rather than gain power through the use of language with homophobic intent, it is actually homophobia that is stigmatized by the vast majority of fans who effectively self-police those views that fall outside of the collective online majority" (Cleland *et al.* 2018: 105).

If attitudes are becoming more enlightened, and there is substantial empirical evidence to suggest that they are, why then aren't more male football players declaring their sexual identity (such declarations are much more common among women players)? Typically blame has been placed on the fans when in fact it resides much more with those running football, as is so often the case. Hitzlsperger said that it would have been impossible for him to come out when he was still playing, "not because of the fans or the other players, but because of the media" (quoted in Cleland *et al.* 2018: 96). The evidence from research shows that social media have contributed to an environment of acceptance, perhaps to an extent that players do not appreciate. Print media often lag behind changing attitudes but catch up with their readers eventually.

Too often "fans are stigmatized as homophobic when in fact an overwhelming majority are very liberal and permissive in their views" (Cashmore & Cleland 2012: 383). Why should that be the case? According to Cashmore and Cleland, "Fans suspect that they are stigmatized as homophobes because it suits the interests of clubs and agents. Their view is that clubs and agents protect their own interests and dissuade players from coming out, while accusing fans of being the main inhibitors" (Cashmore & Cleland 2012: 384). In fact it could be in the commercial interest of clubs to have openly gay players, but their approach to marketing is often rather conventional and cautious once it goes beyond identifying new forms of sponsorship.

The onus should be "placed on the internal culture of football (i.e. players, agents, managers, clubs and football's national, continental and international governing bodies) to provide an environment that supports those active players who want to come out" (Cleland 2018: 420). Some steps have been taken, but they are relatively limited and do not add up to a coherent and effective strategy. In the context of this book, the question that arises is whether this is an issue that could form part of a stronger regulatory framework. The challenge is to avoid overburdening such a framework with too many disparate tasks leading to none of them being tackled adequately. In the meantime, this is an issue where fan organizations can work effectively with their clubs.

The FA launched a Transgender and Transsexual Policy in 2014. Caudwell provides a study of the experiences of "Paula" who self-identified as "transgender, transsexual and queer" (Caudwell 2017: 28) and supported Norwich City. She had to negotiate her own participation, including dealing with being "outed" on a fan forum. She had to deal with "the known discriminations of sexism, racism and homophobia that are ever-present in and around football stadia". She did provide "insights of her positive experience of inclusion, which are largely encouraging. However, the experiences are contingent on her football fan friends" (Caudwell 2017: 42). Some fans at least are more interested in someone's football identity than their sexual identity.

An issue that remains outstanding is playing international football in countries that have anti-gay laws with severe penalties. Homosexuality is illegal in Qatar, but when Sepp Blatter was asked about this in 2010 he tried to make a joke of it and suggested that gay fans should abstain from sex if they attended the World Cup there. Such attitudes aside, there is a broader reluctance in football to tackle such issues when they threaten considerable commercial revenues. Fair and equitable treatment should be given a higher priority than money.

Conclusions

The labour market in football is in many respects uncertain and haphazard in large part because although a greater quantity of more sophisticated information is available to decision-makers than in the past, making good use of that information is not straightforward. There are many uncertainties and information asymmetries persist. The labour market for player wages does work reasonably efficiently, but it has outcomes that are widely criticized because of the very high levels of payment received by some players. However, as Maguire points out, "The fundamental economic concept of supply and demand applies to footballers in terms of their employment price in the form of the wages they command" (2019: 72). The transfer market is less efficient and prone to intuitive decisions that have a limited or flawed evidence base. However, in part this reflects the short-term pressures for success created by owners and fans.

Player migration is not a new phenomenon, but it has increased in extent and the range of locations from which players come, although old colonial relationships have a significant impact on flows. It does not lend itself to a simplistic analysis in terms of globalization, although it should be noted that it is much easier to move capital around to buy clubs than it is for the majority of players to do so. Dazzled by the stories of the few players who have made the grade, which are covered extensively in their home countries, young players from Africa in particular fall prey to unscrupulous agents who abandon them when they arrive in Europe.

The exploitation that occurs in relation to player migration reminds us that in political economy terms a labour market cannot simply be judged in terms of whether it matches supply and demand in an efficient way. As Polanyi reminds us, labour cannot be treated simply as a commodity without depriving it of its moral value. In his analysis commodities are "defined as objects produced for sale on the market" (Polanyi 1944: 72). Labour is a fictitious commodity because it is something that has not been produced to be sold on a market. It is morally wrong to treat human beings as objects whose price will be determined entirely by the market. Labour "cannot be shoved about, used indiscriminately, or even left unused without affecting the individual who happens to be the bearer of this peculiar commodity" (Polanyi 1944: 73). To relate this to football, just think of a young player who has spent the years of his or her youth in an academy with the aspiration of earning his or her living as a footballer to be told that he or she is to be let go and not offered a professional contract. That is the fate of most such young players and they are often poorly equipped for a life outside football.

Polanyi emphasized that the economy is embedded in social and political relations. Hence, there are broader societal considerations that need to be taken into account in assessing how labour markets work. Evidence suggests that racism in football has declined over time, but it has far from disappeared altogether and there are some indications of a recent resurgence. The lack of BAME managers and the underrepresentation of ethnic minorities in the fan base remain causes for concern. There is a risk that the football authorities become complacent, thinking that it is a matter of identifying rogue fans and excluding them. They are also too readily reliant on the argument that it is a wider societal problem that just happens to manifest itself in football.

Homophobia among fans has declined substantially, and there is evidence of self-policing. However, male gay football players remain reluctant to come out, even after they have retired. The football authorities do not seem to be aware of how much attitudes among fans have changed. The broader issue that arises is how far regulatory interventions can tackle issues of this kind.

Football is in many ways a closed world, but it is always susceptible to an unanticipated exogenous shock, as with the outbreak of the Covid-19 pandemic in 2020. The full effects of this on football may take years to work through. As far as the labour market is concerned, transfer values are likely to fall, posing challenges for those clubs that have relied on player sales as a key source of income. Player wages are also likely to fall and some players will fail to secure employment. However, both effects are likely to be more muted in the case of world class players who are valued both for what they offer on the pitch and their contribution to marketing strategies. Top clubs generally have more reserves, or access to financing, to cope with a big fall in income. Challenger banks such as Aldermore became increasingly involved in providing funds for football clubs in the wake of the Covid-19 pandemic because, contrary to what might be assumed, they were seen as secure assets. The pandemic will tend to reinforce existing biases in football that favour wealthier clubs as operators in the labour market and more generally.

Contemporary football focuses on a small number of players who are superstars and are part of celebrity culture. They are valued by clubs not just for their playing ability, but the way in which they can raise the club's profile and sell merchandise. Their lifestyles are not typical of the majority of players and the public may have an exaggerated view of how well off most players are. Some players, especially migrants from Africa, really struggle. However, there is a positive side to the presence of superstars. If they are motivated to do so, they can take a lead on issues such as racism and poverty and help to contribute to positive change. Speaking out on human rights issues may, however, not be welcomed by clubs and among male players being gay remains a taboo subject.

5
FOOTBALL AND GAMBLING

In November 2020 the chairman of the EFL, Rick Parry, said that partnerships with betting companies were worth £40 million and an immediate ban would be "potentially catastrophic" (*Off the Pitch* 2020). His statement emphasizes just how reliant football clubs have become on their financial relationships with betting companies, a relationship that has attracted increasing criticism from advocacy groups and the media and attention from government.

An activity that at one time was seen as a source of innocent pleasure, betting is now recognized as potentially harmful and addictive. Like smoking, alcohol addiction and sugar, betting has become the focus of increased government regulation on its marketing, advertising and tax in recognition of the social harm it can cause (Grant 2018: 52–6). Industries that face such criticism often try to head off direct government intervention by trying to make a case for self-regulation and voluntary levies based on partnership with government. Responsibility for reducing harm, they argue, should rest with the individual addict rather than the industry or society more generally.

The betting industry's political vulnerability was apparent with the success of the campaign against fixed odds betting terminals (FOBTs). Campaigners against them described them as the "crack cocaine" of gambling, arguing that the quick-fire plays and the high stakes involved encourage customers to chase losses. The gambling industry argued that use of FOBTs could be a symptom rather than a cause of problem gambling. The government secured substantial tax revenues from the machines while the industry claimed restrictions on the machines would result in the closure of betting shops. Despite the efforts of the industry, the advocacy campaign was successful and the maximum stake was reduced to £2 (Grant 2018: 56–60).

There has been a long relationship between football and betting. At one time the football "pools" were a significant part of people's lives in the UK. "As late as 1998, 34% of all adults were players" (Forrest 1999: 161). Coupons would be carefully filled in seeking to predict draws, later score draws, in the hope of winning a life-changing prize. There were other chances to win smaller amounts on the coupon, such as the "Easy Six," which in fact consisted of six of the most difficult matches to forecast. When the results were announced on Saturday evening, the coupon would be carefully checked to see if there was any hope of a prize. Invariably there was not, but it was one of the rituals of everyday life for many people, offering hope of an escape from the humdrum and the tedious.

The introduction of the treble chance, a selection of eight draws, in 1946 created a long-odds and high-prize game. The publicity given to big winners, and their subsequent difficulties as some of them splurged the money, only served to increase the attraction of taking part. In 1961 a Yorkshire housewife called Viv Nicholson won £152,319 on the pools. That would be around £3.4 million at today's prices, a relatively small sum compared with the winnings available on the National Lottery today but a small fortune in 1961. When asked what she was going to do with the winnings, Nicholson declared that she was going to "Spend, spend, spend". This was what she did, eventually ending her life in a state of penury. Her story became the subject of a television programme and a musical. A number of lottery winners have bought or contributed substantial sums to their football clubs, although John McGuinness did not realize he would be responsible for the debts of Livingston FC and saw his windfall of over £10 million wiped out (Lottoland 2020).

"Spot the ball" competitions in newspapers were also popular and were judged to involve an element of skill, although in practice, as with the pools, success often depended on making an unexpected prediction. The broader significance of these activities was that they wove football into the fabric of everyday life, giving it an appeal beyond what was largely a working-class and masculine demographic.

In the late 1930s the EFL tried to thwart the pools by delaying publication of their fixture lists, but the promoters of the pools found ways around this obstacle and the league eventually gave up their attempt to challenge their existence. In 1959 the High Court ruled that the English and Scottish football leagues enjoyed copyright in their fixture lists as it involved skill in their construction. The pools companies then agreed to pay the leagues a royalty of 0.45 per cent a year or a minimum of £245,000 (£5.47 million in 2019 prices). In 1972/3 this deal was extended for 13 years at a value of £23 million (£280 million in 2019 prices). Although dwarfed by the sums raised by contemporary broadcasting contracts, it was still a significant contribution to revenues.

The introduction of premium bonds by the UK government in 1956 produced some competition as stakes were retained, although in practice they were eroded by inflation. They also lacked any participant element, which was provided by the creation of the National Lottery in 1994. The popularity of the pools had delayed the introduction of a state lottery, but once it started operating the higher cost base of the football pools made it difficult for them to compete.

Forrest (1999: 162) notes that "by 1996–7 the cumulative decline had reached nearly 60% with gross revenue down from over £900m to about £400m p.a." The "pools" still exist in the UK, but as a shadow of their former selves.

It should be emphasized that football "pools" are not a purely British phenomenon: "Football pools are marketed, typically by national lottery operators, in many jurisdictions around the World, including Singapore, China and Argentina, as well as in Europe" (Forrest & Pérez 2015: 472). In Europe, per capita sales are largest in the Nordic countries, but the largest market in absolute terms is Spain, where sales were €360 million in 2012. *La Quiniela* was established in the 1946/7 season and is run by the national lottery operator. The introduction of a lotto game in 1985 led to an initial sharp fall in coupon sales and revenue but this recovered substantially and since the late 1990s a steady state has prevailed. Garcia and Rodriguez (2007: 336) note the significance of "the active role of the player in *La Quiniela*, which goes beyond the illusion of control in the lotto game where players just decide which numbers are chosen. In *La Quiniela* the player may use the information about the performance of the teams in the past in order to make conscious choices." The gamblers "also have additional fun when following the matches on the radio or TV to see how many correct forecasts they have made" (Garcia & Rodriguez 2007: 349).

The "pools" belonged to a more innocent age of small stakes in betting. There were occasional attempts to ban them by opponents of gambling, but they quickly failed. In George Orwell's *1984*, a largely faked lottery is portrayed as a means of sedating the proletariat, and some left-wing commentators considered that the big prizes available were a diversion which, if they were won, distorted lives. However, these arguments never gained much traction as the "pools" were seen as a largely harmless activity enjoyed by many. Big companies such as Littlewoods were making good money out of them, while Labour MPs recognized how much their voters enjoyed them. The government benefitted from a pools betting tax introduced at a 10 per cent rate in 1948 and peaking at 42.5 per cent in 1982. The pools thus enjoyed unshakeable support from a triangle of monopolistic companies, the Treasury and enthusiastic consumers.

Today sports betting is an international industry that is increasingly online. It is estimated to account "for two-fifths of annual gross gaming revenue", but due to "The lockdown in Northern European markets in the spring of 2020 and the cancellation of the Euro 2020 finals is calculated to have led to a loss of between 42 per cent and 60 per cent of gambling revenues" (*Financial Times* 2020). Football and gambling have developed a symbiotic relationship in which betting firms are a significant source of revenue for clubs that act as gambling's "brand ambassadors". Domestically, however, there is increasing concern about problem gamblers and the risk of children being attracted to betting through its association with football.

Problem gambling

Discussing problem gambling is far from a straightforward matter. There are issues about definition, methodology and data sources. Indeed, the industry would claim that many of the statistics produced are unreliable and do not provide a good basis for policy decisions. It is evident that there are real difficulties in measurement, but it is undeniable that there is a social problem with gambling that requires more effective intervention than has taken place so far. Indeed, in the context of the Covid-19 pandemic the sports minister, Nigel Huddleston, requested that betting firms do more for problem gamblers to stop them spiralling into addiction.

In general terms there has been a debate between medicalized and public health understandings of problem gambling with public health approaches gaining ground, in part as a result of debates initiated in Australia which has a particularly high per capita spend on gambling. In 2019 the UK Gambling Commission launched a new strategy to tackle the range of harms that gambling can cause: "A key driver was the increasing recognition that these harms constitute a public health problem" (Gambling Commission 2019: 8).

Even so, these approaches are not mutually exclusive, and each may have something to contribute. The medical model focuses more on the individual gambler and their supposedly pathological behaviour. It is a medical disorder that can be identified by clinical tests. Hence, "theoretical models that conceive problem gambling as an addiction, mental disorder or impaired control are likely to regard it as a dichotomous phenomenon, as being either present or absent in an individual gambler" (McMillen & Wenzel 2006: 147).

The public health view is that "problem gambling occurs when gambling gives rise to *harm* to the individual gambler, families, other groups and the community as a whole". Problem gambling may be episodic and follow multiple pathways, and Australian work has developed an epidemiological framework for problem gambling (Productivity Commission 1999: 6.20). Some of the variables, such as venue features, may be particularly relevant in Australia with the "pokies" or gaming machines being a distinctive phenomenon. For the purposes of this discussion and its relationship with football, four independent variables are of particular relevance:

- The individual gambler's characteristics and behaviour.
- Support services for gambling addiction.
- Industry behaviour and response.
- Government policies and approach.

It should also be emphasized that the majority of gambling activity has nothing to do with football, although the available evidence suggests that it is a source of gambling activity that is increasing, particularly online. It is especially prevalent in parts of East Asia, where Premier League matches have a particular attraction as they are seen to be immune from any form of match fixing, so figures from the UK only tell part of the story. In Ethiopia, improvements in telecommunications infrastructure and the relaxation of a ban on broadcast advertising of gambling has led to sports betting shops springing up across the country (*The Economist* 2019a). Kenya and Uganda are countries where many young men have an obsession with football and they have been targeted by gambling companies (Davies 2020a).

Data from a large-scale survey in 2010 suggests that problem gamblers in Britain spent the largest percentage of their gambling expenditure on dog races (27 per cent) followed by FOBTs (22 per cent) (Orford *et al.* 2013: 9). More up-to-date data reveals a different picture, and there is particular concern about the attraction of football betting to minors. Figures released by the Gambling Commission covering the period March 2018 to April 2019 showed that 37.1 per cent of £14.4 billion spent by Britons on gambling was on remote casino betting and bingo with 22.7 per cent accounted for by "betting" that would include football and other sports such as horse racing. According to Global Betting and Gambling Consultants, in the UK the gross gambling yield from football (the sum of bets placed minus winnings) rose from £908.5 million in the year to April 2016 to £1.4 billion in the year to April 2019.

Even though the figures from the British Gambling Prevalence Survey, which surveyed 7,756 people, are dated and must be treated as approximations, the conclusions are clear: "[Problem] gamblers make a far greater contribution to total gambling attendances and losses than problem gambling prevalence figures would suggest. There are certain forms of British gambling to which problem gamblers may be contributing as much as 20–30% of all days play and spend and moderate risk gamblers a possible further 10%–20%" (Orford *et al.* 2013: 4).

In 2020 the National Audit Office (NAO) produced a report on gambling regulation in relation to problem gambling and protecting vulnerable people (National Audit Office 2020). In their presentation of key facts, they estimated the total gross gambling yield in 2018/19, excluding the National Lottery, as £11.3 billion. There had been a 57 per cent real terms increase in gross gambling yield over the previous decade, mostly due to a large increase in licensed online gambling. The Gambling Commission estimated that there were 395,000 problem gamblers in Britain, of which 55,000 were aged 11 to 16. It should be noted that many in the industry question the source and reliability of these figures, which are derived from bi-annual health surveys. The number of at-risk gamblers, who might be experiencing some negative consequences, was estimated at 1.8 million. Again, these figures cannot be treated as precise and one has to place in the balance the pleasure that many people derive from responsible gambling.

What was striking was that there was estimated to be a 56 per cent increase in gambling operators' spend on advertising and marketing between 2014 to 2017, mostly from increases in online and social media advertising.

The NAO defined problem gambling as "gambling considered disruptive and harmful to a person's health and well-being" (National Audit Office 2020: 5). The Gambling Commission estimates that about six additional people are directly affected by each problem gambler. Problem gamblers can develop an addiction which can then lead to financial and relationship issues and a deterioration in mental health. The reference to mental health problems as a cause reminds us that some attention has to be paid to the individual's propensity to develop an addiction issue as well as the social context in which they make decisions. The fundamental concern is whether the gambling industry's search for custom leads them to encourage, or at least not sufficiently discourage, problem gamblers because they are big spenders.

Football and gambling companies

Why has there been a close and, until recently, growing relationship between football and the betting industry to the extent that some have talked of "the gamblification of sport"? As Hancock and Ahmed (2019a) note, "Football shirts are attractive billboards, allowing betting companies to reach hundreds of millions of fans around the world." Perimeter advertising, particularly the kind that electronically reproduces moving messages, is also significant. These adverts could even be seen when matches behind closed doors were shown or streamed during the Covid-19 pandemic.

A study of three episodes of the BBC's flagship programme *Match of the Day* "found that gambling logos or branding appeared on screen between 71% and 80% of the show's running time" (Davies 2020a). Three full matches on Sky Television were also examined, but there was less advertising of risky products there than on the BBC highlights programme. "Across both kinds of broadcast, online gambling constituted the majority of brands advertised … The majority of all advertising seen while watching both highlights and live matches was for online gambling viewed on billboards" (Cassidy & Ovenden 2017: 18). References to responsible consumption were absent, which demonstrates "that in the UK, exposure to risky product advertising has become part of the experience of watching sport without the voluntary restrictions which apply to produced commercials" (Cassidy & Ovenden 2017: 19).

In Asia the branded shirts display logos to fans regardless of local laws, such as the one that bans online gambling in China, and the same applies in Australia where there is a ban on betting groups advertising on television during sports matches. In the UK, "[a]nalysis of 44 programmes from the Premier League and Championship found they featured an average of 2.3 gambling adverts, four times as many as for alcohol" (Davies 2020a).

VIP customers are particularly important to betting firms. VIP schemes "target the people who lose the most money and offer them rewards". VIPs claimed that "they were frequently offered football tickets in exchange for their custom" (Davies 2020a). A report obtained from the Gambling Commission "showed the industry's reliance on VIP schemes … these schemes drive profit for the industry" (APPG 2020: 11). By default some of these VIPs will be addicts as well as high rollers. When the Gambling Commission investigated the way in which Betway had handled seven customer accounts, predominantly treated as VIPs, it was noted that some of these customers "had been the subject of police investigations, it was established that stolen money have been spent online with Betway". This was not happenchance, as the Commission "found systematic failings in the way Betway identified and interacted with customers who were at higher risk of money laundering and problem gambling" (Gambling Commission 2020a).

None of the big six clubs has a betting industry sponsor, although Tottenham Hotspur has in the past. It is typically smaller Premier League clubs, and some in lower divisions, who have such sponsors (see Table 5.1). In 2020 half of the 20 teams in the Premier League and just over two-thirds (17) of the 24 clubs in the Championship had gambling company logos on their shirts. Stoke City are owned by the Coates family, who also own Bet365, hence the Bet365 stadium. The EFL has a sponsorship contract with SkyBet worth up to £4 million a year. Even though the shirt deals offered to Championship clubs are typically worth less than £10 million a year, they are usually more generous than those offered by other well-known companies. In the Premier League it was estimated in 2019

Table 5.1 Betting shirt sponsors of Premier League clubs, 2019/20

Club	Shirt sponsor
Aston Villa	W88
Bournemouth*	M88
Burnley	LoveBet
Crystal Palace	ManBetX
Everton	SportPesa
Newcastle United	Fun88
Norwich City*	Dafabet
Watford*	Sportsbet.io
West Ham United	Betway
Wolves	ManBetX

Note: *Relegated. The promoted teams did not have betting shirt sponsors.

that of the £350 million annual income from shirt sponsors, £69 million came from betting companies. At that time it was thought that about £40 million a year went from the gambling sector to the Football League and its clubs.

The FA agreed a six-year deal in 2017 with IMG which allowed the sports agency to sell online streaming rights to gambling companies. The deal allowed Bet365 to show FA Cup matches on its website and mobile app. To watch, fans had to have a funded account or have placed a bet on any event in the previous 24 hours. This was a surprising initiative given that the FA had attempted to distance itself from gambling by pulling out of a £4 million sponsorship deal with Ladbrokes Coral in 2017. The FA's explanation was that the deal with IMG was agreed before it had made a clear decision on its relationship with betting companies.

Football comes under pressure

The betting industry has found itself increasingly under pressure, often from those who might have been well disposed to it in the past. The Conservative Party manifesto for the 2019 general election was short on detail but it pledged to continue to take action on gambling addiction, noting that the Gambling Act was becoming an analogue law in a digital age.

The Gambling Related Harm All-Party Parliamentary Group has some 50 members and in June 2020 they published a highly critical, detailed and wide-ranging report on online gambling harm (APPG 2020). It should be noted that APPGs are informal groups of both Houses of Parliament and have been subject to some criticism for being vehicles of particular interests and points of view with lobbying firms or groups providing the secretariat (Grant 2018: 28).

This is not the case with this particular group, but it is funded by David Webb who set up the anti-FOBT Fairer Gambling Group, which played a pivotal role in the campaign on that issue. Webb's history was as a professional poker player and casino game investor. He was the inventor of Three Card Poker, a game that is played worldwide on casino tables and is an expert in understanding gambling game content and gambler behaviour (Grant 2018: 57). He made £15 million from selling his Prime Table Games business to Las Vegas casino group Galaxy Gaming and has also successfully litigated against the biggest manufacturer of FOBT machines, winning damages of $315 million, subject to an appeal. Webb's history led to allegations from some parts of the bookmaking industry that he was looking after the interests of casinos, hoping to lure them away from high street bookmakers rather than seeking to protect problem gamblers. It may, however, represent a Damascene conversion leading to a poacher turning gamekeeper.

The Football Supporters' Association stated that football clubs had to do more to educate their fans about the risks of gambling. Their chief executive, Kevin Miles, pointed out that "Football clubs are not like any other business – they are an integral part of many match-going supporters' lives and have a duty of care" (Football Supporters' Association 2020). A survey carried out by the Football Supporters' Association in conjunction with GambleAware found that only 10 per cent of fans felt their club were doing enough to warn of the risks of gambling. Only 23 per cent of respondents were (or would be) happy for their club to be sponsored by a gambling company. Of course, one might get a somewhat different answer if one had a series of questions, which suggested a range of hypothetical foregone revenues if a sponsorship was dropped.

Nevertheless, fans were particularly critical of betting companies sponsoring individual players. Particular controversy was caused by the relationship between the online casino 32Red and Derby County which many felt took gambling's relationship with football to a new level. In 2019 the company inserted a "star player" clause into the contract which provided the club with an additional £1.5 million. Former England player Wayne Rooney wore the number 32 shirt after his arrival at the club.

There is particular concern about the relationship between gambling and young players and supporters. The FA introduced a worldwide ban on betting on football for all those involved in the game down to step four of the non-league system (with different rules at step five and below). Participants covered by the ban are prohibited from betting, either directly or indirectly, on any football match or competition that takes place anywhere in the world. This also includes a worldwide ban on betting on any other football-related matter. For example, the transfer of players, employment of managers or team selection. The passing of inside information to somebody that uses the information for betting remains prohibited.

A teenage Leeds United player, Joran Stevens, was banned for six weeks in 2019 for betting on football, a clear contravention of the rules. The independent commission's ruling stated that the player "was heavily influenced by the presence of the gambling industry in football". Professor Jim Orford, founder of Gambling Watch UK, argued that the incident "shows that the relationship between gambling and football is out of control. Alarms should be ringing for the football authorities" (Ziegler 2019a). Gambling companies often use subtle forms of marketing. For example, "a logo for the online casino 888 featured as the answer to a Spot the Difference competition aimed at young Birmingham City fans" (Davies 2020a), and "Young people are at football matches not enjoying the game but engaged in a 90 minute non-stop high speed gambling experience, live betting on the next goal or corner" (APPG 2020: 12).

Tottenham Hotspur were reprimanded by the Advertising Standards Authority (ASA) in 2019 for allowing a player under 25 to appear in a tweet linked to a betting site, conduct that was judged to be a breach of the rules and socially irresponsible. In September 2019 Tottenham Hotspur had to end a multi-million pound sponsorship agreement with the Russian firm 1xBet covering Africa after a *Sunday Times* investigation revealed a string of violations, including bets on children's sports. In 2020 the ASA banned a YouTube video launched by West Ham's sponsor Betway because it featured the 20-year-old midfielder Declan Rice.

In 2020, José Mourinho, the Tottenham Hotspur manager, was urged to end a lucrative personal advertising deal with the major betting company Paddy Power. Mourinho featured in online adverts offering "100 free spins" to new clients. Gambling Commission data revealed a surge in casino games during the Covid-19 lockdown, often associated with problem gambling. Matt Gaskell, clinical lead for NHS Northern Gambling Services, said that footballers and managers should be banned from such campaigns: "The message is that 'this is an ordinary business' and it needs to be replaced with a public health protection model" (quoted in Ungoed-Thomas 2020). A spokesman for Mourinho said that the FA and Tottenham were aware of his partnership with Paddy Power before he took on his role at the club and no concerns were raised. Some might consider that to be itself reflective of prevalent relaxed attitudes towards gambling within football.

Government ministers have talked the talk on gambling and football, but whether they have walked the walk is open to question. In January 2020 Nigel Adams, then a minister of state at the Department of Digital, Culture, Media and Sport (DCMS), said that the FA had been told "in no uncertain terms" to reconsider its grant of streaming rights to gambling companies. Nothing was off the table, including a withdrawal of government funds. The FA indicated it would review its media rights deals when they expired in 2024. Government action was subordinated to a review of the 2005 Gambling Act which was inevitably delayed by the other issues that it had to deal with in 2020.

The extent to which the Covid pandemic response had occupied the DCMS was emphasized by its permanent secretary, Sarah Healey, when she gave evidence to the Public Accounts Committee in April 2020, admitting "We have not announced a timetable for that review". Translated out of Whitehall jargon, this meant that nothing or very little was happening and it had been kicked into the long grass. Alert to this possibility, the chair asked, "Is it likely to happen in this Parliament?" Healey's reply was that it was a manifesto commitment and was something that would be prioritized (Public Accounts Committee 2020: Q47–8). That could be interpreted as meaning that something would happen within the five-year lifetime of the parliament elected in 2019. In practice, much will depend on the stance taken by ministers and whether they think action will enhance their reputations or whether it could be more trouble than it is worth.

The industry response

The gambling industry is concerned about the criticism and reputational damage it is facing, and the possibility of severe curbs being applied to its marketing and advertising, not least in terms of its relationship with football. Interviews conducted by *Financial Times* reporters revealed "a fierce debate … on how to head off a larger regulatory backlash and show gambling groups and clubs are responding to public concern about their close financial ties" (Hancock & Ahmed 2019b).

There has been no agreement, however, on the best approach to take. CVC holdings, one of the world's largest online gambling groups and the owner of Ladbroke Coral, called for a ban on betting groups sponsoring football clubs, as has already happened in Italy. It should be noted that Ladbrokes sponsors the Scottish Football League. It has been suggested that large established companies could benefit from such a move as it would create a new barrier for market entrants.

In 2019 the Remote Gambling Association and Association of British Bookmakers were wound up and replaced by the Betting and Gaming Council, a new UK-facing operator body that aims to act as the industry's mouthpiece. The Betting and Gaming Council aims to ensure operators offer a safe and entertaining gambling experience for customers. It seeks to set high standards for tackling gambling-related harm, and build consumer and public trust in the sector, in part through a code of conduct for its members. The challenge with such a collective approach is that the consensus position may be affected by the slowest ship in the convoy in terms of the firm most reluctant to change. The UK has been categorized as a company rather than an associative state in which direct government–company contacts are often more important than mediation by associations as in Germany (Grant 1993: 14–15) and more may be achieved by industry leaders setting an example.

One of its first challenges was the Covid-19 crisis and its response attracted wide criticism. With more people at home, this increased the risks of exposure to online gambling harm. In response to concerns the Betting and Gaming Council put forward ten pledges to improve protections for online gamblers during the lockdown, but "Unfortunately, all of these pledges were very weak; a number need further explanation and others are obligations that are already set out with the Licence Conditions and Codes of Practice (LCCPs)" (APPG 2020: 19). In a letter to the chief executives of the five major betting companies sent in April 2020 the junior sports minister, Nigel Huddleston, urged them to go beyond the pledges made by the Betting and Gaming Council. In particular, he suggested that "safer gambling" messages attached to advertising should be made more prominent (Davies 2020c).

In the absence of relevant professional expertise and extensive evidence-based studies, it is difficult to assess the impact of "responsible gambling" campaigns. The "When the fun stops, stop" campaign at least appeared to have a clear message with some potential impact (GambleAware 2020). The effectiveness of the campaign was challenged by experimental work undertaken by researchers at the University of Warwick (Farey-Jones 2019).

The industry did announce that they would end television and radio advertising during the pandemic and replace these ads with "safer gambling messages", although there was some anecdotal evidence that they increased social media advertising. In any event, some Betting and Gaming Council members continued to air adverts after the agreed withdrawal date of 7 May 2020. It is, of course, not easy for a trade association to control the profit-seeking behaviour of its members. Moreover, it was suggested that the "safer gambling messages" were in effect another form of advert. They "promoted the brands both verbally and visually at least once, but often multiple times", and the "taglines in the ads were specifically related to gambling – and often prompt people to enjoy the company's products and visit their website" (APPG 2020: 20–1).

GambleAware is registered as a charity and states that it is "wholly independent and has a framework agreement with the Gambling Commission to deliver the National Strategy to Reduce Gambling Harms within the context of arrangements based on voluntary donations from the gambling industry" (GambleAware 2020). In June 2020 the Betting and Gaming Council made a pledge of up to £100 million of funding over a four-year period to fund treatment services for people experiencing gambling harm, effectively funded by the five largest gambling companies. Some would prefer it to be funded by a mandatory levy on gambling activities, including GambleAware itself, although they argue that the voluntary donations model has worked well enough for ten years. The APPG thinks that a levy of at least 1 per cent on gross gambling yield should be used to fund an independent Research, Education, Treatment and Prevention Council (APPG 2020: 63–4). In a response to criticisms of GambleAware made by the APPG in its interim report, it "refuted the accusation that the industry influences GambleAware but added that as an organisation, there was little they could do to stop this perception" (Hughes 2020).

The big five betting companies are aware of the pressure that the industry is under and have attempted to strengthen self-regulation, although not to an extent that has satisfied the sector's many critics. A systematic government response to these criticisms has been delayed, but the breadth of support that advocates of reform have attracted mean that it is likely to happen eventually. It would undoubtedly have a far-reaching impact on football funding.

The regulatory framework: not fit for purpose?

The principal regulatory body for the sector, the Gambling Commission, has attracted considerable criticism. The NAO 2020 report to some extent pulled its punches, suggesting that the problem resided not so much with the Commission itself but the context in which it operated, which is certainly part of the story. It noted that "[t]he Gambling Commission is a small regulator in a challenging and dynamic industry" (National Audit Office 2020: 11). Emphasizing the new risks emerging from technological developments, it argued that "The Commission's ability to ensure consumers are protected by these new risks is constrained by factors outside its control, including inflexible funding and a lack of evidence on how developments in the industry affect consumers." It implied that the legislative framework was inadequate, stating that "The Commission is unlikely to be fully effective in addressing risks and harms to consumers within the current arrangements" (National Audit Office 2020: 11).

The APPG was more forthright in is criticisms: "It is our view that the Gambling Commission is not fit for purpose and we recommend an urgent review of the Gambling Commission and its capacity to effectively regulate the burgeoning online gambling industry" (APPG 2020: 18). The APPG alleged that when they met the chief executive of the Gambling Commission, Neil McArthur, "in some cases he was unable to answer even the most basic of questions about the work of his organisation. The APPG expressed its concerns about the capacity of the regulator as it is currently formed to keep pace with the industry it is tasked with regulating" (APPG 2020: 17).

As was noted above, the ASA has exercised its regulatory functions in relation to advertising by the industry with some effective interventions. The FA also has regulatory functions in relation to the sector and these are considered below.

A major challenge is represented by the links between gambling and organized international criminal activity, in particular money laundering. In 2020 the online bookmaker Betway, a sponsor of West Ham United, was ordered to pay £11.6 million by the Gambling Commission for failing to ensure that money deposited by gamblers was not the proceeds of crime: "In one instance, the operator failed to carry out source of fund checks on a VIP customer who deposited £8m and lost over £4m over a four-year period" (Gambling Commission 2020a). The company failed to check how he could afford to bet so much, which is a condition of a gambling licence. It was even raised with the company's board, but they decided not to intervene. They only stopped taking his money when they were approached by the police who were investigating the customer.

In another case, "Betway did not carry out effective social responsibility interactions with a customer who deposited and lost £187,000 in two days" (Gambling Commission 2020a). The company also allowed an unemployed customer to deposit £1.7 million and lose more than £700,000 over three years. Unsurprisingly, the Gambling Commission concluded that "Betway had ineffective controls to identify and interact with customers who may have been risk of suffering gambling harm or money laundering" (Gambling Commission 2020a). It was concluded that "the repeated and systemic nature of Betway's failures and the involvement of senior and middle management meant that other customers were likely to have bet with stolen money or not been stopped from losing money despite demonstrating gambling problems" (Ellson 2020). Betway cooperated with the investigation and accepted that there were shortcomings in its policies and procedures.

The personal consequences of gambling addiction were tragically illustrated by the case of Chris Bruney, who committed suicide because he could not control his gambling habit and saw no other way out. He had managed to step away for a while but was attracted back during the 2014 World Cup by a firm called Winner that offered him various incentives to gamble. The company (PTES) trading as Winner surrendered its gambling licence before the Gambling Commission completed a review of the case. The Commission found that "PTES was guilty of serious failures in relation to anti-money laundering and social responsibility obligations. These failures also amounted to a neglect to uphold the licensing objectives in relation to prevention of crime and protecting vulnerable people from being harmed or exploited by gambling" (Gambling Commission 2020b).

The Gambling Commission felt unable to levy a fine of £3.5 million because parent company Playtech had shut the subsidiary concerned. Playtech, which had annual revenues of £1.3 billion, made a contribution of £620,000 to charity. A media outcry "forced Playtech to agree to pay the full £3.5m. What sort of regulator would fail so lamentably to bring sufficient pressure by itself?" (Lawson 2020).

The Gambling Commission: fit for purpose?

Criticisms of the regulatory arrangements for gambling focus on the resources available to the Gambling Commission and the response it makes to the considerable challenges presented by contemporary gambling practices. The overall conclusion that the media drew from the NAO report was that "The Gambling Commission is outpaced and outgunned by betting companies" and "that the watchdog is struggling to protect people from gambling-related harm" (Davies 2020b).

The specific problems associated with the Gambling Commission highlight a fundamental dilemma with any form of regulation. Campaign groups and parliamentary committees often call for the toughest possible regulations with heavy fines and prohibitions from operating. However, is it necessarily the most effective way of securing desired outcomes? Could more be achieved by working with the industry but with the threat of greater intervention in the background? What is required is a blended approach with a combination of more effective regulation and working with industry leaders.

Lesson learning is always important in relation to regulation and the NAO thought that there were lessons that could be learned from other regulators; for example, "there could be league tables of performance on treating customers fairly and awards for good practice" (National Audit Office 2020: 32). None of this would particularly affect football, unlike the APPG's view that all gambling advertising, marketing and inducements should be ended (APPG 2020: 12).

The FA and football clubs

Unlicensed football data is a growing problem. It is a serious concern because it is linked with betting in unregulated markets and could ultimately lead to the greatest concern of all for the football authorities: the risk of match fixing. In the UK data from league matches is controlled by Football Dataco, which it then sells to bookmakers that provide data to punters, allowing them to make bets during games. Bet365 has stated that 77 per cent of sports revenue came from bets placing during play: "Real-time updates on goals, tackles and refereeing decisions can be valuable to betting firms, as there is often a lag of 4 to 10 seconds for punters watching on TV". There could be up to 20 scouts from unauthorized data providers at any given league match sending information to betting firms operating in markets where gambling is restricted or illegal. Scouts can be paid £60 to £90 a game, but the data is still offered to betting companies at a knockdown price. As a consequence, Football Dataco has employed security guards to scan the crowd for scouts, but this has led to incidents in which innocent fans texting have been thrown out of grounds (Meddings 2019).

An unusual match-fixing scam that has been tried in the past, usually unsuccessfully, is floodlight failure. The scam worked because of bookmakers who run their operations around a handicap system where a team is given a half goal or one-goal head start. Punters backing the team that beats the handicap can double their money. In 1999 an Asian betting syndicate brought about floodlight failures at West Ham's Upton Park and Selhurst Park, then being used by

Wimbledon. The plot was revealed when an attempt was made at then Premier League club Charlton Athletic to instigate a floodlight failure, and a conviction was secured against a known fraudster with links to Triad gangs. A Charlton security guard also admitted a conspiracy to cause a public nuisance (BBC 1999). The *Calciopoli* scandal in Italy affecting Serie A and some Serie B teams in 2011/12 was a rather different attempt to fix match outcomes as it involved clubs securing "favourable" referees.

The FA is also concerned with enforcing the rules that seek to prevent players, managers, officials and club staff betting on games. The ban also covers passing on inside information such as injury or team news. Breaches often occur in the non-league system. In 2020, Isthmian League North side Soham Town Rangers saw their management team and three players guilty of betting breaches. One player had placed 6,514 bets on matches over a five-year period and was fined £4,000. At Chatham Town a player received an 18-month suspension and a £500 fine while the assistant manager of Berkhamsted was suspended from all football activity for 18 months, with 11 months suspended for two years, and a £500 fine. The vice-chairman of Soham Town commented: "I don't think they took [the rules] seriously. Betting can be very addictive" (quoted in Richardson 2020).

Former Liverpool strike Daniel Sturridge had a fine doubled to £150,000 and a ban extended from six weeks to four months after the FA appealed against the original decision. His contract with a Turkish side was then terminated by mutual agreement. Sturridge faced various charges that he had passed on inside information over a potential transfer in 2018. The FA alleged "that Sturridge's friends and family had stood to make more than £300,000 had bookmakers not refused some of the bets they sought to make on the player's potential moves" (Joyce 2019). The player commented: "I'm going to continue to campaign for professional footballers to be able to speak to their families and close friends freely, without the real risk of being charged" (BBC 2020b). The FA, however, is determined to enforce its betting rules.

Conclusions

A comprehensive report on gambling by a special House of Lords Committee was issued in July 2020. It produced an alarmed reaction from football clubs concerned about the threat to their shirt sponsorships. The committee emphasized the interdependence of football and betting and recommended: "Gambling operators should no longer be allowed to advertise on the shirts of sports teams or any other part of their kit. There should be no gambling advertising in or near any sports grounds or sports venues, including sports programmes" (House of

Lords 2020a: 171). They were, however, prepared to allow the EFL until 2023 to phase out shirt sponsorships.

The committee made clear its dissatisfaction with the existing regulatory arrangements:

> [The] almost universal adoption of the smart phone and other devices which enabled gambling 24/7 – whenever and wherever the gambler wanted, totally unsupervised. Gambling operators have made hay exploiting the laissez faire regime that has existed hitherto, while successive governments and regulators have failed to keep up with the revolution in the UK gambling sector. Our report demonstrates the wholly reactive nature of regulation since gambling was liberalised.
>
> (House of Lords 2020a: 4)

The committee chair, Lord Grade, stated: "Urgent action by the Government is required. Lax regulation of the gambling industry must be replaced by a more robust and focussed regime which prioritises the welfare of gamblers ahead of industry profits" (House of Lords 2020b).

Football continues to have a relatively relaxed attitude towards their close relationship with gambling companies. When the Northern Premier League chairman announced a BetVictor sponsorship for their leagues he argued that it was the toughest sponsorship market on record and that both the EFL and other non-leagues had betting partners. He declared: "I'm not about to enter the moral debate over gambling" (quoted in Richardson 2019). Of course, no credible person or organization is calling for gambling to be prohibited, simply that the controls on betting need to be tightened to minimize their social harm. From the evidence to date it is unlikely that football and the betting companies will be able to put their own houses in order to an acceptable extent. As the title of the House of Lords' report notes: "It is time for action." Government will eventually have to intervene to impose a new regulatory framework and it will involve some financial penalties for football, particularly smaller clubs.

6
WOMEN'S FOOTBALL

A record 11.7 million viewers tuned in to see England's 2019 Women's World Cup semi-final loss to the United States; 38,262 supporters watched the North London derby between Tottenham Hotspur and Arsenal in November 2019. In the summer of 2020 Women's Super League (WSL) clubs made a number of signings of key players from the United States and from leading French club Lyon. Chelsea completed a world record deal of around £300,000 for Danish attacker Pernille Harder. It could justifiably be claimed that "women's football is going through seismic change on an unprecedented scale, as men's clubs and commercial partners finally begin to get serious about it" (Brewin 2020: 55).

Referring to women's football implies that it is something unusual and different from the men's game. A controversial question is, "why should women's and men's football be kept separate? ... What is it about sociocultural understandings of women's and men's bodies that mean it is impossible for them to appear – officially – on the same field of play?" (Caudwell 2011: 339). As it is, the whole history of women's football "is a story of repression and exclusion" (Koller & Brändle 2015: 276). This is in large part because the presence of women in football is seen to challenge traditional notions of masculinity. One of the oldest clichés in football is that it is a "man's game". Hence, "the foundational fact that football was a locus of masculine self-representation changed very little. Football remained a starkly masculine sport" (Koller & Brändle 2015: 266). Many of the standard treatments of the economics of football either do not mention the women's game at all or only do so in passing.

Even when women have been present, they have often been largely invisible, as was the case for female fans for much of the period when football was a popular spectator sport. After a brief period when women's football developed in the late nineteenth century and then during and after the First World War, it only started to revive after around 1970 in line with the development of "second wave" feminism, the first wave belonging to the late nineteenth and early twentieth centuries. This second wave was stimulated by movements for socio-political change in areas such as civil and human rights, and the expansion of higher education: "there was a resurgence of feminist ideas that had been in currency during the pre-war period" (David 2016: 32). Football was one of the spheres of life that was influenced with bans on women's football being lifted in France and Germany in 1970 and in England the following year.

Although its popularity both for participants and spectators has grown, its marginality was illustrated by its vulnerability during the Covid-19 crisis. A survey published by the players' organization FIFPro in November 2020 found "that in 47 percent of the countries surveyed women footballers had wages cut or suspended. In 40% of countries, players received no mental or physical health support. In 69% of countries, communication with players was regarded as poor or very poor" (Kunti 2020). In the UK the girls' academies were controversially closed in the second coronavirus lockdown in 2020 by the FA, but the boys' academies continued to operate, which highlights the disparity between the provision for female and male players even at the junior level. Women's teams are still often seen by clubs as luxury optional extras. "In a matter of three decades, women have successfully entered the male world of Association football", but despite achieving formal equality "there can be no question that women's soccer exists in a marginalized niche compared to the men's game" (Markovits & Rensman 2010: 206).

In this chapter I consider women as players and officials, but also as spectators (a more passive role) and fans (a more active one). The way in which the partners and girlfriends of male players are portrayed in the media highlights the general inequalities surrounding women and football. The term "WAGS" (wives and girlfriends of players), first introduced by British journalists during the World Cup in Germany in 2006, is fundamentally sexist. First, the women are defined in relation to their partner and not as individuals in their own right, and the term became a derogatory epithet synonymous with them being mere consumers of fashion and cosmetics.

My analysis starts by examining how and why the women's game was first established and then suppressed by the football authorities. There are important differences in the way in which the women's game has developed in various parts of the world. It has flourished particularly in Northern Europe where public and official attitudes towards new gender roles have been relatively progressive. For a combination of reasons, it was initially most successful in the United States and it has also made progress in China. Considerable resistance has been encountered in Africa and Latin America, but above all in Islamic countries where even the admission of women to games has been a political issue, although there have been some positive improvements.

The emergence and suppression of the women's game

The first women's games and rioting

Women's teams first emerged in the UK in the 1880s, but they were often associated with scenes of considerable public disorder that required the intervention of the police. Lancashire was one of the original sites of the men's game, supplying five of the 12 original members of the Football League when it was formed in 1888. It was also one of the areas where the women's game emerged, one ground that was used being that of the Cheetham Football Club at Tetlow Fold in Manchester: "For some time past [women's] football matches, or rather exhibitions, have been held in Lancashire, the players being dressed in 'tights' of gaudy colours" (*Dublin Daily Express* 1881).

An England versus Scotland match was held there in June 1881 with a 7.30 pm kick off and the following report comes from a Manchester paper, which was reproduced in Dublin:

> The players, attired in a costume which is neither graceful, nor very becoming, were driven to the ground in a waggonette and, as was expected, were followed by a crowd largely composed of youths eager to avail themselves of the opportunity presented for a little boisterous amusement. Very few persons paid for admission to the grounds, but a great multitude assembled in the ground and struggled for a sight of what was going on within the enclosure, whilst an equally large number gathered on the higher ground on the other side of the field for a similar purpose. [...]
>
> A number of police constables were present to maintain order and prevent anyone entering without paying, and for about an hour while the so-called match was being played they succeeded. There were frequent attempts, however, to elude the constables. At length a great rush was made by those occupying the higher land, and the football ground was speedily taken possession of by the mob. Apprehending a repetition of the rough treatment they have met with in other parts of the country, the women no sooner heard the clamour which accompanied the rush than they also took to their heels, and ran to where their waggonette was standing. This they reached before the crowd could overtake them, amid the jeers of the multitude and much disorder they were immediately driven away. (*Dublin Daily Express* 1881)

The moving spirit behind these and other games was a Scottish suffragist and footballer called Helen Matthews (Tate 2016: 7). Relatively little is known about her, although she appears to have been a born around 1857/8 and a photograph of her in football kit standing on a ball can be found online (Wilkes 2011). She operated under the pseudonym "Mrs Graham" and her team was sometimes referred to as "Mrs Graham's XI".

She organized a women's international between England and Scotland at Easter Road, Edinburgh in May 1881. This news was greeted with concern in some parts of Scotland: "This is women's rights with a vengeance. We certainly often hear of them trying to don the apparel in private, but such pretensions to public notoriety have always been remarkably absent in Scotland. We want no such importations here" (*Jedburgh Gazette* 1881). The match seems to have been played without any trouble even if newspapers viewed "the game as little more than a curio – an entertainment somewhere between a fashion parade and a contemporary (if mild) Victorian freak show" (Tate 2016: 7). Thus an English Midlands paper noted that the players were dressed "in the correct and manly costume apropos to the pastime. The affair, however, was not voted a success, an almost entire absence of females among the spectators being considered proof that these exhibitions cannot become popular" (*Tamworth Herald* 1881).

A subsequent match at Shawfield, Rutherglen, near Glasgow ended in scenes of considerable disorder, described in one contemporary report as "a display of ruffianism" (*Greenock Advertiser* 1881). (Shawfield was later the home of Clyde FC before their move to the new town of Cumbernauld.) About 400 spectators paid to get in, but an even larger number did not and "they were certainly not of the class of people who usually patronise the game of football" (*Manchester Evening News* 1881). The so-called "rougher element" laughed, hooted and cheered, and swear words could be regularly heard above the noise. After an hour or so the ropes, which were all that separated the players from the crowd, were cut and they invaded the field, placing the players in danger. The police staged a baton charge and rescued the players with some difficulty. They were then assisted to their omnibus, "the police being compelled to use their batons freely to beat off the determined assaults of the infuriated ruffians by whom they were surrounded". According to contemporary accounts, one or two players were nevertheless roughed up and one fainted: "As the bus left the field, the players were hissed by the crowd" (*Manchester Evening News* 1881). After these scenes and similar ones at other locations, it was evident that women's football was not welcomed by many males and it disappeared for over a decade.

Women's football in the 1890s

The adoption of cycling by women created something of a moral panic, but it also raised questions about how women should dress, leading to the formation of the Rational Dress Society. Without that organization, "no woman would have dared step on to a football pitch clad in anything other than corsets and skirts" (Tate 2016: 60). A key figure was the president of the British Ladies' Football Club, Lady Florence Dixie. Her life was dominated by "Suffragism, rational dress and a passionate love of sport" (Tate 2016: 81). She anticipated what would happen a century or more afterwards when she said, "Looking ahead, I see arising on the golden hilltops of progress above the mists of prejudice, football will be considered as natural a game for girls as for boys." There was no reason why football should not be played by women provided they dressed rationally. Her "lithe, agile teams … actually allow the calves of their legs to be shown and wear caps and football boots. Terrible! Is it not?" (Dixie 1895).

She had no time for rugby, which she did not regard as a form of football but "harum-scarum scrummage. In Association football, a player must be light and swift of foot, agile, wiry, and in good condition; and are these physical requisites just the very characteristics of good health most to be desired for women?" She saw "no reason why football should not be played by women and played well". If women played football, they would enjoy better health and it would assist in "destroying that hydra-headed monster, the present dress of women" (Dixie 1895).

A search of the British Newspaper Archive for 1894/5 produced a considerable number of references to the emergence of the game. Some were match reports, others were considerations of the suitability or otherwise of women playing football. Views were more mixed than perhaps one might have expected. The correspondence columns attracted letters from both men and women expressing their views on the subject, generally hostile. Some of the articles treated the subject seriously, others as a source of amusement. There was quite a lot of attention to the clothing worn by the women and some reporters managed to include a double entendre referring to portions of the women's anatomy.

One of the origins of the women's game appeared to be that an increasing number of women enjoyed watching football matches and decided they would like to play themselves: "At a good many football matches around London the attendance of women is pretty large" (*Chichester Observer* 1894). This was also happening in northern locations such as Hull where it drew criticism from the "Princess" who urged women to discontinue their attendance of football matches as they were supposed to epitomize gentleness, sympathy and tenderness. She noted disapprovingly: "It has been remarked of late that more girls are seen on the grounds, and that they apparently follow the game with great interest. Football may or may not be a 'manly' sport, but it is certainly not one which women ought to take a pleasure in witnessing" (*Hull Daily Mail* 1893).

This advice appears to have fallen on deaf ears as it was announced in 1894 that a team of ladies was being formed in North London by an "enterprising organiser" (one Alfred Hewitt Smith from Crouch End). They would be professionals as they would receive a share of the gate money which was esti-mated to be substantial. There was some uncertainty about whether the referee would be man or a woman, but it was felt to be appropriate to find a woman referee if at all possible.

The secretary of the British Ladies' Football Club, named as Miss Nettie Honeyball, made it clear that they wanted to be taken seriously: "We have been very hard at work ... we practice twice a week and the girls can never get enough of it". Subsequent research established that "Nettie Honeyball never really ex-isted". She was just a suitable figurehead, "a fiction invented by Alfred Hewitt Smith and his younger sister Phoebe" (Tate 2016: 80). In any event, it was claimed that there were 26 members between the ages of 15 and 26, three of whom were married, and it was taken very seriously: "We have speed and skill ... This is no girlish folly. The British Ladies' Football Club is a stern reality" (*Edinburgh Evening News* 1895). Effective use was made of media publicity: "[The] public prints have been liberally supplied with photographs of lady football players taken in appropriate and not inelegant costume" (*Paisley and Renfrewshire Gazette* 1895). These were described by Miss Honeyball as blue serge knickers of the divided skirt pattern, along with caps and specially made boots.

In March 1895 a North versus South (actually North versus South London) match was held at Hornsey, attracting 10,000 spectators (some published ac-counts said 12,000). Once again it was argued that the colours of the shirts and knickerbockers worn by the players were of more interest than the actual play. The North won by seven goals to one, largely because they had a quality keeper in Mrs Graham, "being one of the three players who had any glimmering notion of the correct thing to do" (*Globe* 1895). She was, of course, the ubiquitous suf-fragist Helen Matthews.

Also singled out for praise was the North striker Miss Gilbert, "a slender young woman whom the spectators soon learned to address affectionately as 'Tommy'". This could be interpreted in more ways than one and as far as some of the crowd were concerned her gender was ambiguous: "One small player's agility and knowledge of the game marked her out for distinction, but the crowd resolutely refused to believe she was a girl, and she was continually greeted with cries of 'Tommy, you are a boy'" (*Paisley and Renfrewshire Gazette* 1895). Subsequent debate in the press revolved around the issue of whether she was Miss Daisy Allen (or Miss N. Gilbert) or the son of one of the players. When one spectator asked if the "little un" was a girl, he received the confusing reply, "Yes, he is" (Tate 2016: 78). One report disparagingly concluded: "The rest of the play-ers from time to time displayed an intelligent curiosity in the movements of one another, and rarely affected any close acquaintance with the rules" (*Globe* 1895).

A report of a match in Lanarkshire which originally appeared in the London *St. James's Gazette* was much fuller and more positive in its tone. It was one of a series played in Scotland with six old pence being charged for admission. The best approximate estimate that can be made of this in 2019 prices making use of the Bank of England inflation calculator is around £5.50. Despite the poor state of the pitch, the game was played at a fast pace and was described as a "stirring contest". The players were mainly mill workers and looked "brawny enough". Following an early corner, Lucy Coombes and the visitors' keeper became involved in what was described as an "altercation" in which faces were scratched. However, this was following by some "excellent dribbling … and a beautiful run by Kate Jackson", both teams being loudly cheered by the crowd. The forwards showed "excellent judgment" in passing.

Following another contested corner, Lucy Carmont shot over the crossbar and this led to a fight behind the goalposts involving several players. After a "fine display of passing" the team in red shirts and white knickerbockers scored to loud applause. At this point there was still 15 minutes to play, "but the game came to an unexpected conclusion owing to the excitement of the spectators, who had been encroaching on the players' space for some time. They broke through the ropes and an indescribable scene of confusion followed: the players being subject to rough treatment" as they retreated to the pavilion. There were supposed to be further matches, but after these scenes of disorder the authorities intervened to stop them (*Sheffield Weekly Telegraph* 1895).

In reports and correspondence to the press a number of arguments were used against women playing football. Some of them were just sexist assertions of an unadulterated kind. A former player with Nottingham Forest asserted that "their proper sphere is the mill, the shop, domestic service or home duties, and doing their level best in this direction they can remain useful and ornamental, and can always clothe themselves in the garments that modesty demands" (*Nottingham Journal* 1895). A female correspondent writing to a woman's magazine was indignant that its report of a women's football match "expressed no sentiment of disapproval of such an unwomanly undertaking". Apart from being "a repulsive exhibition", she also argued that "it must be remembered football is unlike every other game in that it is considered rough and dangerous, even for men; and therefore is doubly unsuitable for women" (*Women's Signal* 1895).

A more specific criticism was that crowds attended for coarse amusement and that once the novelty wore off, they would cease to attend: "No doubt the spectacle of twenty-two young women with flowing locks and clad in appropriate costumes, indulging in violent exercise has its elements" (*Paisley and Renfrewshire Gazette* 1895). A correspondent referring to "footballing women" as "the latest terror" expressed his hope "that the public generally will not support these degrading exhibitions, although no doubt the baser instincts of certain classes will be attracted by the chances of 'sport' at the expense of the women" (*Westminster Gazette* 1895).

One view was that the issue of women being allowed to play football was the result of the efforts of "a small clique of advanced women". Some saw it as a consequence of what they saw as the deplorable activities of lady cricketers or racing cyclists. The view was taken that it was a craze and interest in it would soon subside. Although there were reports of matches in subsequent years, 1895 seems to have been something of a peak. In part this was because the game was weakened by factional disputes between Lady Dixie and "Mrs Graham": "Whatever its merits, women's football was now turning into a sorry farce" (Tate 2016: 85). However, in 1902 the English FA found it necessary to prohibit its member clubs from playing against women's teams (Pfister *et al.* 2002: 68).

Of other European countries, while German women were encouraged to be physically fit to produce strong offspring, "there was absolutely no question about the fact that the football field was no place for women" (Pfister *et al.* 2002: 67). Anticipating later action in England, "The exclusively male members of the Dutch FA banned a women's game between Sparta Rotterdam and an England XI in 1896, following it up with a ban on women's football at all Dutch FA-affiliated stadiums" (Goldblatt 2007: 180). In France, women's football developed towards the end of the First World War, particularly in the Paris region. The Fédération des Sociétés Féminines Sportives de France was founded in 1917, "and organised a championship for teams from Marseille, Reims, Paris and Toulouse" (Williams 2013: 19). As well as works teams on the English model, there were "football-ing sections of more middle-class women's sports clubs" (Goldblatt 2007: 181). English and French women's teams played a match in Paris in 1920 before a crowd of 12,000. In the United States, women's football "did not really commence until the last two decades of the twentieth century, at which point the sport's evolution accelerated quite dramatically" (Markovits & Hellerman 2003: 16). An attempt to start a women's league in 1894 was unsuccessful. In China in the 1920s women's football "was played by women in a number of coastal cities" (Zhao *et al.* 2012: 2372). Nevertheless, the early story of women's football is very much a British one.

The First World War and the resurgence of the women's game

The First World War brought new if not lasting opportunities for women, including playing football. Women were needed to work in munitions and other factories, leading to a blurring of traditional gender roles. The fact that the men's game had been suspended in 1915 meant that women playing football presented no direct threat, and "Whereas the first women football players were looked upon as a curiosity and the games they played were treated as some kind of fairground spectacle, women's football developed during the First World War into a popular sporting event" (Pfister *et al.* 2002: 68). Additional legitimacy was derived from the fact that games were played to benefit war charities: "In this context playing football was not seen as a sign of moral decadence but as evidence of the patriotism of the women playing football" (Pfister *et al.* 2002: 69).

The best-known team, Dick Kerr's Ladies, was based at a Preston engineering firm, and "By the start of 1918, women's football was embedded in the working class munitions heartlands of northern England" (Tate 2016: 139). It was sometimes referred to as "Munitionettes football". By the end of 1920, Dick Kerr's Ladies had raised £15,000 for ex-serviceman's charities (approximately £675,000 at today's prices).

Once the war was over the charitable justification for women playing football could no longer be used, and given that the standard of play was high it was also seen as a threat to the men's game. This was underlined when 53,000 attended a match involving Dick Kerr's Ladies against St Helens Ladies at Goodison Park, Everton on Boxing Day 1920. A further 14,000 were locked out. The gate money amounted to £3,100 (approximately £140,000 in 2019).

In December 1921 the FA brought women's football to an effective end for half a century by ruling that clubs under their control, that is, any club engaged in serious competition, should not permit the use of their grounds for football matches between women footballers, "mainly because the game was unsuitable for women". They added a subsequent ruling banning referees from taking charge of women's games. The opinion of "the doctor Dr Elizabeth Sloan Chesser" was quoted in support. She claimed that "there are physical reasons why the game is harmful to women. It is a rough game at any time, but it is much more harmful to women than to men. They may receive injuries from which they may never recover" (*Lancashire Evening Post* 1921). That could also apply to male football players. The implicit argument here may be that the reproductive capacity of women, and hence their supposedly primary role as mothers, could be compromised, but there was no evidence for such an argument.

The FA also stated that complaints have been made about women playing football; no doubt part of this was economic, but the reservations were more deeply rooted. Although the following statement applies particularly to Germany, it could also have resonated in Britain: "It was much more the case that women playing sports touched on deep-seated convictions regarding the 'nature' of the sexes and their roles in society, as well as their service to the *Volkskörper* (the body of the people)" (Koller & Brändle 2015: 285).

The FA resolution also referred to the appropriation of receipts to other than charitable objects and took the view that "an excessive proportion of receipts are absorbed in expenses and an inadequate percentage devoted to charitable objects" (*Lancashire Evening Post* 1921). The FA had become increasingly concerned about the financial probity of women's football and Tate takes the view "that the FA's concerns about money were grounded in some sort of fact" (Tate 2016: 220). The FA dropped hints that it was going to act, but the leading figures in the women's game do not seem to have mobilized quickly or effectively enough to put their case. It was not an easy task as newspaper editorials which helped to shape opinion were generally not on the side of women football players: "On the one hand women football players were criticised for their lack of skill; on the other hand, if they did demonstrate ball-playing qualities, they were attacked for their lack of femininity" (Pfister *et al.* 2002: 70).

The women's game made an initially robust response to the FA ban: "It is stated that the opposition of the Football Association seems only to have increased the determination of the girls to play football" (*Lancashire Evening Post* 1921). New leagues of ladies' clubs were formed in the Doncaster and Coventry areas. However, there was divided opinion about the best way forward. Some clubs considered that there should be modified rules including "the elimination of charging, latitude with regard to hands for protective purposes, a smaller playing area, and a lighter ball" (*Lancashire Evening Post* 1921).

When 57 clubs met at Grimsby, the view that the game should be adapted to make it "more suitable for women" was challenged. "We want to play real football. If we alter the rules it will not be real football" was the predominant view. A compromise was reached which involved the use of a lighter ball and a reduction in the size of the playing area. Referees would have "a wide discretion with regard to handling and charging" (*Nottingham Evening Post* 1921). The difficulty was that by making changes of that kind, they were effectively conceding the argument that women could only play a modified form of football. The insistence of the English Ladies' Football Association that its members should only play against other clubs affiliated to it was also divisive.

In any event the FA ban had a devastating effect. Dick Kerr's Ladies were able to continue playing because they had access to their own recreation ground. It remained "one of the last stubborn outposts of the women's game" (Tate 2016: 266). They subsequently lost the use of the recreation ground and were renamed Preston Ladies and survived until 1965. More generally, "The years from 1923 onwards were not kind to women's football. Teams which had once been strong and well-supported gradually shut down" (Tate 2016: 265). From then on, "Cut off from formal systems of coaching or finances, the game was reduced to a peripheral and rather odd-looking subculture" (Goldblatt 2007: 181).

Later, "British women's football enjoyed a small renewed boom in the period after the Second World War, although it was not comparable to the growth experienced between 1915 and 1922" (Koller & Brändle 2015: 281). An informant stated: "I can remember everyone going to see it in the Hartlepool of my childhood. It was obviously big in the area during and after the war – my mother-in-law even played when she worked in the shipyard. So far as I know this was not true in East Lancashire when we moved there" (private communication 2020).

Women as spectators

Women continued to be present in football as spectators: "Half of the passengers on the trains that carried supporters of Bolton Wanderers and the team from Portsmouth to London for the cup finals ... in 1929 were women" (Koller & Brändle 2015: 272). I have talked to an elderly lady who attended Charlton matches with her father in the 1920s. Women may have been a minority of supporters at matches, but they were not invisible or silent. My own mother regularly attended Charlton Athletic home games. She was convinced that referees had a systemic bias against Charlton and made her views known in no uncertain terms at the first indication of an unfavourable decision, inviting the referee to make a speedy return to his home town.

Jean Tindell recalls how a lifetime as a keen home and away supporter of Charlton began in 1946. Her mother had left home and she was living with her father. She was then a schoolgirl and her father wanted to see Stanley Matthews play at The Valley. He decided to take his daughter with him, but the neighbours said "You can't take a girl to football. We'll look after her. Naturally I thought that [if] it was somewhere I should not go then it had to be worth going. When the game was over I excitedly asked, 'Daddy, can I come again?' I was hooked" (Tindell 1996).

Away games involved overnight travel in unheated coaches which often broke down or could not return because the driver was drunk as a result of the hospitality offered by the home side. Local residents would invite away fans into their homes for warmth and food. When she ran out of money on the return journey, male supporters would buy Tindell food. A photograph accompanying her article of some 25 away fans on the terraces in Sunderland shows that 12 of them were women, wearing club scarves but also quite fashionably dressed. The author's recollection is that supporters accepted women as fans, including single women like Tindell.

American exceptionalism

The United States provided the major impetus in the revival of women's football. The national team (Team USA) has been a strong force in the Women's World Cup, which it has won four times. Promising players from Europe have sought college scholarships in the United States, a phenomenon captured in the film about women's football, *Bend It Like Beckham*, and "At the end of the [twentieth] century, almost a third of all the women registered as football players in the world came from the United States" (Koller & Brändle 2015: 291). According to FIFA, the US has 1.6 million registered female players, more than the next eight best countries in terms of female players combined. An invitation international tournament, the slightly oddly named SheBelieves Cup, has been hosted in the United States since 2016.

Part of the reason for this dominance seems rooted in the fact "that the earliest and most consistent leading powers of women's football – the United States and its two fiercest rivals, Norway and China – represent countries in which the men's game has played a secondary role at least" (Markovits & Hellerman 2003: 14). In the case of China, the game began to develop in the late 1970s as part of the Chinese government's "Open Policy" and gained in popularity in the 1980s. Early successes appealed to patriotic feelings, as happened in the United States, and "By the 1990s Chinese women dominated Asia's football and became known as the 'Iron Girls' [*tian liangzhi*] of Asia". They won silver medals at the 1996 Olympic Games and at the 1999 World Cup, victories that "stimulated an unprecedented interest in women's football throughout China and put female players a little nearer to the sport's centre stage" (Jinxia & Mangan 2002: 1). The precursor of the Women's World Cup, the first Women's World Championship under the auspices of FIFA, was held in Guangzhou in southern China in 1991.

However, this progress was seen to be at the expense of the men's game which declined as the women's game improved. In 2001 I visited the People's Republic of China on behalf of the EU and was taken to see training facilities used by the men's national team. I was not impressed by their standard and considerable efforts have been made since then to make China a world football power. As far as women's football was concerned, the 1990s represented the peak of international success. The national team failed to qualify for the Women's World Cup and the 2012 London Olympic Games. The China Football Association took the view "that the way forward for the women's game was to establish a sound foundation by popularising football among teenage girls" (Zhao *et al.* 2012: 2382). They listed five realistic proposals as part of a long-term strategy. In 2019 the electronic payments company, Alipay, announced a ¥1 billion ($145 million) ten-year deal with the Chinese women's football team.

The story of women's football in China has been a long road, but a more winding one than in the United States. The more general point is that women's football was most successful in its late twentieth-century development "in countries where football was not completely occupied by men, and thus did not fully constitute … 'hegemonic sports culture'" (Markovits & Hellerman 2003: 14). Women's football in the USA did not present any threat to the leading sports of American football, baseball, basketball and ice hockey. It did, however, run the risk of being a tolerated niche activity.

In 1998 I visited a remote college town in the American Midwest to give a presentation and was given a tour of the campus. There was an excellent American football stadium and it was explained that the team was very important to alumni who were prepared to fund it generously. Round the back was a very basic football pitch and it was explained that this was one way of the college discharging its legal obligations to women's athletics. Title IX of the Education Amendments Act of 1972 (itself an amendment to the Civil Rights Act of 1964 and subsequently strengthened in 1988) is a federal law that states: "No person in the United States shall, on the basis of sex, be excluded from participation in, be denied the benefits of, or be subjected to discrimination under any education program or activity receiving Federal financial assistance." Intercollegiate sport has a level of spending and significance in the USA that it does not enjoy in Europe, and "The growth of women's football as an intercollegiate sport since the early 1980's has been truly phenomenal" (Markovits & Hellerman 2003: 20). It has been estimated around 20 per cent of all US high school females play football.

Another important aspect of the development of women's football in the United States was its popularity as a participant sport. It was seen as safer for children than American football or even "little league" baseball or softball. This led to the much commented on "football mums" phenomenon, which was actually rather patronizing terminology as it could be read to imply that football's popularity stemmed from the anxieties of overprotective suburban women. According to Markovits and Hellerman, "During the last two decades of the twentieth century, football became the second favourite participatory team sport, trailing only basketball and surpassing baseball by a wide margin" (Markovits & Hellerman 2003: 17). In fact, football was slightly ahead in the under-18 and under-12 age groups.

In any form of sport in any country, nothing succeeds like success. When participants in less well-known sports win a gold medal at the Olympics there is a surge of interest. American culture places a particular premium on success. The success of the women's team has made "their fans feel proud for being American in a sport where being American had not been a major source of pride and satisfaction" (Markovits & Hellerman 2003: 25). The broader social and political context should not, however, be neglected. Despite the persistence of sexism and misogyny in American public life, there has been substantial support from both women and men for women's football. The women's movement, for all the constraints on its influence, has had a substantial influence on public perceptions on appropriate roles for women in the USA, but there is still much to be achieved.

The hosting of the 1999 Women's World Cup in the USA attracted a big television audience and led to the formation of the first professional league. The first season in 2001 saw bigger than expected average attendances of 8,000, but television ratings were below what Turner Broadcasting hoped to achieve and the television contract was terminated. Attendances started to fall, expenditure could not be kept sufficiently in check and the league collapsed in 2003. It came back as the Women's Professional Football League in 2009 with a three-year television deal involving a Sunday night slot. It folded in 2012 and its successor from 2013 was the National Women's Football League (NWSL), initially with eight teams, increasing to ten from 2021. Eight of the nine teams playing in 2020 ranked among the top 20 women's teams in the world according to the football consultancy 21st Club.

Six teams in 2021 will be affiliated with men's teams in the USA and one with Olympique Lyonnais, the highly regarded French team. They paid $3.15 million to acquire NWSL's Seattle-based team Reign in 2019, subsequently OL Reign and playing its games in Tacoma, Washington. The French club's women's team is said to have an annual budget of €7–8 million, with players paid up to €10,000 a month: "Though this is far less than the club's male footballers, it is among the highest wage offered to female players anywhere in the world" (Ahmed 2019c). The objective is to have the two best women's teams in the world, in Europe and the USA.

In 2019, 28 members of the women's national team sued US Football for institutionalized gender discrimination, arguing that they did not receive equal pay and resources with their male counterparts. Between the years 2013 and 2016 "the male players earned on average $236,320, while the women earned a maximum of $99,000" (Myers 2019a). To some surprise the action was thrown out by a US district court in 2020, although a complaint about inferior travel and accommodation was allowed to go to trial, and the main action could be appealed. One proximate factor was that the men's team has been so bad in recent years that they have actually been paid less.

The lawsuit has been "a public relations nightmare" for US Football and it may well be settled out of court. Former US Football president, Carlos Cordeiro, "was forced to resign in March [2020] when US Football's legal team got overzealous (or, in plainer terms, sexist) in their defence against USWNT's [the United States women's national soccer team's] lawsuit, and sponsors became alarmed" (Murray 2020). Women football players have aligned themselves with the #MeToo movement. Co-captain Megan Rapione provoked a Twitter outburst from President Trump when she declared that she would not be going "to the f***ing White House" (Ahmed 2019d).

Women's football in difficult contexts

For all the challenges it faces, women's football has received broad support in the USA, and "In Northern Europe, the egalitarianism and social engineering of social democratic governments has helped promote women's football" (Goldblatt 2007: 698). However, in many parts of the world there is much more resistance to women playing or even watching football. Despite encouragement from FIFA, "many national federations – particularly outside Europe and North America – barely fund it. Professional leagues are still new and non-existent in many countries and many of the women playing [at the 2019 World Cup] are semi-professionals who hold down other jobs" (Jenkins 2019).

There has been a challenging environment in some Southern European and Latin American countries. Playing numbers in Southern and Eastern Europe are lower than in the north. "Forty years ago Italy was a leading light in the women's game", but sexist officials managed to curb progress with the head of the country's amateur football association telling a meeting with colleagues: "We can't talk constantly about paying money to this bunch of lesbians" (Myers 2019b). The 2019 World Cup, when Italy reached the quarter finals, boosted interest, with 24.4 million Italians watching the women's team with an average audience share of 31.8 per cent for the main terrestrial channel, RA1, showing live women's football for the first time. The 2019 World Cup "represented a huge, potentially mind-changing triumph on the landscape of traditionally male-chauvinist and sexist Italy" (Agnew 2019). Based on her time at Juventus, Aluko describes the Serie A *femminile* league as "competitive and growing", and notes that, "In March 2019, a record crowd of just under 40,000 fans watched us beat our rivals Fiorentina when we played at the Allianz Stadium for the first time" (Aluko 2019: 464).

The women's team in Argentina has faced ingrained sexism and a lack of support from the Argentinian Football Federation (AFA). Their guide to the 2018 World Cup included advice on how to pick up Russian women, and "The Argentinian women's team has been shockingly neglected by its federation and treated with downright hostility at times" (Elsey & Nadel 2019). The women's team has been supported by the feminist movement in the country. Following public pressure, the AFA announced the professionalization of the women's league in 2019: "The 16 clubs must each sign at least eight players on professional contracts, although most salaries will be just a few hundred dollars a month" (Kuper 2019).

Africa "inherited the male culture of European football". Even in urban centres, traditional attitudes about the role of women can persist, but "Nonetheless, in Nigeria, Ghana and South Africa the women's game has grown" (Goldblatt 2007: 880). The Confédération Africaine de Football has created a women's development department. Cameroon won the African women's team of the year title after a long period of domination by Nigeria. When Nigeria was eliminated from the 2019 World Cup, "the players staged a sit-in in their hotel simply to be paid" (Kuper 2019). South Africa started an amateur women's league in 2019 with the first game played in Soweto: "The start of the Safa Women's National League (SWNL) is a glimpse of light in a long, dark tunnel in women's football" (Makwena 2019). Namibia successfully hosted the African women's championships in 2015: "Finances have been their Achilles heel over the years, with the men's game gobbling up the largest portion of investments, leaving the women to feed off crumbs" (*Namibian* 2020). However, the executive of the Namibian Football Association is being supportive and has promised $500,000 from the FIFA Covid-19 relief fund.

It has been a struggle for women in Islamic countries even to be allowed to watch games. It was permitted in Saudi Arabia from 2018, but women sit in the family section separated from men. In Iran a woman committed suicide by setting fire on herself after she was threatened with prosecution for entering Tehran's Azadi stadium dressed as a man. This increased the pressure on the government to lift the ban on women attending matches, with FIFA threatening to suspend Iran because of its male only policy. In 2019 some 4,000 women watched a World Cup qualifier against Cambodia, and "Iran has now lifted the ban on national games but its policy on league matches remains unclear" (Khalaj 2019).

Women playing football is a controversial issue, but there are some signs of change in Saudi Arabia after a period when it was an underground activity seen as unacceptable by adherents of conservative Wahhabism, the country's dominant form of Sunni Islam. The Riyadh women's league had seven teams in 2019: "They play nine-a-side, largely in women-only facilities so that they can wear normal kit including shorts rather than be covered head to toe" (Dickinson 2019).

There is undoubtedly an elite group of women's football nations, while the game struggles in the Global South. Seven of the eight quarter finalists in the 2019 World Cup came from Western Europe and the United States, the Americans beating Thailand 13–0 earlier in the competition. The six European nations with more than 100,000 or more registered women footballers reached the quarter finals of the World Cup (England, France, Germany, the Netherlands, Norway and Sweden). The strength of the men's game in countries such as England and Spain permits the cross-subsidization of women's teams by leading clubs. They also have existing fan bases which can be attracted to support the women's team.

In the past women players have suffered considerable hardship. Fara Williams was homeless for seven years at the start of her England career and lived in a hostel. Her former club, Reading, now has a club house where a few women players can live: "If players now were to have a similar situation to mine, they would be housed more easily with the funding available in women's football" (Flanagan 2019). A top-level player at a club like Arsenal with an England contract could earn £200,000 a year, but some male players could earn that in a week: "The combined salaries of the 1,693 women playing in the top seven football leagues add up to $41.6m, just slightly less than the $41.7m salary paid to Neymar by Paris Saint-Germain" (*The Economist* 2019b). According to the players' global union FIFPro, a survey of 3,600 players in women's leagues around the world showed they earned just $600 a month on average (Ahmed 2019c).

Progress and a new challenge

The impact of the 2019 Women's World Cup

The Women's World Cup provided a big boost to the women's game, primarily as a television event, which is how the greatest numbers of people watch football. A number of countries broke viewing records for women's football. The semi-final featuring England was the most watched television programme of the year up to June with a peak audience of 11.7 million, and "Some 14m Americans saw their team beat the Dutch 2–0 to win their fourth title … more than tuned in to most basketball and baseball league finals" (*The Economist* 2019c).

Such events may, of course, not have a lasting effect once the excitement has subsided. The 1994 men's World Cup in the USA was a success financially and in many other ways, but it did not have a transformative effect on US football. In relation to the impact of the 2019 Women's World Cup, three dimensions need to be examined: attendances at league games, sponsorship and broadcasting.

One of the difficulties faced by the WSL in England, which only became professional in 2018, is that many of the games are played in inferior stadiums that are difficult to reach. For example, Arsenal normally play their games at Boreham Wood and Tottenham Hotspur at Barnet's ground. Manchester City does have a purpose-built stadium next to the Etihad which is also used by the development squad. In the 2019/20 season some clubs experimented with holding key games in their main stadium. The record attendance was 38,000 at the new Tottenham Hotspur stadium for their game against Arsenal. The Manchester derby at the Etihad attracted 31,213 fans. In the preceding season average crowds were just 833, but the average home crowd in the truncated 2019/20 season was 3,401. This is more than the National League at the top of the non-league pyramid (2,174) but below League Two of the Football League (4,698).

As far as sponsorship is concerned, Barclays Bank became the first title sponsor of the WSL in 2019 in a three-year deal worth £10 million which provided clubs with a £500,000 prize pot: "The women's game is luring brands which have been shut out of the sport because of the way sponsorships of women's teams were bundled with those of men's sides" (*The Economist* 2019c). However, the sums made available are well below those in the men's game. The chemicals firm Arkema bought the naming rights to the French women's league. At €1 million a year (£870,000) over three years it was "peanuts compared with the €15m [£13 million] a year the men's league receives from its main sponsor" (*The Economist* 2019c). Nevertheless, consultancy Brand Finance has estimated that there is €1 billion (£870 million) of untapped sponsorship opportunity for women's leagues and clubs generally.

Broadcasting deals are of key importance. Under the present arrangements for the WSL, BT Sport and the BBC only cover the production costs at around £50,000 per match. In France, the pay-TV broadcaster Canal+ has paid €6 million (£5.2 million) over five years to show matches in the country's women's league: "At about £1 million per year, that is one ninth of what Sky and BT Sport pay the Premier League to show a single game live" (Ziegler 2019b). Nevertheless, audience figures have improved, although they are still relatively small. BT Sport saw a 52 per cent increase for its live coverage, with 85,000 viewers at its average peak. The Women's Football Show, which was being shown on BBC4 at 7.00 pm on a Sunday evening, "peaked at more than a million viewers" (Hudson 2019). The FA was hoping to secure some terrestrial coverage for the WSL from 2020 onwards.

Covid-19

FIFPro saw an "almost existential threat to the women's game" from the Covid-19 pandemic: "Due to its less established professional leagues, low salaries, narrower scope of opportunities, uneven sponsorship deals and less corporate investment, the fragility of the women's football eco-system is exposed by the current situation." Inferior contracts and the absence of basic worker protections "leaves many female players – some of whom were already teetering on the margins – at great risk of losing their livelihoods" (FIFPro 2020).

In practice leading clubs are unlikely to abandon their commitment to the women's game which is one way of signalling their commitment to inclusivity and diversity. This is in spite of the fact that only one WSL club made a profit in 2019, Manchester United, which made £51,000 in its first campaign as a relaunched Championship team. Other than that, "The losses ranged from £36,000 (Aston Villa) to just over £1 million (Manchester City and Everton), and they are set to increase in 2020 following a frenzied period of investment and a calendar struck by the pandemic" (Brewin 2020: 59).

There are greater challenges outside the top leagues where teams either have a loose link with established clubs or no connection at all. The women's team at Charlton Athletic is allowed to use the men's training ground, but the cost of running the club was subsidized by a different owner at a cost of £50,000 a year until the new owner of the men's team acquired the women's team in 2021. In the summer of 2020 the women's team had to reach out to supporters of the men's team for financial assistance via the Supporters' Trust.

Paradoxically, the women's game in the USA was able to reap some benefits from the Covid-19 crisis as it was the first professional team sport to start playing, albeit in a makeshift Challenge Cup. The absence of ticket sales was offset by the presence of three new sponsors: Procter & Gamble and its "Secret" brand, Google and Verizon. The league saw a window of opportunity to win new fans from other sports, and "Television ratings for its opening match more than tripled the league record" (Gerano 2020). The launch of Angels City (an interim name) in Los Angeles would bring the number of WSL teams to ten from 2022. It was backed by tennis star Serena Williams and Hollywood actress Natalie Portman among others.

Conclusions

Some of the overt sexism that surrounded the women's game in the past has diminished, although it is more of an obstacle in some countries than others and never absent anywhere: "On the whole, blatant and overt forms of misogyny and sexism are not tolerated: however, it would be inaccurate to claim that misogyny and sexism have been eradicated" (Caudwell 2011: 330). Former England international Eniola Aluko has written at length about her long battle to get the FA to take her grievances seriously, culminating in a financial settlement and later a full and unreserved apology (Aluko 2019).

A more positive development is that women officials, although still relatively rare, are now more accepted in the men's game. That said, I have personally heard sexist comments about a female referee at a non-league game. The real pioneer in women's refereeing was Wendy Toms, "who endured the media spotlight every time she was promoted to a higher division and treated almost as a freak" (Rudd 2019). A fitness test originally devised for men has been changed to one that takes account of women having less muscle mass. Previously, "plenty of female referees were not being allowed to progress through the men's game because they were simply unable to meet this arbitrary standard of fitness that had been conjured up many years previously" (Dunn 2019: 147).

Koller and Brändle wrote the original German version of their analysis in 2002 and may have been understandably pessimistic when they argued that "The basic connotation of football as masculine has proven even more persistent than the individual concepts of masculinity" (Koller & Brändle 2015: 293). Football is, of course, conditioned by societal conventions, but it can also help to reshape those conventions. Koller and Brändle's (2015: 294) claim that "The future of the gender order in football may well be identical to the gender order in society as a whole" may be argued to be too sweeping a conclusion. Women's football may help to change society's perceptions rather than being constrained by them.

7
REGULATING FOOTBALL

As the preceding chapters may have suggested, the regulation of football is not very effective. Football has largely regulated itself, reflecting the extent to which it is a closed policy community with its own norms, values and largely unchallenged assumptions. It sees itself as a special world that can isolate itself from wider societal trends with external interventions regarded as unwanted and inappropriate. "In a country obsessed with football" (Cameron 2019: 571), politicians are often willing to tolerate this distinctiveness if they can bask in the reflected glory of success by national and club teams and pretend that they are "one of the lads" by supporting a particular team. This can, of course, lead to mistakes. David Cameron insisted that he was an Aston Villa fan, but mistakenly identified himself as a West Ham supporter in the 2015 general election campaign (Cameron 2019: 571–2). This led to social media jokes about "West Ham Villa" and "Aston United". Politicians also appreciate hospitality offered at big matches. This combination of internal self-satisfaction, cosy relationships and external benign neglect has meant that in general the governance of football is inadequate at a national and international level.

Government and legislative interventions have been largely ad hoc with calls for the game "to get its own house in order". It rarely does and no systematic pressure is placed on it to do so. The EU did start to use its capacity and mission as a regulatory state at one stage, but this faded with personnel changes and the arrival of new and more pressing challenges. FIFA has been beset by problems of corruption, while UEFA has been unable to put in place an FFP system that can withstand legal challenges. At a national level, the FA has been seen as ineffective and conservative while the EFL seems unable to deal with "rogue owners". The US commissioner and franchise system centralizes control in a way that means a lot depends on the probity and good judgement of the person in charge.

Explaining the relative absence of the state

It is possible to offer a theoretically grounded explanation of the relative absence of the state from football, or indeed sport more generally. There have been moves towards greater involvement, but these have been spread across a number of distinctive policy areas and there is an absence of any coordinated strategy. The Covid-19 pandemic did lead to calls for a "reset" of football finances amid arguments that the current business model was not sustainable (House of Commons 2020). However, there has been no shortage of calls for change over recent years, but they have not produced much in the way of action. Pressure could mount, but that requires identification of a feasible model for change, as discussed in Chapter 8.

Here comes the regulatory state – or does it?

Before proceeding further, it is necessary to explore what is meant by the concept of the "regulatory state" and how it might apply to football. The first point to bear in mind is that this is really an ideal typical model that attempts to capture long-term shifts in the nature of the state and its relationship with society. In practice the regulatory state will coexist with other forms of the state, reflecting its protean character.

Even so, it is possible to present a narrative about the state experiencing a number of historical stages. Originally it was a "laissez-faire" state with the functions of providing defence against external enemies, maintaining law and order and collecting the revenue needed to perform those functions. The state never stood completely aside from the market because it provided a currency, and it had a long-standing interest in the standards of goods and the conditions under which they were sold. In the nineteenth century there was increasing interest in the conditions under which people worked, pollution of the environment and the promotion of public health to tackle diseases like cholera. The First World War required the mobilization of society on an unprecedented scale and some of the relationships that were developed between government and business persisted into the interwar period and led to interventions such as that which saw the formation of Imperial Chemical Industries as a "national champion" to remedy defects in the chemical industry identified in the war. A rudimentary welfare state also emerged. The "New Deal" in the USA involved more radical and extensive interventions than in the UK.

Nevertheless, these interventions fell far short of the "command" or "control" state that developed after the Second World War, exemplified by an extensive programme of nationalization, the provision of social security and the creation of the National Health Service. The partial disappearance of this Keynesian welfare state does not require further explanation here, although many accounts tend to downplay the impact of globalization on domestically driven attempts at autonomous economic policy as distinct from the policy preferences of the Thatcher government.

The emergence of a regulatory state does not mean that state power necessarily diminishes, but its form changes. It becomes less direct but can also be more penetrating. Moran (2000: 2) suggests that in the shift from a command state to a regulatory state, "this new order of command actually marks a different kind of command – in many ways more pervasive than the old, defunct order of command". One must be careful about characterizing the regulatory state as a withdrawn, distant state that stands in the background offering guidance and a modicum of empowerment to approved intermediaries but leaving civil society to do the heavy lifting, sometimes expressed in a distinction between "steering" and "rowing": "The story cannot just be about shifting from rowing to steering, but about the state acquiring new means of control over areas of civil society, like sport and financial regulation, which hitherto largely operated independently" (Moran 2015: 406)

So why has football been left to its own inadequate devices? According to Moran (2003) sport regulation is a self-referential system. Until the 1960s sport was rooted in a tradition of voluntarism that was "paradigmatic of the British tradition of self-regulation" (Moran 2003: 87). If regulation of football could be achieved without and outside the state by self-appointed elites, the decision-making load on the state was reduced. However, from the 1990s onwards external systems of values started to impinge on these hitherto autonomous worlds, leading to the erosion of self-regulation.

Sport started to be seen as something that contributed to an external social purpose. As well as being a significant economic activity (which contributed to exports and tax revenues), sport helped to "achieve wider purposes of social policy, like promoting public health and combating social exclusion" (Moran 2003: 91). In particular, this fitted with some central policy objectives of New Labour. What this meant was a focus on how football could be utilized as a mode of community action to help achieve public policy objectives, combating knife crime becoming central after 2010. Clubs often have quite strong community involvement schemes and can appear to be effective mechanisms for delivery. They were able to congratulate themselves on how such involvement with government policy put them in a good light. Having received visits from the Chancellor of the Exchequer, the health secretary, Prince William and a Home Office delegation, Charlton Athletic felt able to claim that "[s]uch heavyweight and high profile visits have positioned the club and the Community Trust as a highly imaginative pathfinder contribution that can be used as an excellent model of best corporate social responsibility practice". In particular, the club's activities were seen as offering "an innovative way of meeting the Government's social objectives and the new Respect Policy" (Charlton Athletic 2005).

These engagements with social policy diminished in importance after the change of UK government in 2010. Yet self-regulation remains a strong force in football despite Moran's predictions. It is here that policy community theory with its notion of strongly patrolled boundaries to exclude outsiders from decision-making becomes relevant. Arguments about expertise acquired by experience are used to resist exogenous pressures. This is in spite of a frequent lack of the political sophistication that permitted agriculture to maintain a policy of exceptionalism and special treatment for so long. Football clubs are not generally politically sophisticated actors. I remember being asked to brief a Premier League manager about a projected tour of China and Japan, only to be greeted with the observation that the empress of China had recently had a baby.

Even so, a blunt "clear off" strategy can bring its rewards. An indignant Premier League chairman thus said of the European Commission: "It cannot be right that the Commission should seek to challenge our right to enter into genuine commercial agreements for the sale of our broadcast rights because they do not like the outcome. We must use every means at our disposal to protect the game in this country from such outside interference" (quoted in Grant 2007: 71). Government has many other problems to deal with, and faced with such stances the temptation is to resort to a depoliticization strategy to deal with football-related issues. Hence, the penetration of the regulatory state into football remains more limited than in other economic and social arenas.

This was apparent under New Labour when there was serious discussion of introducing an independent regulator, a suggestion robustly opposed by leading Premier League clubs. Tony Blair was told by then special adviser James Purnell that this was a bad idea that would antagonize football by imposing something suggestive of a Soviet nanny state. Football hated outsiders "questioning, influencing or instructing them about their business". What, then, was the answer? Government should "support self-regulation to change football's culture" (Bower 2003: 206). How can one change a deeply embedded culture by resorting to those who are its defenders and beneficiaries? That remains a highly pertinent question.

The world of the self-regulators

A common complaint by football fans is that the FA and the EFL are not "fit for purpose". It is important to be clear about what those purposes are. The FA is the national governing body for English football. The EFL is a limited company which runs a competition on behalf of its shareholders, the clubs. It is in effect a trade association for the clubs. It is certainly not a fans' representative body and, although it carries out regulatory functions, it lacks the mission, capacity and resources required by an effective regulatory body.

The FA

The FA is the governing body of English football. Unfortunately it has not discharged this task in a way that has been found to be particularly impressive. This was evident in terms of its weakness in the face of the formation of the Premier League, which the FA saw as a way of weakening the position of the Football League with which it had had a poor relationship on issues such as club versus country. The subsequent operation of the Premier League and the huge sums of money it generated led to an undermining of the FA's authority.

In many respects the FA was a helpless bystander while the decisions that mattered were made by the Premier League. It has tried to address governance issues, "but at its heart the governing body looks even weaker, less capable of doing what is necessary, than when it made the fateful, fatal howler of backing the Premier League breakaway back in 1991" (Conn 2005: 350). It looks like a body that lacks confidence combined with a failure of imagination: "[The] FA has shown itself unable to govern independently because it has become inexorably controlled by the Premier League and is bedevilled by the conflicts of interest around its top table" (Conn 2005: 370).

In its written evidence to the House of Commons committee inquiry into the collapse of Bury FC, the FA's stance could be described at best to be one of wringing its hands in despair, but also of seeking to wash its hands of the matter and pass the buck elsewhere. Shrugging its shoulders, it stated, "there will always be clubs that trip up along the way". Owning a club meant "owning a business in an extremely competitive market". For its part the "FA does not seek to compel action" (House of Commons 2019a). Others needed to come up with answers, in particular the clubs by empowering their league board.

The Owners' and Directors' Test is administered by the FA for the Premier League and the EFL for its leagues, the objective being to enhance the image and reputation of the game. Any person with a "disqualifying condition" is prevented from becoming involved in the ownership and management of a club. The list of "conditions" is a long one and includes disciplinary action by a professional body, such as the Law Society; an unspent conviction involving a number of matters, including corruption; having an equivalent conviction outside the UK; being subject to a disqualification order as a director; and various forms of insolvency. These are all tests of an individual's financial probity based on whether they have been caught in some form of misconduct. It does not relate to their future intentions for the club or what their business plan might be.

In practice, applying these tests can encounter difficulties, as was evident in the case of a projected Saudi takeover of Newcastle United. Despite a finding by the WTO that Saudi broadcasters had engaged in football piracy, the Premier League emphatically denied that there had been any pressure from ministers to approve the deal in the interests of the UK's relationship with Saudi Arabia. The Premier League had not made a decision after four months, leading to the consortium withdrawing its bid.

The collapse of Bury FC

The case of Bury shows the limits of what the football authorities can do once a club has spiralled into debt. Bury was acquired by a property developer, Stewart Day, in 2013 and he took out a number of loans with the club used as security. Steve Dale bought the club for £1 in December 2019, after passing the Owners' and Directors' Test. He was then required to provide the EFL with a business plan up to June 2020 and a commitment to provide proof of the funding required as underwriting for that plan.

During the following seven months he not only failed to do so but he also presided over a club that was unable to pay wages on a number of occasions. Furthermore, the club was subject to winding-up petitions presented in the High Court by Her Majesty's Revenue and Customs and a former employee, and was being pursued by other clubs for outstanding debts. Dale eventually (on 19 June) launched a company voluntary arrangement (CVA) in an attempt to satisfy the club's many creditors. He claimed that the problems he uncovered were more serious than had been revealed during due diligence on his purchase of the club.

The House of Commons committee concerned with sport started an inquiry into the events at Bury, but this was brought to a halt by the 2019 general election. The chair of the committee, Damian Collins MP, stated: "Systematic and structural problems are responsible for the tragic expulsion of Bury FC from the League this year. These failures were avoidable, and it is essential that the authorities urgently overhaul their framework if they wish to avoid the same fate befalling other clubs." The committee considered that the EFL must share the blame for having allowed the situation at the club to deteriorate for so long. They set out a number of recommendations including a proposal that the FA, EFL and Premier League should establish a supporters' ombudsman to hear concerns about how clubs are being run. (Such a person would have wider functions than the existing ombudsman discussed below.) A reformed Owners' and

Directors Test would disqualify a buyer with a record of corporate insolvency. Clubs would be banned from borrowing against fixed assets such as stadiums. There should be a licensing system for professional English football clubs, as recommended in the committee's 2011 report on football governance (House of Commons 2019b).

The EFL commissioned an independent review of its actions from Jonathan Taylor, QC. It contended that the league spent significant time and effort monitoring the situation at Bury FC and applying its regulations to try to force the club and its owners to meet their commitments. It was concluded that while it could always be argued, with the benefit of hindsight, that more could have been done, any additional action would not have made any difference to the eventual outcome, which was ultimately caused by a lack of owner funding. Damian Collins MP dismissed the report as a "complete whitewash". He also described the QC-led probe as "inadequate" and added that it was "the final insult" for the club's supporters who have been "let down every step of the way" (*Political Economy of Football* 2020f).

The events surrounding Wigan Athletic being placed into administration in 2020 once again put the spotlight on the EFL's Owners' and Directors' Test. The sequence of events baffled even experienced administration practitioners. In 2019 International Entertainment Corporation (IEC), a Hong Kong-listed operator of hotels and casinos, controlled by the poker player Stanley Choi, bought Wigan for £22 million from long-standing owner of the club Dave Whelan. IEC appeared to make a decent profit, selling the club to Next Leader Fund, led by Au Yeung Wai Kay, a largely unknown Hong Kong businessman for around £40 million in June 2020. Both takeovers were approved by the EFL. The new owner then put the club into administration, citing the effects of the pandemic.

On the face of it, Au Yeung's conduct is difficult to understand: "At first in partnership with Choi, he paid £17.5m, giving IEC more than they paid for the club, and also ensured their £24m loan was repaid. But then, on the day he took ownership after this £41m purchase, he decided not to fund it and to put the club into administration, so losing control, the £17.5m, and probably the £24m too" (Conn 2020). Unsubstantiated explanations were put forward about why this might have occurred.

The limits of the EFL's rules

Rick Parry made some illuminating comments about the limitations of the EFL tests with regard to Wigan. He said, "He [Choi] passed the tests. You can criticise them and say they need to be beefed up, but he did pass the test." Parry admitted that the test had its limitations: "Our test, bluntly, is limited, it's an objective test, there are limited grounds to turn down an owner. It is a test that, by definition, the more foreign owners you have the more difficult it is to apply because of the amount of information that is available" (BBC 2020c). The EFL does not have an investigatory capacity and had to rely on self-certification in this instance.

In any case, Parry argued that the real problem was not the test, but the lack of sustainability in the business strategies of Championship clubs. He commented: "It's no use just talking about owners' and directors' tests as if that is going to solve all of the problems. You really need to go back to why did we end up with Chinese owners in the lower reaches of the Championship in the first place?" (BBC 2020c). Unfortunately this implies that foreign owners are the real problem whereas there can be just as many problems with domestic owners, as was evident from unfolding events at Charlton Athletic in 2020/21, which saw the club at risk of expulsion from the EFL. In that case, although there was involvement from Abu Dhabi and Romania, two of the purported owners came from the Manchester area.

The Championship has a version of FFP similar to that of the Premier League called the "Profitability and Sustainability Rules". The assessment is carried out in March (rather than December). The maximum loss limit is now £13 million per Championship season (or £5 million a season if the owner does not inject equity to cover losses). Losses are assessed over three seasons (rather than just over the single, previous season). The assessment of each club's finances is a combination of a historic assessment (looking at figures for the two previous completed seasons) and an assessment over the season currently taking place. Clubs are permitted to exclude some expenditure (youth development spend, charitable community spend and women's football spend). For a Championship club this rarely exceeds £500,000 per season (and is usually less).

Clubs sought to find creative ways around the rules. Three clubs – Aston Villa, Derby County and Sheffield Wednesday – sold their stadiums back to the owners and then leased them back. It is possible to make a profit in terms of the difference between the sale price and the book (not market) value of the asset. There was suspicion that the sale price had been inflated above the market value. In effect, clubs "have simply shifted large amounts of money from one of their bank accounts to another, but their respective clubs have had a FFP boost as a result" (Maguire 2019). One of the puzzles is that the rules were changed in 2016, although no one seemed to notice at the time. Previously, counting profits made on the sale of tangible fixed assets had not been allowed: "Why the change was allowed to go through has never been explained, although we have heard on the grapevine that the EFL simply cut and pasted the Premier League P&S [profit and sustainability] rules (which have always allowed asset sales) without looking at the small print for any changes, unlike the accountants and lawyers at Derby" (Maguire 2019).

Leaving aside the ability of those who read the small print to avoid the rules, the impact on Championship finances has fallen far short of what was hoped for. As Rick Parry, the chair of the EFL, has admitted: "The Championship is a financial nonsense" (BBC 2020c). Championship clubs have been losing on average a total of £1.5 million every day. Not a single club made a profit in 2017/18 and total losses are around £400 million. Kieran Maguire has reported, "In the last five years Championship clubs' income was up 53 per cent, wages were up 55 per cent and losses up 106 per cent" (quoted in *Political Economy of Football* 2019d). Wages are now the highest ever in the Championship compared to income: 107.5 per cent in 2018 (the average wage is £15,000 per week). The Championship competes with some of the big five European leagues for transfer spending.

Clubs in League One and League Two operated within a spending constraint framework termed the Salary Cost Management Protocol (SCMP), which was temporarily replaced in 2020 by a salary cap, but it is worth discussing as it arguably had some advantages over the new scheme (see Chapter 8). The SCMP limited spending on player wages to a percentage of a club's turnover. In League One clubs could spend a maximum of 60 per cent of their turnover on wages; in League Two the limit was 55 per cent. The wages of coaching staff are not included. There are no restrictions (in themselves) on the amount a club can lose or spend on transfer fees. Initially introduced into League Two in 2004/05 for guidance purposes, sanctions for breaching the SCMP thresholds were introduced during the 2011/12 season, with Swindon the first club to be sanctioned under the rules.

The process was interactive with clubs providing the Football League with projections for the spending for the coming season. During the season the clubs provided regular updates on their turnover and wage bill. Any club that was forecasting a wage spend within 5 per cent of the figure would be scrutinized more closely. Where a club was on course to exceed the limits, the Football League would apply a transfer embargo. Crucially, a club does not have to overspend to incur the embargo, it only needs to be shown to be heading for an overspend. This interactive approach enabled clubs to increase their wage bill if their circumstances improved: a successful cup run will generate increased income and the Football League may be able to sanction additional wage spend. Because the SCMP does not rely on the retrospective scrutiny of club accounts, it was also extremely effective at stopping overspend before the spending actually occured (something that has been a problem for the Championship's version of FFP).

The definition of turnover is important as it defines the maximum wage spend that is permitted. The EFL turnover figure included donations from the owners to the club and injections of equity. Loans from club owners are understandably not included in the turnover figure as these would result in growing club debts. In League One and League Two, a wealthy owner could therefore fund the club spending in a way that is not permitted in other divisions.

The EFL was reviewing its financial sustainability rules in 2020 and the outcome remains to be seen. However, tweaking the rules is not really the answer. The EFL is not best suited to devise, apply and enforce these rules. How that task might be undertaken differently and more effectively is discussed in Chapter 8. The salary cap was replaced by the SCMP in 2021 after an arbitration panel ruled against its use.

The Independent Football Ombudsman

The office of the Independent Football Ombudsman (IFO) was created in July 2008 by the English Football Authorities (the FA, the Premier League and the EFL) with the agreement of government. It is the successor body to the Independent Football Commission (IFC), which operated from 2002 to 2008 as an integral part of football's self-regulatory system. The IFO was established by the football authorities to receive and adjudicate on complaints that have failed to be resolved by football clubs or the football authorities. Furthermore, if the football bodies have dealt with a complaint in full, then the IFO can review whether due process has been followed and the complaint handled properly. The ombudsman in 2020 was Professor Derek Fraser, who also served as chair of the IFC from 2001. He is a Birmingham City fan and formerly vice-chancellor of the University of Teesside.

The IFO is seen to act as a check and balance and is the final stage within football's complaints procedure. In February 2016 the IFO was officially recognized as an Approved Alternative Dispute Body under the 2015 Alternative Dispute Consumer Regulations. The vast majority of complaints are resolved at an early stage, but anyone who feels dissatisfied with the outcome of a complaint they have submitted to a football body, such as a football club or governing body, can refer it to the IFO for investigation. The IFO will not accept a complaint unless the provider of the goods or services has had the opportunity to resolve the complaint. The IFO has no remit for incidents that occur on the field of play or for referee performance.

The IFO "receives about 2,000 messages each year, over 90% of which are submitted by e-mail. Most of these do not lead to a formal investigation or adjudication by the IFO", largely because they are outside its remit, such as complaints about referees. In 2020, "The cases which were disputes between 'consumer' and 'trader' (as defined by the Regulations) and were investigated by the IFO totalled 31 in the year under review. Of these 24 were adjudicated by a formal published

Adjudication Report and 7 were concluded by a letter to the complainant" (IFO 2020a).

The IFO deals with a great variety of cases, which include sanctions imposed on supporters, stewarding and access issues at matches and demands for refunds and compensation, together with claims that there were shortcomings in the way the governing bodies have been exercising their powers. In 2020, "the main issue was the imposition of sanctions on supporters following accusations of mis-selling of tickets, commonly referred to as 'ticket touting'. A familiar theme was also problems at matches due to standing supporters and the lack of appropriate response by stewards and stadium managers" (IFO 2020a).

There have been occasional complaints by fans that the IFO is not "fit for purpose", particularly when they have been unhappy about the way in which their complaint was resolved. However, given the propensity of fans to complain, the IFO has got off relatively lightly. I return to how it should fit into the wider architecture of regulation in Chapter 8.

The European Union

Until the Treaty of Lisbon came into force in 2009 the EU did not have a specific competence that allowed it to involve itself in matters of sport. This did not, of course, prevent the ECJ from identifying a space where it could pronounce on sporting issues while recognizing sport's particular characteristics, most importantly as far as football was concerned in the Bosman judgement. What Bosman did was to place "a model of *conditional autonomy* at the heart of EU sports law – sporting autonomy is respected on condition that it is shown how and why chosen practices are needed to govern sport" (Weatherill 2020: 10).

What is more, competition law and policy offered a route for the Commission into football and one that it was prepared to use in the early years of the twenty-first century. This active phase of policy led to the possibility of fragmenting the broadcasting of games in Britain, undermining what was then a BSkyB monopoly and hence the whole Premier League model. In 2003 the Premier League sold its rights to BSkyB without waiting for formal approval from Brussels. The Commission was outraged by this flouting of its authority.

In December 2002 the Commission reached the preliminary conclusion that the joint selling of Premiership television rights was "tantamount to price-fixing" (O'Connor 2002). Mario Monti, the competition commissioner, was concerned the structure of the UK auction process could strengthen the dominance of BSkyB at the cost of other operators and new media outlets. Recently approved television sales schemes for the Champions League and the German league left room for such new media, which had been a central concern of Mr Monti, as well as dividing the rights into several different packages. The Commission was worried that the Premier League scheme, which divided rights into four packages, might have had only a superficial effect as BSkyB won all the live game rights.

Mario Monti had been facing problems in his fight against cartels, and the Premier League offered the prospect of a high-profile win. He declared, "The announcements so far made by the Premier League suggest that BSkyB will have an even greater monopoly over live television rights than was the case in the past. This is bad for competition on broadcasting markets, and is bad for consumers" (quoted in WG Football Page 2003). If the Commission had forced the Premier League to restructure the rights on offer and deprive BSkyB of exclusivity, the pay-TV group would have substantially lowered its offer. Such a move could have caused chaos among England's top football clubs. Many had already budgeted for the next three years on the assumption that the £1.02 billion would be paid in full. The difficulty for the Premiership is that there were at that time no real rivals to BSkyB, with cable services having only a weak share of the market. The auction was therefore something of a charade.

It is believed that UK politicians at the highest level made it clear that any undermining of BSkyB and the Premier League was unacceptable. As a short-term strategy the Commission insisted on the sublicensing of a limited number of games. None of the bids received for the less exciting games achieved the reserve price agreed by BSkyB and the Commission. The Commission had been outmanoeuvred by BSkyB and its strategy had failed. The Commission persisted with the idea of a 50/50 split between Sky and other companies in two years of negotiations. What it ended up with, under pressure from the UK government, was a much less radical solution. This resulted in a new company, Setanta, receiving two unattractive packages in the 2007–10 contract period, and just one after 2010. Setanta eventually collapsed with its channels going off air in 2009 and most of the rights sold off to ESPN.

If nothing else, this episode led football clubs and authorities to accept that the EU had powers it could use to intervene in their affairs. There was "a grudging acceptance by sporting bodies that it was politically impossible for them to extract a promise of absolute autonomy from the EU" (Weatherill 2020: 18). In the discussions running up to the Lisbon Treaty, EU sporting bodies came to accept that they could not keep the European institutions out of their affairs as they would prefer. Given the impossibility of achieving total autonomy, a second-best solution was to devise a strategy of cooperation with the Commission. This was particularly apparent as competition law issues continued to be raised where there was an uncomfortable and potentially serious tension between some of the rules and practices of football and understandings of what constitutes fair competition, notably in relation to FFP.

It is important to consider the nature of the explicit competence on sport given to the EU in Article 165 of the Treaty on the Functioning of the European Union. Clause 1 states: "The Union shall contribute to the promotion of European sporting issues, while taking account of the specific nature of sport, its structures based on voluntary activity and its social and educational function." The opening phrase is deliciously vague: what could promotion consist of? However, it is a positive word, as are the later references to voluntary activity and the societal contribution of sport. However, the key phrase is: "taking account of the specific nature of sport". This wording recognizes that sport is an arena that deserves special treatment. Clause 2 thus refers to "promoting fairness and openness in sporting competitions", which could be used as a defence for their special features. Clause 3 is an anodyne statement about the benefits of cooperating with all and sundry. Clause 4 is significant because it limits legislative intervention to "incentive measures" rather than penalties. It is a strategy of carrots rather than sticks.

In 2014 the European Commission and UEFA signed an Arrangement for Cooperation between them. This declared that they wanted to "strengthen their relations" and "cooperate in a regular and constructive manner" through a dialogue that included an annual meeting between the relevant director-general in the Commission and the general secretary of UEFA. Much of the agreement was a rather general statement of good intentions, but it was significant that it recognized "responsible self-regulation" as the means of pursuing goals such as financial stability and better governance. It also acknowledged that, "subject to compliance with competition law", measures to encourage greater rationality and discipline in club finances such as FFP were a means of contributing to sustainable development (Commission of the European Communities 2014: 2–3).

Competition law remains the elephant in the room: "The legal status of FFP is unclear. UEFA, however, has shrewdly attempted to avert the need to defend its rules in court" (Weatherill 2020: 21). However, given the truce with the Commission it is unlikely to be brought into court at the European level. That does not, of course, prevent an individual or corporate entity launching an action in a national court of a member state.

Financial fair play

FFP was introduced by UEFA in 2009 with the rules set out in 2010. It was intended to curb some of the worst financial excesses of the game. It was hoped to introduce more discipline and rationality in club football finances; to encourage clubs to operate on the basis of their own revenues; to encourage responsible spending for the long-term benefit of football; and to protect the long-term viability and sustainability of European club football. The rules "are built around two main areas: an obligation for clubs, over a period of time, to balance their books (first assessed in the 2013/14 season) and an obligation for clubs to meet all their transfer and employee payment commitments at all times (first assessed in the summer of 2011)" (UEFA 2020). UEFA considers that some of the most excessive loss-making by clubs has been restricted.

It should be noted, as was evident in the Manchester City case, that UEFA is reliant on the clubs concerned to supply information about possible breaches of the rules. In other words, there is a classic regulatory asymmetry of information problem. The judicial authorities think that it is reasonable to ask clubs to provide additional information and evidence during proceedings. However, the extent to which a football club "can be required to provide accounting evidence from its sponsors is less straight-forward". Whether clubs "are required to provide information derived from third parties depends on the specific circumstances of the case" (CAS 2020: 76).

In a critique, Szymanski (2014: 218) argues that "[c]loser inspection of the stated objectives suggests that it is more about efficiency than fairness". What the rules did was to substitute one form of inequality for another and they were even unlikely to achieve efficiency. What FFP did was impose "some very specific restrictions on competition" (Szymanski 2014: 227). Franck (2014), in contrast, argued that criticisms overlooked the impact of the rules on managerial decision-making: "By introducing hard budget constraints, FFP restores the incentives for 'good management' in an industry that has degenerated into a zombie race with an ever-increasing number of technically bankrupt participants, which rely on getting rescued by state subventions and/or private money injections year after year" (Franck 2014: 211).

There was concern that whereas smaller clubs complied with UEFA rulings on FFP, big clubs employed legal teams to challenge UEFA's decisions or used creative schemes to avoid punishment for overspending. Efforts by some of Europe's biggest teams to circumvent FFP put the future of the regulatory regime in doubt. This in spite of the fact that UEFA claims that it was a success, with clubs making a combined profit of €600 million in 2017 compared with a combined loss of €1.7 billion in 2011. In 2019 PSG successfully challenged an investigation into the club's claimed breaches of FFP rules in the past. AC Milan and Galatasaray have also lodged successful appeals against UEFA in FFP-related cases. They took their cases to the Court for Arbitration of Sport in Lausanne where they won on procedural grounds.

PSG faced the threat of sanctions by UEFA after a preliminary investigation in 2018 showed that sponsorship contracts valued by the Qatari-owned club at €200 million were "overstated". UEFA's investigatory arm was reported to have hired sports consultancy Octagon to conduct an independent review of

PSG's sponsorship contracts amid concerns that some of the money had come from "related parties": entities with financial or other links to the club's owners. Contracts under review include those with Qatar National Bank, Bein Sports and Qatar Tourism Authority.

In June 2019 UEFA's Club Financial Control Body (CFCB) closed its investigation into PSG over alleged breaches of its FFP regulations. However, nine days later the chairman of the CFCB requested that the decision be reviewed. Following that review in September, UEFA concluded that PSG's conduct did indeed warrant further investigation and deemed the case open once more. PSG filed an appeal to CAS seeking to have the decision annulled, claiming UEFA had breached its own rules, which state that it must reopen any investigation within ten days of the chairman's request to review: UEFA had taken two months. CAS found in PSG's favour. Some considered that UEFA had surrendered without a fight.

This may have made UEFA more determined to secure a win against a major club in its pursuit of Manchester City. Smaller clubs were often treated relatively leniently. For example, in the summer of 2020 Marseille was fined €3 million but allowed to keep its Champions League place after breaching an FFP settlement. In the case of Manchester City, UEFA saw its sanctions overruled by CAS leading to social media claims of "FFP – RIP". In fact the lesson to be drawn was that UEFA needed to be smarter in following its procedures to the letter.

The key substantive issue before CAS was whether disguised equity funding was provided to Manchester City "through Etihad and Etisalat and whether this was properly reflected in the information provided by MCFC [Manchester City Football Club] to UEFA for licensing and monitoring purposes" (CAS 2020: 49). Leaked emails were published by the German magazine *Der Spiegel* in November 2018. They appeared to show that Sheikh Mansour had funded the sponsorship by Etihad, which City presented as a commercially credible deal, arguing the Abu Dhabi airline, and all the other sponsors, are not technically "related" to the owner. The leaked emails showed that Manchester City had a case to answer but were not sufficient to support a finding that Manchester City provided incorrect information to UEFA. The panel was satisfied that the allegations made "were particularly severe". They concerned equity funding being disguised as "sponsorship contributions over a significant period of time". This led to an influx of income "with the consequence that [the club] could spend significantly more money (£200m) that it would have been unable to spend without such arrangements" (CAS 2020: 57). However, any breaches before 15 May 2014 were barred by the relevant procedural rules. Breaches relating to the financial statements for 2012 and 2013 were time barred. Moreover, financial statements filed in 2014 related to 2013 and were therefore time barred.

The majority of the CAS Panel found that the Etihad sponsorship agreements were negotiated at fair value. There were only two specific instances in which

Manchester City failed to comply with its duty of cooperation. The main charges in relation to disguised equity funding were dismissed. The charges, however, were not frivolous and there was a legitimate basis for prosecution. There was a failure to cooperate with the investigation, and the failure to produce the original versions of the leaked emails was particularly serious. Manchester City was allowed to remain in the Champions League and its fine was reduced to €10 million.

Failed world governance: FIFA

One might hope that, as the world governing body of football, FIFA would be able to provide guidance on appropriate regulatory frameworks for the game, and even help to put them into effect. In fact it has been unable to put its own house in order. It has been beset by serious problems of corruption for three decades with numerous senior officials demonstrated to have lined their own pockets through bribes, embezzlement and some very dubious decisions about the allocation of World Cup venues. Investigators had been raising concerns about FIFA for some time, but it was the award of the 2022 World Cup to Qatar in 2010 that focused attention on the organization's decision-making and eventually led to criminal indictments.

UEFA was also implicated in the decision to hold a World Cup in Qatar. This was a decision that was met with surprise given the high temperatures and allegations of human rights abuses involving imported labourers. Nine days before the decision UEFA president Michel Platini, who had previously supported a US venue for the 2022 tournament, lunched at the Elysée Palace in Paris with then French president Nicolas Sarkozy. Among other guests was Qatar's crown prince Sheikh Tamin Bin Hamad Al Thani (now the emir): "Platini denied that Sarkozy ordered him to support Qatar to enhance French business" (Simpson 2020: 83).

In 2015, after a preliminary investigation, the FIFA authorities initiated disciplinary proceedings in respect of an alleged salary supplement of two million Swiss francs (CHF) that Mr Platini had received in 2011, in the context of a verbal contract between him and FIFA's president, Sepp Blatter, for activities as adviser between 1998 and 2002. He was initially given an eight-year suspension from all football-related activities at national and international levels and was fined CHF 80,000 by the adjudicatory chamber of the FIFA Ethics Committee. The sanction was upheld by the FIFA Appeal Committee, which reduced the length of the suspension to six years. Platini appealed against this decision to CAS. He alleged, in particular, that the articles of the FIFA Code of Ethics relied upon had not been applicable at the time of the relevant acts and that the sanction appeared excessive. The CAS rejected this complaint but reduced the suspension period from six years to four and the fine from CHF 80,000 to CHF 60,000. Subsequent appeals to the Swiss Federal Court and the European Court of Human Rights were unsuccessful.

As for FIFA, it was "brought low by proven corruption on a dizzying, entrenched scale" (Conn 2017: 7). It "crumpled into a mire of corruption and lies" (Conn 2017: 1). The US indictment traced this corruption back to 1991, and "In May 2015, FIFA's top executives were arrested after allegations of bribery, fraud and money laundering were made" (Boudreaux *et al.* 2016: 866). Fourteen defendants were arrested for racketeering, money laundering and other serious offences. The US Department of Justice alleged that £200 million had been taken in bribes over 24 years. US officials stated that the "indictment alleges corruption that is rampant, systemic and deep-rooted, both abroad and here in the United States. It spans at least two generations of football officials who, as alleged, have violated their positions of trust to acquire millions of dollars in bribes and kickbacks" (quoted in Conn 2017: 171).

One consequence of this scandal was that FIFA budgeted lower marketing rights for 2015–18, as many sponsors (Sony, Emirates, Castrol, Johnson & Johnson, Continental) did not renew due to the various corruption scandals. However, to some extent this was compensated for by new sponsors from China and Russia.

These events fatally undermined the position of the powerful FIFA president, Sepp Blatter, and the organization banned him from football for eight years in December 2015, reduced to six years by its appeals committee. Blatter had authorized a CHF 2 million payment to Platini weeks before he had endorsed him for a new term as FIFA president. Blatter appealed to CAS but the panel found against him and dismissed his appeal, describing the sanction applied to him as "reasonable and fair" (CAS 2016: 66). It found that while Mr Blatter may have believed that he had a debt to Mr Platini, "the fact is that this was not a debt of FIFA and FIFA did not owe the CHF 2 million to Mr Platini". They found Mr Blatter's conduct to be "reckless, or at least profoundly careless, as he approved the payment without checking the written contract" (CAS 2016: 59). The panel had no doubt that this was "an undue gift" (CAS 2016: 60).

The CAS Panel drew attention to FIFA's special responsibility to safeguard the integrity and reputation of football worldwide and this special responsibility was borne in particular by the FIFA president. Given that, like all courts, it uses restrained language, the CAS Panel delivered a blistering rebuke to Blatter:

> Mr Blatter as FIFA president was the top person in the world of football. There is no higher position in football and the FIFA president must especially be aware of and conduct himself in accordance with his

duties and responsibilities ... The standard of conduct required under the [FIFA Code of Ethics] should be and should be seen to be applied to the FIFA President as rigorously, (and) if not more rigorously than that applied to anyone else bound by the FCE. (CAS 2016: 66).

After these events one might have hoped that FIFA would take special care to ensure that it adhered to the highest standards of probity. Gianni Infantino, formerly at UEFA, became FIFA president in 2016 vowing to clean up the organization. He attracted criticism "for his attempts to curb the independence and strength of internal ethics bodies" (Jones & Ahmed 2020). FIFA officials admitted that a step backwards in recovering its reputation occurred in July 2020 when prosecutors in Switzerland launched criminal proceedings against Infantino in relation to an alleged secret meeting with Swiss attorney general Michael Lauder. Both men emphatically denied any wrongdoing.

It was claimed that numerous secret meetings took place between the pair to discuss whether "sensitive investigations against football's governing body have all but derailed the chances of those in FIFA suspected of corruption being successfully brought to trial in Switzerland". It was alleged that leaked emails "showed that Mr Infantino had intended to lobby Mr Lauber to drop investigations into his conduct while he was legal affairs director at UEFA" (Jones & Ahmed 2020). Stefan Keller was appointed as special prosecutor to investigate the matter. Concerns were also raised about Mr Lauber's links to Russian officials and he was already facing impeachment proceedings in the Swiss parliament.

One of the difficulties with FIFA is that it has never really been accountable to anyone. The member associations have been too preoccupied with pursuing their own agendas, whether securing a future World Cup or FIFA payments for their facilities or training programmes. The development budget for 2019–22 is $2.3 billion. Staff members have often seemed to give the first priority to safeguarding their own positions. Although they cooperated fully with the US investigation, the Swiss authorities have not vigorously investigated FIFA in the past as an organization constituted under Swiss law, although clearly this relaxed stance is changing. FIFA still falls far short of what one would hope for in a body supposed to promote the integrity of world football.

Weak governance

The unavoidable conclusion is that the governance of football falls short of what is necessary at the national, regional and global levels. In part this is because the governing bodies are relatively weak compared to the other actors they have to deal with: clubs, leagues and players. They are often outsmarted by them and their lawyers. State interventions have occurred, but they have been sporadic and unsystematic. There has been too much respect for the cloistered nature of the world of football and its supposedly special nature. There are many arguments and appeals that football can use to keep outside intervention at bay.

However, it is clear that football is not going to sort things out if it is left to its own devices. A different kind of regulatory framework is clearly required, but actually designing an effective set of arrangements as distinct from a token facade is no easy task. It is this task that is considered in Chapter 8.

8
FINDING SOLUTIONS: A NEW REGULATORY FRAMEWORK

To place this chapter in an analytical context, we need to consider two alternative versions of economics. Conventional or mainstream economics has developed a set of theories and terminologies based around such concepts as rational utility maximizing actors, supply and demand, and efficient markets. In the wake of the global financial crisis the adequacy of mainstream economics has been widely challenged. The central doctrines of economics "have encouraged the deregulation and de-institutionalization of markets, especially financial markets, thereby increasing volatility" (Skidelsky 2018: 384). An alternative perspective focuses on the reduction of inequality and the promotion of a more fulfilling life, which may not be captured by statistics such as growth in GDP.

Mainstream economics is not irrelevant or outdated, to discard it would be to lose valuable insights and ways of thinking about problems, but it is insufficient. Skidelsky admits that economics is "micro-efficient, but macro inefficient" (Skidelsky 2018: 387). A risk arises in aggregating micro decisions into a belief that a macro model can be built on "the optimizing decisions of well-informed, forward-looking rational agents, subject only to the logic of competitive markets" (Skidelsky 2018: 386). Behavioural economics, using the insights of psychology and experiments on cooperation, offers a corrective to oversimplified assumptions of rationality, but can lead to behaviour being labelled as irrational when it "may be perfectly reasonable in the circumstances" (Skidelsky 2018: 389).

Some classic concepts of economics have been shown to be applicable in this book. Football shows a tendency towards oligopoly as far as the big clubs are concerned. What has emerged "is a handful of really big winners with quasi-monopoly status at the top, and a very long tail with everyone else earning a fraction of their returns" (Lonergan & Blyth 2020: 99). There is cartel-like behaviour in an attempt to erect barriers to new entrants and to a significant extent competition law has been evaded. All this might suggest the familiar phenomenon of market failure and the need for a resort to the usual corrective remedies.

Notions of market failure are not irrelevant, but in football one is dealing with a market with some very unusual characteristics.

In particular, there is the absence of a normally functioning exit mechanism for market participants. Football businesses rarely go bust: "Despite being incompetently run, they are exceptionally stable businesses" (Kuper & Szymanski 2012: 81). Nearly half the top global companies in 1912 had disappeared by the mid-1990s. Almost "every English professional club has survived the Great Depression, the Second World War, recessions, corrupt chairmen, appalling managers and the current economic crisis" (Kuper & Szymanski 2012: 89). Reckless behaviour is not disciplined by the market, particularly given the way in which generous insolvency laws can be used as a reorganization device: "Of the forty-eight English clubs that underwent insolvency proceedings between 1982 and 2010, all have survived" (Szymanski 2015: 213). An economist with no attachment to the game might conclude that there are too many producers (clubs) for all of them to be viable. They might recommend a franchise system in which clubs had to bid for the right to compete in a league as in the MSL.

The myth of the "total fan"

As well as the producers, one has to consider the consumers, albeit disempowered as individual actors in the market and difficult to organize politically because of their heterogeneity. According to research by Kantar Media, "about 36 per cent of Britons call themselves football fans. That's more than 20m people". Yet prior to the pandemic, in a week where every English and Scottish professional club played at home once, "only about 1.8m attended a game" (Kuper 2020b).

There is more churn in support for a club than diehard fans are prepared to concede. It is empirically false "that you can change your job, your spouse or your gender, but never your football team". Kuper illustrates his point by noting that "if Reading host Preston one season, and then again the next, about half the seats in the stadium will be occupied by different people the second time around" (Kuper 2020b). Some fans change club because they change location, but you can easily find a new local side without moving home. There are 43 professional clubs within 90 miles of Manchester. It has "always been the case that the majority of people who go to English football matches only go once in a while, and are often quite fluid about who they choose to watch" (Kuper & Szymanski 2012: 251).

Even so, it is difficult to think of an activity that commands the same level of "emotional, social and political commitment" (Szymanski 2015: 144). This observation particularly applies to the minority of lifelong one-club fans who are the most passionate and vociferous. The football fan is a very special kind of consumer and any regulatory solutions have to take this into account. It is necessary to set aside a model of the consumer as logical thinker processing information to make purchasing decisions about tangible goods based on such factors as price and quality. Such a model does not help with understanding emotional responses to leisure activities where it is difficult to assess the likely quality of an event ahead of actually experiencing it. Even then, perceptions may vary widely: for example, some may see mud as an acceptable or even enjoyable part of attending a major festival such as Glastonbury. New models are needed to understand what changes consumer perceptions: "Consumption has begun to be seen as involving a steady flow of fantasies, feelings and fun encompassed by what we call the 'experiential view'" (Holbrook & Hirschmann 1982: 132). There is considerable empirical evidence that consumers are placing more value on an experience than possession of a material brand. Research by Barclaycard found that "half of consumers would rather spend money on entertainment and events than material items" (Barclays 2018).

Attendance at a football match can provoke a wide range of emotional responses: anger, delight, joy, surprise, frustration and anxiety, to name just a few. One of the attractions of football is the way in which a competitive match can ebb and flow, evoking a range of emotions from optimism to despair. One of the most exciting types of game is when a team that looks as if it is hopelessly defeated makes a late fight back to draw or win. Excitement is a key feature of watching football: a survey of nearly 7,000 fans looking forward to the 2020/21 season found that 54 per cent were excited and these findings related to non-league football. Of those fans intending to return after the pandemic, 72 per cent said that their reason for returning was that being a fan is part of their identity (Lyons 2020). The psychological and social costs of losing that identity can be high. For many people "it is a primary source of identity, or a crutch to get through life" (Kuper 2020b): "[The] fact remains that football clubs have near-irreplaceable value to identity, pride and hope in communities across the country, and losing them will have real consequences" (Fairley 2020).

There is thus a need for a much broader understanding of the consumer to inform the design of a regulatory framework. It does make the task more complicated than dealing with a consumer of water or energy, where there is no emotional attachment to the provider and it is possible to make a calculation of what constitutes value for money for the consumer and a fair return to the producer. This in turn needs to be placed within a broader understanding of the economic and political forces at work in the world in an era in which globalization may have been disrupted, but has not disappeared. There is, of course, an immediate challenge here: domestic or at best regional systems of regulation have to cope with a sector that remains highly globalized.

The world economy has grown, but so has inequality. Capital has taken a bigger share of economic output and wages have stagnated. People have to work longer and harder to earn a sufficient income and some hope of a pension that will support them when they have stopped working, but "Economics as it stands can't seem to explain why the pressures of life appear to be intensifying, at the same time as income per capita is rising" (Lonergan & Blyth 2020: 5). So if "economics describes the way the economy is supposed to work, angrynomics reveals what we actually experience and why it matters to us" (Lonergan & Blyth 2020: 7).

Lonergan and Blyth refer to angry football fans at a number of points in their book as exemplars of tribal anger. Anger can be directed at a number of targets: opposition players, the manager, match officials, opposition fans. Many fans, however, spend as much time on social media and fan boards hiding behind pseudonyms criticizing other supporters or their own players in often as vehement terms as they do for the opposition. One recurrent phenomenon is the "scapegoat player" who is often blamed for all the shortcomings of the team. He may not be the best player in the team, but all his errors are catalogued and any successes are dismissed as a fluke. Very often the candidate is a defensive midfielder as this is a role that often involves keeping possession by playing the ball sideways or backwards whereas many fans want relentless attacking football as a spectacle.

Sometimes anger is directed at highly paid players of the club, but this type of criticism comes more often from outside football. Nevertheless, there is an issue that arises from the fact that fans are often more passionate than the players. However much they kiss the badge, for the player it is a job that forms part of a career. When players move on, they are often criticized for disloyalty, yet fans would readily seize a better employment opportunity in their own lives. Fans may be alienated from distant owners, but as long as they continue to fund the club generously they are at worst indifferent and may even be appreciative. However, if one is trying to construct a "responsive" form of regulation, the special character of fans as consumers is a challenge that cannot be evaded. They are more emotional and less rational than the consumer buying a commodity.

Is there a German Sonderweg?

It is a general characteristic of the public policy debate in Britain to see Germany as an example from which lessons can be drawn. This is understandable given the success of the German economy and the way in which, for example, it has developed systems of training that have produced high levels of skill. *Modell Deutschland* had to deal with the challenges of unification, Europeanization and the eurozone crisis, unprecedented levels of immigration by refugees, globalization and the rise of far-right parties, and at times it has looked fragile. Nevertheless, it has proved to be resilient and Germany was widely praised for its initial response to Covid-19, while the German economy and German football made a relatively rapid recovery.

However, one has to be careful about how one interprets differences of culture and structure. One of the difficulties is that some key German terms do not translate readily into English. Consider, for example, the widely used and shared term *Ordnungspolitik* that describes an approach to politics that is based on rules established by law. The problem is that this appears "to be a concept that is difficult to appreciate for observers outside of Germany. It is significant that the difficulty of explaining the concept of '*Ordnungspolitik*' in English – or, for that matter, in French, Italian, Spanish or any other language begins with the fact that there exists no equivalent term into which it could be readily translated" (Vanberg 2014: 1). The important point is that the German ordoliberal tradition, emanating from the Freiburg School and seeking to provide a constitutional order that would guarantee economic freedom, is very different from the more liberal, individualistic approach to be found in Britain. The UK experienced an industrial revolution driven by individual entrepreneurs, whereas Germany had more of a developmental state guided from above.

Associations as well as the state play an important role in exercising social discipline, so German football authorities face fewer ideological impediments than their counterparts in Britain. Again, there are some linguistic challenges. The term *Verein* or association has several meanings in German and is a somewhat imprecise term: "'*Verband*' is similar to '*Verein*' but tends to be used more in reference to formal, means-oriented associations that combine common or mutual interests, like business associations' (Anheier & Seibel 1993: 11). Somewhat confusingly, the German Football Association is a *Bund* or federation.

Culture can be an elastic variable and one can manipulate it to get the explanation that one wants. Structures, however, condition and influence the behaviour of the actors that operate within them. Consider the German *Handwerk* or artisan system. In order to operate in a number of sectors of the German economy, mainly in the construction sector but also including undertakers and hairdressers, small firms have to meet a number of quality standards including levels of skill. The principal governing legislation is the 1953 *Gesetz zur Ordnung des Handwerks*, but the "system has more or less continuously evolved since the late nineteenth century" (Streeck 1989: 62). The general point to be derived here is that German firms accept as normal a degree of discipline administered by associations, which is a product of both culture and structure. This is also evident in the obligatory membership of chambers of commerce. In the UK that would be seen as unwarranted external interference in the autonomy of a firm's decision-making.

German football is nevertheless widely admired, not least by supporters' organizations elsewhere, because it is claimed "that financial regulation effectively limits the incidence of financial distress among football clubs, in contrast to other countries" (Szymanski & Weimar 2019: 54). Szymanski and Weimar identified 119 insolvency events among the top five tiers of the German football pyramid since 1994: "When looking at the incidence of insolvencies of the football pyramid from 1992–2002, the frequency in Germany (22) was very similar to England (19) and France (24)" (Szymanski & Weimar 2019: 61). Since then the number in Germany has dropped and that in England has increased, mainly because of insolvencies in the second tier: "While there has been much talk of a German football 'Sonderweg' (special, unique path) based on financial regulation and measures, such as the 50+1 rule, we find little evidence to believe that Germany is a unique case" (Szymanski & Weimar 2019: 65).

As was noted in Chapter 3, determined individuals and firms have been able to evade the 50+1 rule. Replicating the 50+1 rule in England attracts considerable support, but its translation to a different environment is not the straightforward, readily applicable solution presented by its advocates. In 2021 the rule was under review by the German federal cartel body (the Bundeskartellamt) and there was a suggestion that it might be replaced by a 80+1 rule to allow greater external investment.

Modifying existing arrangements

Strengthening the Owners' and Directors' Test

It is often less costly to build on existing arrangements rather than create new ones. It is therefore important to consider proposals for strengthening the Owners' and Directors' Test. It should be noted, however, that a more stringent test might mean that no one could be approved to take a club out of administration or financial difficulties. This would increase the risk of clubs disappearing altogether.

In the summer of 2020 a petition was launched by Wigan fans to Parliament calling for the test to be given a statutory basis. One cannot see government being keen to take this idea up, but in any case would it really improve matters unless the nature of the test was changed? One difficulty with the test at the moment is that it does not provide a means of dealing with individuals who have not experienced a disqualifying event of any kind but whose general standard of conduct falls well below the highest standards of probity. However, it would be difficult to find a legal framing that could determine whether someone was "dodgy" in the sense that they have worked within existing rules but bent them to their favour.

It has been suggested by the chairman of Crystal Palace that the EFL's capacity should be strengthened through the creation of a separate regulatory department: "The EFL must invest in a regulatory department which properly monitors real-time spending instead of the 'black box' one now in place, which serves only to tell us what caused a crash after it has happened" (Parish 2020). More resources would enable the EFL to deal with matters more thoroughly and expeditiously. Its average monthly number of employees in 2019 was 89, not a large number considering the range of tasks undertaken. Notwithstanding the league's claim to be a governing body for its member clubs, it is a private limited company and not well suited to undertaking a regulatory function when it is evident that many of its priorities are understandably commercial ones.

One of the shortcomings of the test at the moment is that it is a snapshot that looks at the record to date of the purchasers and their financial means, but offers no mechanism for reviewing their conduct after they become owners. Potential owners should be required to set out their overall strategy and vision for the club, including how they intend to involve supporters. They should be required to lodge a performance bond, a common practice in industries such as construction. It is a surety bond issued by an insurance company or bank to guarantee completion of a project. It is a formula that could be applied to football.

The involvement of supporters is not a straightforward matter. Every club in the EFL has a supporter liaison officer whose responsibilities are not only to act as a point of contact for supporters but also to deliver the club's policy with regard to its stakeholders in so far as that policy concerns supporters, and to liaise with the club's management with regard to supporter issues. Clubs generally have liaison committees or forums with supporters, but the range of matters discussed is often limited to issues such as catering on match days. One cannot reasonably expect them to discuss the performances of the individual players or the manager.

Some clubs have experimented with having a fan on the board. However, many clubs have quite a complex board structure, and fans can find themselves on a body that is legitimizing rather than decision-making. They are also bound by considerations of commercial confidentiality like any other director and this limits the feedback they can give to fans.

Although there have been calls for a complete reset of football finances, more modest steps may be achievable and feasible. For some commentators, it is simply a matter of the Premier League giving more money to the EFL. In 2020 it gave around £400 million a year, although £273 million of this was swallowed up by parachute payments. Of course, conventional economics would ask why a successful group of businesses should cross-subsidize failing ones? Even if one dismisses that argument, the question remains what a fair formula for redistribution would be. The Premier League admits that it benefits from a strong pyramid underneath it, but it is not easy to devise a methodology to quantify that benefit.

Parachute payments

Some commentators, including the House of Commons DCMS committee, would like to abolish parachute payments, first introduced in the 2006/07 season to provide a soft landing after relegation from the Premier League. The amount received, payable for a maximum of three years, is based on the Premier League's broadcasting revenues. They certainly have a highly distorting effect on competition in the Championship and encourage clubs without them to overspend to close the gap and win promotion. However, if they were abolished clubs in the Premier League would be reluctant to offer contracts of more than one year to players. The Premier League takes the view that if they did not exist promoted clubs would not invest in players and might not be competitive. Despite relegation clauses in contracts, and the possibility of a fire sale of players, relegated clubs might find themselves in real financial difficulty.

Calculations by the Swiss Ramble blogger looking at recently relegated clubs show a revenue decrease following relegation that ranged from £54 million (West Bromwich Albion) to £63 million (Sunderland), averaging £61 million (50 per cent) in 2017/18 and £56 million (45 per cent) in 2018/19. Given the higher revenue in the 2019/20 Premier League (pre-Covid), due to the new television deal, the reduction is likely to be around £60 million. Obviously, the most significant revenue decrease is in broadcasting, despite the parachute payments, although clubs can also experience major reductions in the other revenue streams. For example, Sunderland's commercial income fell £14 million, while Hull City's match day was down £9 million. On average, broadcasting income drops by around £50 million following relegation from the Premier League. In 2018/19 this went from an average of £103 million to £52 million. This will change following the new television deal in 2019/20, but the magnitude of the fall should be in the same ballpark. In 2018/19 the decrease in wages averaged £42 million (45 per cent), ranging from £38 million at Stoke to £45 million at West Brom. In 2018/19 the three relegated clubs actually improved profitability, as the average losses narrowed from £38 million to £28 million. The previous season, operating losses only rose by £7 million from £11 million to £18 million (*Political Economy of Football* 2020g).

There are clear arguments against abolishing parachute payments. However, it is reasonable to ask whether they need to be paid for three years or whether the total sum paid over (£40 million on average) is excessive. A bigger share of the Premier League's revenues for the EFL might offset the need for generous parachute payments. Kieran Maguire has suggested that there could be a levy on transfer payments or on betting related to football.

Salary caps

Salary cap proposals were brought forward for Leagues One and Two, but were opposed by some of the stronger clubs such as Portsmouth, Plymouth Argyle and Sunderland. They argued with some force that they would be better established as a percentage of a club's turnover. Nevertheless, League One and League Two clubs voted in favour of squad salary caps to replace the SCMP in August 2020. There was overwhelming support in League Two, but in League One the vote was 16 for, seven against and one abstention.

When calculating total salary spending, the "cap" includes basic wages, taxes, bonuses, image rights, agents' fees and other fees and expenses paid directly and indirectly to registered players. There are financial penalties for overspending of up to 5 per cent that would amount to £125,000 in League One and £75,000 in League Two. Above 5 per cent and clubs are referred to a disciplinary commission that will be able to dock points. Their introduction in the Championship is being resisted, although arguably they are needed more there given the out-of-control spending that takes place in that league. In the Premier League they would risk undermining the global attraction of the competition for world class players.

The PFA set out a substantial critique of the salary cap proposals, which they described as illegal and unenforceable. They considered that the proposed rules lacked clear objectives. They claimed, "there is no evidence e.g. supported by financial modelling, of how the regulations will aid future financial sustainability or why they are the appropriate mechanism to achieve the overall objectives (which do not appear to have been defined)". It was unclear how the salary cap had been determined (£2.5 million for League One and £1.5 million for League Two). The issue of an allowance for marquee players appeared not to have been considered. The PFA stated that "The proposed salary caps, if implemented, could potentially reduce the ability of clubs to generate commercial revenue with sponsors and commercial partners now fully aware that clubs wage obligations will in some cases be significantly reduced. This effectively represents a potential loss of revenue to EFL clubs" (Professional Footballers' Association 2020).

The rules appeared to be based on the Premiership Rugby Salary Regulations, but there were a number of differences between the two competitions, not least in the range and disparity of clubs. The PFA noted that the "financial performance of clubs in League One and League Two has remained relatively consistent in the last ten years with revenue growth being matched by increases in staff costs.

Financial disparity is prevalent with the average ratio of top to bottom revenue generators being 7:1 in League One and 3:1 in League Two between 2014/15 and 2018/19" (Professional Footballers' Association 2020). They pointed out that there were more important disparities between League One and League Two with a much higher ratio of highest to lowest revenue generating clubs (7:1) in League One compared with League Two (3:1). They were concerned that the process of developing the new regulations had been rushed through without proper consultation, arguing that it typically took between 11 and 25 months to devise new sporting regulations. In February 2021 an arbitration panel upheld the PFA's complaint that the salary cap was illegal and unenforceable.

Evasion and securing compliance has been a characteristic difficulty with salary caps elsewhere, notably in the USA: "The ultimate goal of the draft rules should be to ensure compliance and we believe it is necessary for the EFL to demonstrate further how they shall monitor and enforce these regulations, before the Clubs carry out a vote on their adoption" (Professional Footballers' Association 2020). It was unclear whether the rules would satisfy competition law scrutiny.

One suggestion might help with distributive issues. Until the 1980s away teams received 20 per cent of the gate. The away team and their fans contribute to the match. One small but meaningful adjustment would be to restore this arrangement, for example on the basis of 50 per cent of the away gate, reflecting the fact that some costs fall on the home club.

Fan ownership

The limits of fan ownership were discussed earlier in the book. Wrexham fans voted overwhelmingly to end fan ownership in November 2020 when two Hollywood actors offered to take over the club and make substantial investments. Experiments are taking place in Scotland with "structured transitions" to fan ownership where one year is allowed so that the new structures can adjust to the challenges they face and develop experience in dealing with them. For example, at Greenock Morton the existing owner has wiped out £2 million of debts and arranged to hand the club over to the fans after one year. The concern about fan ownership is not the competence or skill sets of the fan directors, but their ability to meet the inevitable losses as supporters call for more "investment" in players.

Proposals for regulatory reform

Damian Collins MP and former Sunderland director Charlie Methven have put forward a set of proposals for the regulatory reform of football. They point out that "the EFL itself is a members club which is presided over by executive officers who are given their jobs by the same people they are then supposed to regulate". The first part of their proposal is for a Football Finance Authority (FFA), which would be created by the FA – but working with and backed financially by the government – to provide financial assistance to EFL clubs. Funds would be provided by the FFA to allow clubs to meet their short-term liabilities and provide them with enough breathing space to restructure their finances but could not be used to invest in recruiting new players or improving the club's infrastructure. Rather than being offered as loans these funds would instead be exchanged for a minority shareholding in the club, of between 10 to 49 per cent depending on the level of investment required and the value of the club.

This part of their argument is based on the assumption that following the pandemic, "We may only have a few weeks to save professional football in this country as we know it … If nothing is done, clubs with old and famous names will almost certainly go into administration within weeks" (Collins & Methven 2020). This rather gloomy prediction was not verified by events. No clubs went into administration within their timescale. This is not to say that clubs may not go into administration, indeed it would be surprising if no club did. However, administration is a reorganization device and clubs at the professional level very rarely disappear altogether. In the case of Third Lanark in Scotland, very special factors were at work, notably the avarice of one individual (*These Football Times* 2019). What happened was that clubs made effective use of the furlough scheme while owners dug into their pockets to provide funding. For example, American owner Simon Hallett made a substantial cash injection at Plymouth Argyle. Non-league clubs raised funds from their supporters. In the National League North Leamington FC exceeded a target of £30,000 by raising over £32,000 from supporters.

In any case, it is difficult to see why the FA with its poor governance record should be given the task of creating this new body, albeit in collaboration with the government. For its part, government might not be enthusiastic about using taxpayers' money to support businesses with a dubious financial track record. It was unwilling to do that for much larger companies with a more central role in the economy, despite speculation about possible Treasury schemes. The minority shareholdings would be of little monetary value, even though they envisage the shares subsequently being acquired at a discount by a supporters' trust or the local authority.

Independent directors would be appointed to the boards of clubs as representatives for this minority shareholding. These directors could be nominated by either a registered supporters' trust or by the relevant local government authority, but they must be non-political and subject to approval as "fit and proper" by the FFA. Quite how a local authority representative can be non-political given that they are dominated by political parties is unclear.

In practice fan directors have found it quite difficult to exercise their role (Addick's Championship Diary 2020). It is envisaged that these independent directors would have real-time access to the financial records of their club "and can report their concerns back to the FFA. Clubs that continue to trade outside the rules of the EFL would be put into a form of administration by the FFA, where a credible plan would be implemented by independent auditors to bring the financial affairs of the club back in line with the League's rules" (Collins & Methven 2020).

Quite how the independent directors acting as internal watchdogs would be regarded by fellow directors who had put money into the club is open to question. A company lawyer would need to look carefully at the details of the proposal to ensure that they were compatible with duties of commercial confidentiality. The proposed "form of administration" is rather vague and would presumably require changes to company law. Whether auditors are suitable individuals to sort out the finances of a football club is open to question. What this proposal seems to amount to is a rather convoluted way of avoiding direct government involvement.

Grasping the nettle: why there is a need for a statutory regulator

There is a considerable community and social interest in the financial viability of football clubs. That can best be ensured by a statutory regulator (Ofsoc) on the model of the utilities regulators and funded by a levy on the clubs. The policies of successive governments that have relied on exhortation and the threat of penalties never implemented have not succeeded. The boundaries of the football policy community have been respected far too much.

An independent regulator would face a number of challenges. Accounts of the "capture" of regulators by regulated industries were once part of the stock in trade of analyses of regulation. For a while they fell out of favour, but more attention was paid to them in the wake of the global financial crisis. The regulator would face an asymmetry of information problem as much of what she or he would need to know would be in the possession of the clubs and extracting it would be difficult and time-consuming.

Choosing the director-general of the regulatory office would be of great importance. The person chosen should be a football fan, should have some understanding of accountancy and company law, and possess good communication skills, including media experience. It is possible to think of individuals who would meet those requirements. The funds likely to be available mean that they would have a relatively small staff. It might be possible to train individuals to undertake preliminary sifting of complaints through remote working on a part-time or even a voluntary basis. An advisory board should be made up of the relevant stakeholders in the interests of responsive regulation.

The regulator would be responsible for English football and to keep the workload in check would need to be limited to the Premier League and the EFL. A separate regulator would be needed for Scotland and that person would be encouraged to develop an informal working relationship with their English counterpart to discuss good practice. The devolved administrations and assemblies in Wales and Northern Ireland would need to discuss the arrangements that were appropriate for them. Welsh clubs play in the Premier League and the EFL and would need a regulatory arrangement based in Wales that operated in concert with the English regulator.

Given that an effort should be made to develop a "responsive" form of regulation, the fans would be a challenging stakeholder group to deal with. As has been discussed throughout the book, they are a long way from a traditional economic model of a rational consumer. The expression of emotion and the renewal of identity lie at the heart of support, but can tip over into obsession and the abandonment of normal or indeed reasonable standards of judgement.

The experience of the IFO does give some grounds for hope, although the regulator still receives a number of very specific personal complaints, often relating to ejection from grounds. Some of these were resolved to the satisfaction of the complainant, for example, the "provision of cleaning costs and the reimbursement of postage for a coat damaged by wet paint at Sheffield United". Unfortunately no details are available of a "poor and demeaning experience at the Arsenal shop". The irrelevance of some complaints is shown by the case of "one impassioned complaint from a barber, whose business was closed, querying why the returning Premier League players looked so well-groomed and deducing that they had breached regulations by having haircuts at home during the lockdown". Some encouragement may be drawn from the observation that, in "contrast to the early years of the IFO, the vast majority of issues raised with the IFO do fall within its remit and there are now far fewer expressions of outrage at referee incompetence or player misbehaviour, though these have not entirely disappeared from the IFO mailbox, particularly after controversial matches" (IFO 2020b).

It would be important to make clear what Ofsoc could and could not do. Its remit would principally be concerned with the financial probity of clubs and their owners, including owners' and directors' tests and salary caps. It would oversee the introduction of performance bonds. It would also ensure that good practice was followed in arrangements for liaison with supporters of clubs. It would not be responsible for the conduct of match officials, coaching staff and players or the use of technology. A grey area would be the IFO function of dealing with complaints not resolved within existing complaints procedures. There might be a case for maintaining this as a separate office, which could then deal with matters that were of concern to the individual supporter but did not necessarily raise wider issues. This might help to keep Ofsoc from being overloaded, but the existence of two offices might lead to some confusion, so an alternative would be to constitute IFO as a department of Ofsoc.

One should not allow debate over the details to obscure the need for a new approach to the financial regulation of football that would overcome at least some of the deficiencies of a failing system of self-regulation. A more disciplined and coherent approach is required and that will require government to accept its share of responsibility. That might be seen as a forlorn hope, although government did hint in the autumn of 2020 that it might have to consider such an idea given the delays in the Premier League agreeing to transfer additional funds to the lower leagues. However, that might just be another case of an empty threat designed to generate a response, rather than any systematic commitment to new arrangements.

Conclusions

There are so many conflicting interests in football that designing an effective system of regulation that satisfies all the relevant stakeholders is an almost impossible task. In many respects the fans themselves are the greatest obstacle because the very nature of their identity and experience stands in the way of a rational resolution of contentious issues.

It is also difficult to be confident about the response of football clubs and existing authorities. Their perspective is often too inward-looking or partial, and they have difficulty in grasping the bigger societal picture. Their system of self-regulation is undergoing a relentless process of erosion, but their response is reminiscent of that of residents of properties on the edge of a crumbling cliff. They may feel their walls moving as the tide comes in, and they may be losing their back garden to the sea, but they manage to maintain a state of denial. At best football clubs and authorities are generally reactive rather than proactive.

An even bigger challenge is globalization. Whatever happens in other sectors of the economy and society, it is unlikely to retreat in football. Just as in other arenas, migration flows present some of the greatest challenges to notions of fairness and social justice. UEFA, other regional football bodies and FIFA have not responded adequately to global challenges. Indeed, in some respects their record has been a disgrace. Faced with other challenges, the EU has stepped back to some extent from its earlier interest in football, having achieved a mutually satisfactory *modus vivendi* with UEFA. As the home of the world's richest clubs, the EU needs to step up to the plate once more and develop a more systematic football policy, albeit limited by the exit of the country with the richest league.

A cartoon once depicted a new Subbuteo table football game that included accountants and lawyers as well as players: the genie is out of the bottle and football has changed for good from its sometimes overly romanticized origins. New forms of regulation are needed, but these need not detract from the unique forms of enjoyment the game can provide.

REFERENCES

Abboud, L. & M. Ahmed (2020). "Row over rights: Mediapro vs the beautiful game". *Financial Times*, 13 November.

Addick's Championship Diary (2020). "Giving fans a stake in the club". Last modified 10 August 2020, https://addickschampionshipdiary.blogspot.com/search?q=Giving+fans+a+stake.

Agnew, P. (2019). "Times a changing in Italian women's Football?" Last modified 13 July 2020, https://www.worldfootball.com/features/times-changing-italian-womens-football-408833.

Ahmed, M. (2019a). "Man City stake sale breaks valuation record for a sports group". *Financial Times*, 27 November.

Ahmed, M. (2019b). "Global football league idea 'insane'". *Financial Times*, 7 December.

Ahmed, M. (2019c). "Women's World Cup kicks off with money row". *Financial Times*, 9 June.

Ahmed, M. (2019d). "Kicking up a fuss: Trump tiff politcises women's football". *Financial Times*, 6 July.

Ahmed, M. & J. Burn-Murdoch (2019). "How player loans are reshaping Europe's football transfer market". *Financial Times*, 30 August.

Aluko, E., with J. Le Blond (2019). *They Don't Teach This.* London: Yellow Jersey Press.

Anderson, C. & D. Sally (2013). *The Numbers Game.* London: Viking.

Andersson, T., J. Backman & B. Carlsson (2011). "Sweden: the development of club football on the periphery of Europe". In A. Niemann, B. Garcia & W. Grant (eds), *The Transformation of European Football: Towards the Europeanisation of the National Game*, 187–203. Manchester: Manchester University Press.

Anheier, H. & W. Seibel (1993). "Defining the nonprofit sector: Germany". Working Papers of the Johns Hopkins Comparative Nonprofit Sector Project, no. 6. Baltimore, MD: Johns Hopkins Institute for Policy Studies.

APPG (2020). *Online Gambling Harm Inquiry: Final Report.* Report from the Gambling Related All Party Parliamentary Group. Last modified 17 June 2020, http://www.grh-appg.com/wp-content/uploads/2020/12/Online-report-Final-June162020.pdf.

Arsenal History Society (2019). "When Margate was part of Arsenal". Last modified 16 September 2019, https://blog.woolwicharsenal.co.uk/archives/10444.

Arsenal Supporters' Trust (2020). "Mission statement". Last modified 19 November 2020, https://www.arsenaltrust.org/about/mission-statement.

Away Section, The (2019). "Floodlights: a brief history". Last modified 5 September 2019, https://theawaysection.com/floodlights-a-brief-history/.

Ayres, I. & J. Braithwaite (1992). *Responsive Regulation: Transcending the Deregulation Debate.* Oxford: Oxford University Press.

Baldwin, R. & J. Black (2007). "Really responsive regulation". LSE Law, Society and Economy Working Papers 15/2007.

Banks, S. (2002). *Going Down: Football in Crisis.* Edinburgh: Mainstream.

Barclays (2018). "Experience economy grows as consumers seek out memories in favour of material possessions". Last modified 6 August 2020, https://www.home.barclaycard/media-centre/press-releases/Experience-economy-grows-as-consumers-seek-out-memories-in-favour-of-material-possessions.html.

BBC (2019a). "Robert Maxwell's phantom club, the Thames Valley Royals". Last modified 16 September 2019, https://www.bbc.co.uk/sport/football/22862495.

BBC (2019b). "Manchester City investment from US breaks global sports valuation". Last modified 27 November 2019, https://www.bbc.co.uk/news/business-50570117.

BBC (2019c). "Mesut Ozil: Arsenal–Manchester City game removed from schedules by China state TV". Last modified 16 December 2019, https://www.bbc.co.uk/sport/football/50799009.

BBC (2020a). "Fifa to introduce new agent regulations and modify commission". Last modified 13 November 2020, https://www.bbc.co.uk/sport/football/54834219.

BBC (2020b). "Daniel Sturridge 'devastated' by four-month ban for breaching betting rules". Last modified 13 November 2020, https://www.bbc.co.uk/sport/football/51712017.

BBC (2020c). "Wigan Athletic: EFL chairman Rick Parry says English football has been 'disrespected'". Last modified 4 August 2020, https://www.bbc.co.uk/sport/football/53341269.

Boudreaux, C., G. Karahan & M. Coats (2016). "Bend it like FIFA: corruption on and off the pitch". *Managerial Finance* 42(9), 866–78.

Bow, M. (2019). "Row erupts as watchdog shuns Thames Water's £11bn upgrade". *Evening Standard*, 31 January.

Bower, T. (2003). *Broken Dreams: Vanity, Greed and the Souring of British Football.* London: Pocket Books.

Braithwaite, J. (2019). "Responsive regulation". Last modified 7 October 2019, http://johnbraithwaite.com/responsive-regulation/.

Braithwaite, T. (2019). "Silicon Valley is inflating the football bubble". *Financial Times*, 30 November.

Brannagan, P. & R. Giulianotti (2015). "Soft power and soft disempowerment: Qatar, global sport and football's 2022 World Cup finals". *Leisure Studies* 34(6), 703–19.

Brewin, J. (2020). "WSL: it's a whole new ball game". *Four Four Two*, November, 55–9.

Bridgewater, S. (2010). *Football Brands.* Basingstoke: Palgrave Macmillan.

Brighton and Hove Independent (2019). "Brighton and Hove Albion give local economy £212m yearly boost". Last modified 11 December 2019, https://www.brightonandhoveindependent.co.uk/sport/football/brighton-hove-albion-give-local-economy-212m-yearly-boost-1-9003256.

Brunsden, J. (2019). "Brussels puts football on money laundering watchlist". *Financial Times*, 25 July.

Cameron, D. (2019). *For the Record.* London: William Collins.

Carter, N. (2006). *The Football Manager: A History.* London: Routledge.

CAS (2016). "CAS 2016/A/4501 Joseph S. Blatter v. FIFA, Arbitral Award".

CAS (2020). "CAS 2020/A/6785 Manchester City FC v UEFA, Arbitral Award".

Cashmore, E. & J. Cleland (2012). "Fans, homophobia and masculinities in association football: evidence of a more inclusive environment". *British Journal of Sociology* 63(2), 370–87.

Cassidy, R. & N. Ovenden (2017). "Frequency, duration and medium of advertisements for gambling and other risky products in commercial and public service broadcasts of English Premier League football". Working paper, Goldsmiths College London. Last modified 17 June 2020, http://research.gold.ac.uk/20926/.

Caudwell, J. (2011). "'Does your boyfriend know you're here?' The spatiality of homophobia in men's football culture in the UK". *Leisure Studies* 30(2), 123–38.

Caudwell, J. (2017). "'I love going to watch Norwich': the experience of a transgender football fan". In B. Garcia & J. Zheng (eds), *Football and Supporter Activism in Europe,* 27–44. London: Palgrave.

Charlotte Business Journal (2019). "MLS will announce decision on expansion team in selected city". Last modified 4 December 2019, https://www.bizjournals.com/charlotte/news/2019/12/02/mls-will-announce-decision-on-expansion-team-in.html.

Charlton Athletic (2005). *Charlton Athletic plc: Annual Report and Accounts 2005.* Bexleyheath: Charlton Athletic.

Chichester Observer (1894). "Women at football". 21 November, www.britishnewspaperarchive.co.uk.

City Football Group (2020). "Other club investments". Last modified 11 August 2020, https://www.cityfootballgroup.com/our-teams/other-club-investments/.

Cleland, J. (2018). "Sexuality, masculinity and homophobia in association football: an empirical overview of a changing cultural context". *International Review for the Sociology of Sport* 53(4), 411–23.

Cleland, J. & E. Cashmore (2014). "Fans, racism and British football in the twenty-first century: the existence of a 'colour-blind' ideology". *Journal of Ethnic and Migration Studies* 40(4), 638–54.

Cleland, J., R. Magrath & A. Klan (2018). "The internet as a site of decreasing cultural homophobia in Association Football: an online response to fans to the coming out of Thomas Hitzlsperger". *Men and Masculinities* 21(1), 91–111.

Collins, D. & C. Methven (2020). "A way forward for football". Last modified 10 August 2020, https://damiancollins.com/a-way-forward-for-football/.

Commission of the European Communities (2014). C (2014). 7378 "Draft Arrangement for Cooperation between the European Union and the Union of European Football Associations, Annex".

Conn, D. (1997). *The Football Business.* Edinburgh: Mainstream.

Conn, D. (2005). *The Beautiful Game?* London: Yellow Jersey Press.

Conn, D. (2017). *The Fall of the House of FIFA.* London: Yellow Jersey Press.

Conn, D. (2018). "Manchester United have been owned by the Glazers for 13 years. No wonder they're struggling". *The Guardian*, 16 September, https://www.theguardian.com/football/2018/oct/04/glazers-manchester-united.

Conn, D. (2020). "Brutal and bizarre: the story of how Wigan collapsed into administration". *The Guardian*, 4 August, https://www.theguardian.com/football/2020/jul/02/story-of-how-wigan-collapsed-into-administration-au-yeung-investigation.

Connell, J. (2018). "Globalisation, soft power and the rise of football in China". *Geographical Research* 56(1), 5–15.

Crabtree, J. (2019). "Is it time to declare the end of globalisation?", *Financial Times*, 19 July.

Darby, P. (2007). "African football labour migration to Portugal: colonial and neo-colonial resource". *Football and Society* 8(4), 495–509.

David, M. (2016). *Reclaiming Feminism: Challenging Everyday Misogyny.* Bristol: Policy Press.

Davies, R. (2020a). "How the betting industry has become inextricably linked to football". *The Guardian*, 16 June, https://www.theguardian.com/sport/2020/jan/08/how-the-betting-industry-has-become-inextricably-linked-to-football.

Davies, R. (2020b). "Gambling Commission 'is being outgunned' by betting companies". *The Guardian*, 12 August, https://www.theguardian.com/society/2020/feb/28/gambling-commission-is-being-outgunned-by-online-betting-companies-nao.

Davies, R. (2020c). "UK minister urges betting firms to do more for problem gamblers", *The Guardian*, 21 April.

Deloitte Sports Business (2019). *World in Motion: Annual Review of Football Finance 2019.* Manchester: Deloitte.

Diamond, P. (ed.) (2019). *The Crisis of Globalization: Democracy, Capitalism and Inequality in the Twenty-First Century.* London: I. B. Taurus.

Dickinson, M. (2019). "Women's football drives Saudi change". *The Times*, 6 December.

Dickinson, M. (2020). "Time for solidarity, not salaciousness, over male footballers' sexuality". *The Times*, 16 July.

Dixie, Lady F. (1895). "Football for women". *Pall Mall Gazette*, 8 February, www.britishnewspaperarchive.co.uk.

Dobson, D. & J. Goddard (2001). *The Economics of Football.* Cambridge: Cambridge University Press.

Downing, D. (2003). *England v Argentina: World Cups and Other Small Wars.* London: Portrait.

Dublin Daily Express (1881). "Women's football match". 23 June, www.britishnewspaperarchive.co.uk.

Dunn, C. (2019). *The Pride of the Lionesses: The Changing Face of Women's Football in England.* Worthing: Pitch Publishing.

Economist, The (2019a). "All bets are on". 17 September, 46.

Economist, The (2019b). "Better pay, lesser pay". 29 June, 37.

Economist, The (2019c). "Net gains". 13 July, 61.

Economist, The (2020). "Flat-white world". 7 November, 59.

Edinburgh Evening News (1895). "Women as football players". 8 January, www.britishnewspaperarchive.co.uk.

Ellson, A. (2020). "Betway hit with record £11.6m fine". *The Times*, 13 March.

Elsey, B. & J. Nadel (2019). "How Argentina's women took on blatant sexism to reach the World Cup". *The Guardian*, 14 June.

England, A. & M. Ahmed (2019). "Why the Gulf states are betting on sport", *Financial Times*, 27 November.

Everitt, R. (2019). "A date with my destiny". *Voice of the Valley* 155 (December), 18–19.

Farey-Jones, D. (2019). "Gambling industry's 'when the fun stops' slogan 'doesn't work'". Campaign, 5 August, https://www.campaignlive.co.uk/article/gambling-industrys-when-fun-stops-slogan-doesnt-work/1592996.

Fairley, C. (2020). "Loss and belonging on the terraces". *Hope Not Hate* 42 (spring/summer), 51.

FIFA (2020). "The football landscape". Last modified 12 November 2020, https://www.fifa.com/who-we-are/vision/football-landscape/.

Fifpro (2020). "Covid-19: implications for professional women's football". Last modified 14 July 2020, https://www.fifpro.org/media/mybpsvym/fifpro-womens-football-covid19.pdf.

Financial Times (2020). "Players, fans and gambling groups hail sports return". 27/28 June.

Flanagan, C. (2019). "I'd play for England then it was back to reality at the hostel – I was homeless". *Four Four Two*, July, 108–11.

Football League Paper (2020). "The big interview: Gareth Ainsworth". Last modified 19 March 2020, https://www.theleaguepaper.com/features/11100/big-interview-gareth-ainsworth-wycombe/.

Football Supporters' Association (2020). "Clubs must do more on gambling risks survey". Last modified 16 June 2020, https://thefsa.org.uk/news/clubs-must-do-more-on-gambling-risks-survey/.

Footballex (2019). "Football finance 100". Last modified 16 September 2019, http://myfootballex.com/Footballex_Football_Finance_100_2019_Edition.pdf.

Forbes (2019). "New world club association could shake up football's club politics". Last modified 11 December 2019, https://www.forbes.com/sites/steveprice/2019/11/19/new-world-club-association-could-shake-up-footballs-club-politics/#55c66e2c5b44.

Forrest, D. (1999). "The past and future of British football pools". *Journal of Gambling Studies* 15(2), 161–76.

Forrest, D. & J. Pérez (2015). "Just like the lottery? Player behaviour and anomalies in the market for football pools". *Journal of Gambling Studies* 31, 471–82.

Franck, E. (2014). "Financial Fair Play in European club football: what is it all about?" *International Journal of Sport Finance* 9, 193–217.

GambleAware (2020). "Fundraising". Last modified 24 June 2020, https://about.gambleaware.org/fundraising/.

Gambling Commission (2019). *Annual Report 2018–19*. Last modified 23 June 2020, https://www.gamblingcommission.gov.uk/PDF/Annual-Report1819.pdf.

Gambling Commission (2020a). "Betway to pay £11.6m for failings linked to 'VIP' customers". Last modified 23 June 2020, https://www.gamblingcommission.gov.uk/news-action-and-statistics/news/2020/Betway-to-pay-11.6m-for-failings-linked-to-%27VIP%27-customers.aspx.

Gambling Commission (2020b). "Gambling Commission investigation into failures in player protection at PT Entertainment Services (PTES) leads to company closure". Last modified 23 June 2020, https://www.gamblingcommission.gov.uk/news-action-and-statistics/news/2020/Gambling-Commission-investigation-into-failures-in-player-protection-at-PT-Entertainment-Services-PTES-leads-to-company-closure.aspx.

Garcia, G. & P. Rodriguez (2007). "The demand for football pools in Spain". *Journal of Sports Economics* 8(4), 335–54.

Gerano, S. (2020). "US women's football scores open goal in virus-hit calendar". *Financial Times*, 13 July.

Gheerbrant, J. (2019). "Power of stadiums can be used as a force for good in society". *The Times*, 28 December.

Giulianotti, R. & R. Robertson (2004). "The globalization of football: a study in the glocalization of the 'serious life'". *British Journal of Sociology* 55(4), 545–68.

Giulianotti, R. & R. Robertson (2006). "Glocalization, globalization and migration: the case of Scottish football supporters in North America". *International Sociology* 21(2), 171–98.

Globe (1895). "Women at football". 25 March, www.britishnewspaperarchive.co.uk.

Goldblatt, D. (2007). *The Ball is Round: A Global History of Football.* London: Penguin.

Goldblatt, D. (2014). *The Game of Our Lives.* New York: Nation Books.

Goldblatt, D. (2019). *The Age of Football: The Global Game in the Twenty-First Century.* London: Macmillan.

Grant, W. (1993). *Business and Politics in Britain.* Second edition. Basingstoke: Macmillan.

Grant, W. (2007). "An analytical framework for a political economy of football". *British Politics* 2, 69–90.

Grant, W. (2018). *Lobbying: The Dark Side of Politics.* Manchester: Manchester University Press.

Gratton, C. (2000). "The peculiar economics of English professional football". In J. Garland, D. Malcolm & M. Rowe (eds), *The Future of Football: Challenges for the Twenty-First Century*, 11–28. London: Frank Cass.

Greenfield, S. & G. Osborn (2001). *Regulating Football.* London: Pluto.

Greenock Advertiser (1881). "The Glasgow roughs and the female football teams". 17 May, www.britishnewspaperarchive.co.uk.

Grix, J. & P. Brannagan (2016). "Of mechanisms and myths: conceptualising states' 'soft power' strategies through sports mega-events". *Diplomacy and Statecraft* 27(2), 251–72.

Hancock, A. & M. Ahmed (2019a). "Gambling and football: a relationship under scrutiny", *Financial Times*, 23 August.

Hancock, A. & M. Ahmed (2019b). "Betting groups tackle threat of a football crackdown". *Financial Times*, 24/25 August.

Hirsch, F. (1977). *Social Limits to Growth.* London: Routledge & Kegan Paul.

Holbrook, M. & E. Hirschmann (1982). "The experiential aspects of consumption: consumer fantasies, feelings and fun". *Journal of Consumer Research* 9(2), 132–40.

Hong, F. & L. Zhouxiang (2013). "The professionalisation and commercialisation of football in China (1993–2013)". *International Journal of the History of Sport* 30(14), 1637–54.

Hopkins, G. (2010). *Star-Spangled Football: The Selling, Marketing and Management of Football in the USA*. Basingstoke: Palgrave Macmillan.

Hornby, N. (1992). *Fever Pitch*. London: Victor Gollancz.

Horton, E. (1997). *Moving the Goalposts: Football's Exploitation*. Edinburgh: Mainstream.

House of Commons (2019a). Digital, Culture, Media and Sport Select Committee Inquiry into the Administration of Football Clubs, written evidence submitted by the Football Association.

House of Commons (2019b). "Committee calls for regulatory reforms to English football". Last modified 4 August 2020, https://www.parliament.uk/business/committees/committees-a-z/commons-select/digital-culture-media-and-sport-committee/news/football-administration-correspondence-19-20/.

House of Commons Digital, Media and Sport Committee (2016). "The governance of football inquiry". Last modified 21 October 2019, https://www.parliament.uk/business/committees/committees-a-z/commons-select/culture-media-and-sport-committee/inquiries/parliament-2015/football-governance-inquiry-16-17/publications/.

House of Lords (2020a). *Time for Action*. House of Lords Select Committee on the Social and Economic Impact of the Gambling Industry. London: House of Lords.

House of Lords (2020b). "Statement by the Lord Grade of Yarmouth". Last modified 12 August 2020, https://www.parliament.uk/business/committees/committees-a-z/lords-select/gambling-committee/news-parliament-2019/lords-gambling-report-published/.

Hudson, M. (2019). "Records fall but results matter most". *The Times*, 19 November.

Hughes, S. (2017). "Inside the City Football Group: how Manchester City's network of clubs is methodically taking control". *The Independent*, 7 September, https://www.independent.co.uk/sport/football/premier-league/inside-city-football-group-manchester-citys-network-of-clubs-new-york-melbourne-girona-a7934436.html.

Hughes, V. (2020). "GambleAware responds to All-party Parliamentary Group criticism", https://bestbettingsites.com/news/society/gambleaware-responds- party-parliamentary-group-criticism.html.

Hull Daily Mail (1893). "Women at football matches". 13 March, www.britishnewspaperarchive.co.uk.

IFO (2020a). "Annual ADR Activity Report 2020". Last modified 12 August 2020, https://www.theifo.co.uk/docs/ADR_SCHEDULE_5_2020.pdf.

IFO (2020b). "Annual Report 2020". Last modified 10 August 2020, https://www.theifo.co.uk/docs/IFO_Ann_Rep_2019-20(Web).pdf.

ISL media team (2019). "Ferran Soriano: CFG's objective is to unleash the power of Indian football". Last modified 2 December 2019, https://www.indiansuperleague.com/features/ferran-soriano-cfgs-objective-is-to-unleash-the-power-of-indian-football.

Jackson, J. (2019). "Tired worn Old Trafford, a symbol of Manchester United's faded grandeur". *The Guardian*, 11 December.

Jedburgh Gazette (1881). "Notes: did I really read recently?". 14 May, www.britishnews paperarchive.co.uk.

Jenkins, S. (2019). "Football, not gender politics, is the winner in France". *Financial Times*, 2 July.

Jijon, I. (2017). "The moral glocalization of sport: local meanings of football in Chota Valley, Ecuador". *International Review for the Sociology of Sport* 52(1), 82–96.

Jinxia, D. & J. Mangan (2002). "Ascending then descending? Women's football in modern China". *Football and Society* 3(2), 1–18.

Johnson, M. (2019). "Abuse of Balotelli exposes Italy's race problem". *Financial Times*, 11 November.

Jones, S. & M. Ahmed (2020). "Fifa chief and Swiss federal prosecutor face investigation". *Financial Times*, 3 July.

Joyce, D. (2019). "FA wants long Sturridge ban". *The Times*, 19 July.

Kalimuddin, M. & D. Anderson (2019). "Soft power in China's security strategy". *Strategic Studies Quarterly* 12(3), 114–41.

Kelly, W. (2013). "Japan's embrace of football: mutable ethnic players and flexible football citizenship in the new East Asian sports order". *International Journal of the History of Sport* 30(11), 1235–46.

Kerr, S. & A. England (2019). "Rising star plays a winning game for Abu Dhabi". *Financial Times*, 5 December.

Khalaj, M. (2019). "Iran eases ban on women attending football matches". *Financial Times*, 10 October.

Koller, C. & F. Brändle (2015). *Goal! A Cultural and Social History of Modern Football*. Trans. D. Bachrach. Washington, DC: Catholic University of America Press.

Kunti, S. (2020). "Growth of professional women's game hit hardest by virus, finds FIFPro survey". Last modified 16 November 2020, http://www.insideworldfootball. com/2020/11/12/growth-professional-womens-game-hit-hardest-virus-finds-fifpro-survey/.

Kuper, S. (2019). "Female footballers grab world's attention". *Financial Times*, 28 June.

Kuper, S. (2020a). "Sports clubs get smarter in search for top talent". *Financial Times*, 6 May.

Kuper, S. (2020b). "When Saturday comes". *Financial Times*, 20/21 June.

Kuper, S. & S. Szymanski (2012). *Soccernomics*. London: HarperSport.

Lancashire Evening Post (1921). "Doctor condemns girls playing". 6 December, www. britishnewspaperarchive.co.uk.

Lawson, D. (2020). "Football's back: If only gambling firms weren't". *Sunday Times*, 21 June.

Lex (2019). "Man City/Silver Lake: the football factory". *Financial Times*, 27 November.

Liverpool Football Club (2019). "Liverpool Football Club boosted the Liverpool City region economy by £497m GVA during the 2017–18 season". Last modified 27 November 2019, https://fcbusiness.co.uk/news/liverpool-football-clubs-497m-gva-boost-to-regions-economy/.

Lonergan, E. & M. Blyth (2020). *Angrynomics*. Newcastle upon Tyne: Agenda.

Lottoland (2020). "Lottery winners who bought football clubs", https://www.lottoland. co.uk/magazine/lottery-winners-football-clubs.html. Last modified 19 May 2020.

Lyons, J. (2020). "Fans eager to return". *The Non-League Paper*, 19 July, 4–5.

McMillen, J. & W. Wenzel (2006). "Measuring problem gambling: assessment of three prevalence screens". *International Gambling Studies* 6(2), 147–74.

Maguire, K. (2019). "Selling your stadium to yourself: it's not cricket". The Price of Football. Last modified 4 August 2020, http://priceoffootball.com/selling-your-stadium-to-yourself-its-not-cricket/

Maguire, K. (2020). *The Price of Football: Understanding Football Club Finance.* Newcastle upon Tyne: Agenda.

Makwena, R. (2019). "A new dawn in women's football in South Africa". Last modified 13 July 2020, https://mg.co.za/article/2019-09-02-00-a-new-dawn-in-womens-football-in-south-africa/.

Malcolm, D., I. Jones & I. Waddington (2000). "The people's game? Football spectatorship and demographic change". In J. Garland, D. Malcolm & M. Rowe (eds), *The Future of Football: Challenges for the Twenty-First Century*, 129–43. London: Frank Cass.

Mance, H. (2019). "'I've never received racism outside football'". *Financial Times Weekend Magazine*, 17 June.

Manchester Evening News (1881). "Disgraceful scenes at a women's football match". 18 June, www.britishnewspaperarchive.co.uk.

Markovits, A. (1990). "The other 'American exceptionalism': why is there no football in the United States". *International Journal of the History of Sport* 7(2), 230–64.

Markovits, A. & S. Hellerman (2003). "Women's football in the United States: yet another America 'exceptionalism'". *Football and Society* 4(2/3), 14–29.

Markovits, A. & L. Rensman (2010). *The Gaming World: How Sports are Reshaping Global Politics and Culture.* Princeton, NJ: Princeton University Press.

Meddings, S. (2019). "Our fan in the stand: tipping off the bookies". *Sunday Times*, 18 August.

Montague, J. (2017). *The Billionaires Club: The Unstoppable Rise of Football's Super-Rich Owners.* London: Bloomsbury.

Moran, M. (2000). "From command state to regulatory state?". *Public Policy and Administration* 15, 1–13.

Moran, M. (2003). *The British Regulatory State: High Modernism and Hyper-innovation.* Oxford: Oxford University Press.

Moran, M. (2015). *Politics and Governance in the UK.* Third edition. London: Palgrave Macmillan.

Mourao, P. (2016). "Football transfers, team efficiency and the sports cycle in the most valued European football leagues: have European football teams been efficient in trading players?". *Applied Economics* 48(56), 5513–24.

Murray, C. (2020). "USNWT may have lost the battle over equal pay but they will win the war". *The Guardian*, 4 May.

Myers, R. (2019a). "Stars and gripes". *Sunday Times*, 16 June.

Myers, R. (2019b). "Italy move on from sexism row". *Sunday Times*, 23 June.

Namibian (2020). "Women's football in the frame". Last modified 12 August 2020, https://www.namibian.com.na/92864/read/Womens-football-in-the-frame.

National Audit Office (2020). *Gambling Regulation: Problem Gambling and Protecting Vulnerable People.* London: National Audit Office.

Nottingham Evening Post (1921). "Ladies' Football Association: to play the real game and adhere to the rules". 21 December, www.britishnewspaperarchive.co.uk.

Nottingham Journal (1895). "Women and football". 20 December, www.britishnews paperarchive.co.uk.

Nye, J. (1990). "Soft power". *Foreign Policy* 80, 153–71.

O'Brien, J. (2017). "C. A. Osasuna: identity, ownership and governance in Spanish club football". In B. Garcia & J. Zheng (eds), *Football and Supporter Activism in Europe*, 121–39. London: Palgrave Macmillan.

O'Connor, A. (2002). "Premier League facing censure over TV rights", *The Times*, 21 December.

Off the Pitch (2020). "Gambling sponsorship ban would have 'potentially catastrophic' consequences for English football". Last modified 12 November 2020, https://offthepitch.com/a/gambling-sponsorship-ban-would-have-potentially-catastrophic-consequences-english-football.

Orford, J., H. Wardle & M. Griffiths (2013). "What proportion of gambling is problem gambling? Estimates from the 2010 British Gambling Prevalence Survey". *International Gambling Studies* 13(1), 4–14.

O'Sullivan, M. (2019). *The Levelling: What's Next After Globalization*. New York: Public Affairs.

Paisley and Renfrewshire Gazette (1895). "Should women play football: the attempt a failure". 30 March, www.britishnewspaperarchive.co.uk.

Parish, S. (2020). "The Football League needs a survival plan not a handout". *Sunday Times*, 19 July, https://www.thetimes.co.uk/article/the-football-league-needs-a-survival-plan-not-a-handout-f00xk593v.

Pfister, G., K. Fasting, S. Scraton & A. Vásquez (2002). "Women and football – a contradiction? The beginnings of women's football in four European countries". In S. Scraton & A. Flintoff (eds), *Gender and Sport: A Reader*, 66–78. London: Routledge.

Polanyi, K. (1944). *The Great Transformation*. Boston, MA: Beacon.

Poli, R. (2010). "African migrants in Asian and European football: hopes and realities". *Sport in Society* 13(6), 1001–11.

Political Economy of Football (2019a). "Chelsea business model depends on player sales". Last modified 12 September 2019, https://footballeconomyv2.blogspot.com/2019/01/chelsea-business-model-depends-on.html.

Political Economy of Football (2019b). "Premier League the place to generate cash". Last modified 16 September 2019, https://footballeconomyv2.blogspot.com/2019/01/premier-league-place-to-generate-cash.html.

Political Economy of Football (2019c). "English clubs have coined it in the Champions League". Last modified 18 September 2019, https://footballeconomyv2.blogspot.com/2019/04/english-clubs-have-coined-it-in.html.

Political Economy of Football (2019d). "The crazy world of Championship finances". Last modified 4 August 2020, https://footballeconomyv2.blogspot.com/2019/10/the-crazy-world-of-championship-finances.html.

Political Economy of Football (2020a). "QPR losses are now moderate by Championship standards". Last modified 19 March 2020, https://footballeconomyv2.blogspot.com/2020/02/qpr-losses-are-now-moderate-by.html.

Political Economy of Football (2020b). "Non-league losses". Last modified 19 March 2020, https://footballeconomyv2.blogspot.com/2020/03/non-league-losses.html.

Political Economy of Football (2020c). "Wycombe takeover completed". Last modified 19 March 2020, https://footballeconomyv2.blogspot.com/2020/02/wycombe-takeover-completed.html.

Political Economy of Football (2020d). "Bournemouth reliant on their owners". Last modified 24 March 2020, https://footballeconomyv2.blogspot.com/2020/03/bournemouth-reliant-on-their-owners.html.

Political Economy of Football (2020e). "Hamburg shows limits of German model". Last modified 30 March 2020, https://footballeconomyv2.blogspot.com/2018/05/hamburg-were-longest-serving-members-of.html.

Political Economy of Football (2020f). "Bury review described as whitewash". Last modified 4 August 2020, https://footballeconomyv2.blogspot.com/2020/03/bury-review-described-as-whitewash.html.

Political Economy of Football (2020g). "Which relegated club will take the hardest hit?" Last modified 7 August 2020, https://footballeconomyv2.blogspot.com/2020/07/which-relegated-club-will-take-hardest.html.

Productivity Commission (1999). *Australia's Gambling Industries* (Canberra: Government of Australia).

Professional Footballers' Association (2020). "EFL salary cap proposals". Last modified 7 August 2020, https://www.thepfa.com/-/media/Files/PFA---EFL-Salary-Cap-Proposals.pdf?la=en.

Public Accounts Committee (2020). "Oral evidence: Gambling Regulation – Problem Gambling and Protecting Vulnerable People". HC 134, ordered by the House of Commons to be published 20 April.

Richardson, D. (2019). "This can transform football at our level". *The Non-League Paper*, 14 July.

Richardson, D. (2020). "Rangers accept FA betting bans". *The Non-League Paper*, 1 March.

Ridge, J. (2019). "The Premier League has had 154 managers in the 2010s". *Daily Mail*, 31 December, https://www.dailymail.co.uk/sport/football/article-7802625/Premier-League-104-different-managers-2010s-one-charge-FIVE-teams.html.

Robertson, G. (2019). "Why are terraces so white? Fear of racial abuse turns fans away". *The Times*, 28 October.

Rowe, M. (2018). "The human game: tackling football's slave trade". *Geographical*, 16 July, https://geographical.co.uk/people/development/item/2817-football-trafficking.

Rudd, A. (2019). "Three women who changed face of the 'man's game'". *The Times*, 6 June.

Scholte, J. (2000). *Globalization: A Critical Introduction.* Basingstoke: Palgrave Macmillan.

Sheffield Weekly Telegraph (1895). "A stirring contest". 5 December, www.britishnewspaperarchive.co.uk.

Simpson, P. (2020). "The rise and fall of Michel Platini". *Four Four Two*, March, 78–83.

Skidelsky, R. (2018). *Money and Government.* London: Allen Lane.

Sport Industry Research Centre (2019). "Analysing the value of football to Greater Manchester". Last modified 27 November 2019, http://www.neweconomymanchester.com/media/1404/280613_technical_reportcompressed.pdf.

Steger, M. (2017). *Globalization: A Very Short Introduction.* Fourth edition. Oxford: Oxford University Press.

Streeck, W. (1989). "The territorial organisation of interests and the logics of associative action: the case of *Handwerk* organisation in West Germany". In W. Coleman & H. Jacek (eds), *Regionalism, Business Interests and Public Policy*, 59–94. London: Sage.

Szymanski, S. (2014). "Fair is foul: a critical analysis of UEFA Financial Fair Play". *International Journal of Sport Finance* 9, 218–29.

Szymanski, S. (2015). *Money and Football: A Soccernomics Guide.* New York: Nation.

Szymanski, S. & T. Kuypers (2000). *Winners and Losers: The Business Strategy of Football.* London: Penguin.

Szymanski, S. & D. Weimar (2019). "Insolvencies in professional football: a German Sonderweg?" *International Journal of Sport Finance* 14(1), 54–68.

Tamworth Herald (1881). "Two teams of young women". 14 May, www.britishnewspaperarchive.co.uk.

Tabner, B (1992). *Through the Turnstiles.* Harefield: Yore Publications.

Tate, T. (2016). *Women's Football: The Secret History.* London: John Blake.

Taylor, M. (2007). "Football, migration and globalization: the perspective of history". Idrottsforum.org, Department of Sport Science, Malmo University. Last modified 13 April 2020, www.idrottsforum.org.

These Football Times (2019). "How Scottish football lost Third Lanark". Last modified 10 August 2020, https://thesefootballtimes.co/2019/04/19/how-scottish-football-lost-third-lanark-a-cherished-club-destroyed-by-one-mans-greed/.

Thomas, D. & M. Smith (2019). *Bob Lord of Burnley.* Worthing: Pitch.

Tindell, J. (1996). "The point of no return". *Voice of the Valley* 93 (January): 22–3.

Tomkins, P., G. Riley & G. Fulcher (2010). *Pay As You Play.* London: Gorf Publishing.

Tyrie, A. (2019). "Keynote Speech to the SMF". Last modified 7 October 2019, http://www.smf.co.uk/andrew-tyrie-keynote/.

UEFA (2020). "Financial Fair Play". Last modified 4 August 2020, https://www.uefa.com/insideuefa/protecting-the-game/financial-fair-play/.

Ungoed-Thomas, J. (2020). "José Mourinho urged to cut links with Paddy Power". *Sunday Times*, 14 June.

Van Der Burg, T. (2014). *Football Business: How Markets are Breaking the Beautiful Game.* Oxford: Infinite Ideas.

Van Campenhout, G., J. van Sterkenburg & G. Oonk (2018). "Who counts as a migrant footballer? A critical reflection and alternative approach to migrant football players on national teams at the World Cup, 1930–2018". *International Journal of the History of Sport* 35(11), 1071–90.

Van Campenhout, G., J. van Sterkenburg & G. Oonk (2019). "Has the World Cup become more migratory? A comparative history of foreign-born players in national football teams, c. 1930–2018". *Comparative Migration Studies* 7(2), 1–19.

Vanberg, V. (2014). "Ordungspolitik: the Freiburg School and the reason of rules". Freiburg Discussion Papers on Constitutional Economics, 14/01.

Vandevelde, M. & M. Ahmed (2019). "Silver Lake raises its game in sports". *Financial Times*, 28 November.

Ware, A. (2020). *Inequality in Britain*. Abingdon: Routledge.

Weatherill, S. (2020). "Sources and origins of EU sports law". In J. Anderson, R. Parrish & B. Garcia (eds), *Research Handbook on EU Sports Law and Policy*, 6–23. Cheltenham: Edward Elgar.

West Bromwich Albion (2020). "Jonathan Leko statement following FA verdict". Last modified 16 November 2020, https://www.wba.co.uk/news/2020/march/jonathan-leko-statement-following-fa-verdict.

Westminster Gazette (1895). "Should women play football?". 2 February, www.britishnewspaperarchive.co.uk.

WG Football Page (2003). "Brussels slams TV deal". Last modified 4 August 2020, http://wyngrant.tripod.com/WGFootballPage.html.

Wilkes, D. (2011). "Meet the first female footballers". *Daily Mail*, 9 December, https://www.dailymail.co.uk/sport/football/article-2071996/Meet-Britains-1st-female-footballers-kicked-quite-fuss-knickerbockers.html.

Williams, J. (2013). *Globalizing Women's Football: Europe, Migration and Professionalization*. Bern: Peter Lang.

Wolter, M. (2019). "Migrating for football: the harsh reality behind the dream". InfoMigrants.net, 24 September, https://www.infomigrants.net/en/post/19733/migrating-for-football-the-harsh-reality-behind-the-dream.

Women's Signal (1895). "Should women play football?". 4 April, www.britishnewspaperarchive.co.uk.

Wood, M. (2018). "Does the English Premier League actually need fans in the stadium?" *Forbes*, 29 October, https://www.forbes.com/sites/mikemeehallwood/2018/10/29/does-the-english-premier-league-actually-need-fans-in-the-stadium/#15c629781814.

Zhao, A., P. Horton & L. Liu (2012). "Women's football in the People's Republic of China: retrospect and prospect". *International Journal of the History of Sport* 29(17), 2372–87.

Zheng, J. & B. Garcia (2017). "Conclusions: the rising importance of supporter activism in European football". In B. Garcia & J. Zheng (eds), *Football and Supporter Activism in Europe*, 277–85. London: Palgrave Macmillan.

Ziegler, M. (2019a). "Banned teenager was 'heavily influenced' by betting culture". *The Times*, 11 September.

Ziegler, M. (2019b). "FA wants Women's Super League on terrestrial TV". *The Times*, 28 June.

Ziesche, D. (2017). "Well governed? Fan representation in German professional clubs". In B. Garcia and J. Zheng (eds), *Football and Supporter Activism in Europe*, 89–120. London: Palgrave Macmillan.

INDEX